The Good Life

D1646234

Are we born selfish or primed to help others?
Does stress make people more antisocial?
Can we ever be genuinely altruistic?

This book explores some of the dilemmas at the heart of being human. Integrating cutting-edge studies with in-depth clinical experience, Graham Music synthesises a wealth of research into an explanation of altruism, cooperation and generosity and shows how we are primed to turn off the 'better angels of our nature' in the face of stress, anxiety and fear.

Using fascinating psychological research but rooted in a clinician's understanding of the impact of stress on our moral and prosocial capacities, *The Good Life* covers topics as diverse as:

- the role of parenting and family life in shaping how antisocial or prosocial we become
- how stress, abuse and insecure attachment profoundly undermine empathic and altruistic capacities
- the relative influence of our genes or environments on becoming big hearted or coldly psychopathic
- how our immediate contexts and recent social changes might tilt us towards either selfish or cooperative behaviour.

This book makes a unique contribution to a subject that is increasingly on people's minds. It does not shirk complexity, nor suggest easy explanations, but offers a hard look at the evidence in the hope that we can gain some understanding of how a 'Good Life' might develop. Often personally challenging, intellectually exhilarating and written in an easily accessible style, *The Good Life* makes sense of how our moral selves take shape and shines a light on the roots of goodness and nastiness.

Graham Music is Consultant Child and Adolescent Psychotherapist at the Tavistock and Portman Clinics in London, UK, and an adult psychotherapist in private practice. At the Tavistock Clinic he leads in teaching on attachment, the brain and child development, organises training for therapists and other professionals, and teaches and supervises on a range of psychotherapy training in Britain and abroad. He currently works clinically at the Portman Clinic in forensic psychotherapy and has worked for two decades with the aftermath of abuse and neglect.

The Good Life

Wellbeing and the new science of altruism, selfishness and immorality

Graham Music

Routledge
Taylor & Francis Group

LONDON AND NEW YORK

First published 2014
by Routledge
27 Church Road, Hove, East Sussex BN3 2FA

and by Routledge
711 Third Avenue, New York, NY 10017

Routledge is an imprint of the Taylor & Francis Group, an informa business

British Library Cataloguing in Publication Data
A catalogue record for this book is available from the British Library

Library of Congress Cataloging in Publication Data
Music, Graham, 1957-
 The good life : wellbeing and the new science of altruism, selfishness and
immorality / Graham Music.
  pages cm
1. Altruism. 2. Helping behavior. 3. Cooperativeness. I. Title.
  BF637.H4M875 2014
  158.3--dc23
2013040014

ISBN: 978-1-84872-226-2 (hbk)
ISBN: 978-1-84872-227-9 (pbk)
ISBN: 978-1-315-84939-3 (ebk)

Typeset in Baskerville
by Saxon Graphics Ltd, Derby

Printed and bound in Great Britain by
TJ International Ltd, Padstow, Cornwall

For Rose, an inspiration for the Good Life,
full of passion, care for the world and hope for a
better future. With love and pride.

Contents

Figures

Acknowledgements

As always there are too many people to thank properly, and I apologise for any I have left out. So many have helped me to develop these ideas, have debated, read chapters or the whole text, painstakingly corrected my grammar, pointed out rudimentary errors and tried their very best, often to no avail, to get me to steer a better course. These, who of course are in no way responsible for what follows, include Anne Alvarez, Geraldine Crehan, Sue Gerhardt, Hetty Einzig, Robert Glanz, Sacha Mullins, Ed Hopkins, Juliet Hopkins, Jane O'Rourke, Toby Phillips, Roz Read and Helen Wright. Special thanks to those who went even further beyond the call of duty, particularly Jeremy Holmes, Janine Sternberg and my very good friend Paul Gordon.

A constant theme in this book is the importance of feeling that one belongs. I am a natural outsider rather than a 'belonger', but am very grateful for the health-enhancing support, care and enjoyment gained from a few groups. Huge thanks to my blokes' book club, 13 years as the same eight blokes together, we might not read as many books as some but we have great 'larks', and have shared holidays, weekends, lively nights, laughed loud, argued and are always there for each other; thanks, Alan, Danny, Graham P., Martin, Pits, Rob and Simon. I would also like to thank my colleagues and friends in my mindfulness group, particularly Ricky Emanuel, in whose inspired company I have enjoyed many journeys of discovery, as well as Asha Phillips, Beverley Tydeman, my good friend Andy Metcalf, Beatrice Bartlett and Helen Mueller, who have all helped me in body, mind and spirit. I have also valued the discussions in my evolution and psychotherapy group with John Launer, Bernadette Wren, Daniela Sieff, Michael Reiss, Jim Hopkins and Annie Swanepoel, whose ideas have all fed into this book. Special thanks too for discussions with other friends, such as John Cape, Colin Campbell, Cai Draper, Lucy Draper, Julia Granville, Rob Jones, Simon Lynne, Mike Miller and Helen Odell-Miller.

Big thanks also to Lawrence Dodgson and Teresa Robertson whose illustrations make the text so much livelier. Thanks also to all those from Psychology Press who have worked so diligently to get me to this stage, particularly Russell George, as well as to the very helpful comments by my reviewers, especially William Arsenio. Of course, deep gratitude goes to my patients who have shown me that the ideas in this book have definite substance, that when people feel better they become kinder and more open and generous. Thanks also to my colleagues at the Portman Clinic, the Tavistock Centre and the Anna Freud Centre who have so often been an inspiration.

Finally my biggest debt of gratitude is to my family, especially Sue and Rose, for their extreme forbearance, for allowing this project to leak into holidays, evenings and weekends, and for supporting me in my stressed and less than altruistic states. You really have taught me in the best way possible why the lessons from this book are so important.

Chapter 1

Introduction

This book is about fundamental issues that concern us all. What predisposes us to act kindly? Have we evolved to be selfish or cooperative? How do our moral senses form? What undermines this? How do parenting and family life shape how moral we are? What is the role of our biology or genes? What is the influence of the particular culture that we are born into? Is contemporary Western society, with its individualistic values, leading us to become less moral but more impulsive and selfish?

Questions about whether humans are fundamentally good or bad, selfish or altruistic, go back, of course, as far as known human thought, and have been debated by philosophers for as long as philosophy has been debated. Plato and Aristotle had a lot to say on these matters. The likes of Jean-Jacques Rousseau (1754) argued that people were basically born good and were ruined by society. Others such as the English philosopher Thomas Hobbes (1651) took the opposite view, that society rescued the possibility of a moral life from the throes of our baser instincts. Aristotle particularly described the Good Life, or *eudaemonia*, in terms of a life lived ethically and which also feels good, what these days we often refer to as emotional wellbeing or human 'flourishing' (Seligman 2012). This link between feeling good and doing good is borne out by much contemporary research and is a central thread throughout this book.

I wanted to write this book for a whole range of reasons. Like most people, I am both intrigued and at times unnerved by how I act towards other people. Sometimes I can be kind and generous, but neither to everyone, nor by any means consistently. At times I can be rude and cut-off, even to the people I care about most. How I act depends a lot on my mood: it is best not to ask me for a favour the day before a deadline, or when my football team goes a goal behind with five minutes to go! My actions also depend a lot on my context. I am less likely to smile at the next person I set eyes on, or offer to help someone who looks lost, after I have just been accosted rudely. My background and early experiences, and my culture and social class, have also filled me with a host of expectations, beliefs and biological predispositions to act in certain ways. I explore how new scientific research has drilled down to explain many of the drivers of such behaviours.

Another important motivation comes from my professional life as a psychotherapist working mainly with people who have experienced difficult lives, many of whom have been abused in some way. Some can act aggressively and vindictively, often without compassion or remorse. I have seen at close hand how neglect and abuse can shake a child's faith in the goodness of the world. I see day in day out how children who have been treated appallingly can be unpleasant to others, can steal, lie and be aggressive, but also that some retain and act from more humane areas of their personalities. I have also seen the profound effects of compassionate psychological understanding on children, how they become softer after a good adoption for example, blossoming and becoming likeable, kinder and more generous. I often witness how empathy and caring can flourish through psycho-therapy, and also through mindfulness practices, both of which have benefited me hugely. I have seen what the research is now unequivocal about, that stress has a powerfully negative effect on how nice we are. Any observer of nurseries, family life or work dynamics will see how, after something upsetting happens, people can transform from relaxed, playful and cooperative to tense, angry and aggressive.

This is something psychotherapists have long known about. Donald Winnicott over half a century ago (1958) wrote about what he called 'The Antisocial Tendency' and how this develops in children and adults after neglect or deprivation. John Bowlby's original findings at the Tavistock Clinic about attachment similarly showed how early emotional deprivation was common in the lives of young people in trouble with the law, then called 'juvenile delinquents' (1969). Of course such antisocial behaviour can become entrenched as character traits if countervailing influences are not in place early enough. Contemporary research sheds a powerful light on these issues.

My third area of personal motivation is a more social and political one, concerning how life in the industrial West seems to have been changing in recent decades, and the cost of this, for society as a whole, for the quality of people's lives, and also for the future of our environment. I am thinking about what prominent sociologists (Sennett 2012; Bauman and Donskis 2013) have described about life becoming faster and harsher, with less continuity and security, with community and mutual support seemingly waning, and the individual increasingly deemed more important than the group. Allied to this we have seen an increasing emphasis on material consumption, on status, fame and its symbols. Many have also made a link between business methods, financial practices geared to profit irrespective of human costs, and a lack of concern for the planet's ecosystems (Hare 1999a; Olson 2013). Although we await conclusive research about its effects, it is also likely that living in our new digital age, with constantly 'on' communications, is also having an impact on our brains and our nervous systems (Turkle 2012).

Such issues have sparked a range of debates about morality and the Good Society that I can only touch upon. I do not idealise previous societies, and one only has to think of the worlds of the Aztecs, Genghis Khan, Stalinist Russia, Pol Pot, or any supposed former pastoral idyll to realise the dangers of romanticising the past. I do, though, draw on evidence of some of the ways society has been shifting in recent decades, and also examine research about our evolutionary past, which provides an interesting counterpoint to today. However, this is not done with a view that one kind of society is any more *natural* than any other, nor with a naïve assumption that findings from one culture can just be transplanted into another without much being 'lost in translation'.

There is a powerful discourse that suggests that human beings are primarily selfish and competitive and not naturally fair or cooperative. Richard Dawkins wrote in *The Selfish Gene*:

> If you wish, as I do, to build a society in which individuals cooperate generously and unselfishly towards a common good, you can expect little help from biological nature. Let us try to teach generosity and altruism, because we are born selfish.
>
> (Dawkins 2006)

Much contemporary research suggests that this view of human nature is limited, and underestimates the extent to which we are born primed for altruism, cooperation and generosity. It would of course be naïve to suggest that selfishness, aggression and ruthless competitiveness are not part of our human psychological inheritance, albeit taking different forms in different societies. However, we also have an urgent need to understand what tips the balance of character traits in either a more selfish direction or a more selfless and cooperative one. This includes how we parent our children, and how we organise communities, institutions and society as a whole.

Discourses about whether humans are *naturally* selfish or co-operative are embedded in particular cultural and ideological belief systems and social constellations and can be the site for disputes about how we define what being human is. Some anthropological accounts have suggested that in many cultures the very dichotomy between egotism and selflessness would make little sense, particularly those in which people are much more embedded in systems of mutual obligation.

Paul Anderson, for example, argues convincingly (2008) that the idea of an opposition between selfishness and selflessness is a legacy of market-oriented societies in which individuality is uniquely valued. He and others suggest that this distinction simply does not work for most pre-industrial and sociocentric societies where, for example, personhood is defined partly in terms of group obligations, and where rituals such as gift-exchange are pervasive. This links with Jacques Derrida's argument (1992) that acts such as gift-giving inevitably create a sense of obligation in the receiver. In contemporary societies the commodity market has emerged as a sphere of self-interest the like of which was never seen in previous societies, enabling the very concepts of selfishness and altruism to take on culturally unique meanings.

Cooperation, of course, is in our DNA as much as selfishness, and as Martin Nowak (Nowak and Highfield 2011) points out, genes cannot be selfish, and anyway life on this planet has only thrived because of cooperation, whether between cells that make up an organism or between members of species, tribal groups or herds. Nowak has gone so far as to suggest that cooperation is the third principle of evolution, alongside mutation and selection. Of course some of the most successful forms of life have been extremely cooperative, such as ants and their 140,000 species.

Cooperation also comes with risks, most notably from defectors, cheats and free-riders, who work the system for their own advantage, whether these are rogue cells or people who steal or exploit others.

Long before Dawkins, people argued that humans are 'naturally' aggressive, competitive and selfish and that to live in any kind of harmony a form of social contract is needed to quell individualistic urges. For thinkers such as the English philosopher Thomas Hobbes, anarchy would prevail without such a contract, or a sovereign leader to impose the rule of law.

Sigmund Freud's influential views on human nature, for all their radicalism and innovation, are equally suggestive of a less than flattering version of our nature and dispositions. He argued that we are born with powerful urges and drives, particularly for sex and aggression, and that we are driven by an innate Pleasure Principle which if given free rein, would pose an insurmountable threat to civilisation. His solution was the internalisation of authority, via the parent, initially in the form of the Oedipus complex; in short our fear of external authority mitigates against our anarchic drive for pleasure. Yet for Freud the repression of desire comes at huge personal cost, in particular sexual repression and neurosis of many kinds.

Thinkers such as Freud helpfully keep us aware of our selfish and destructive potential, but also take insufficient account of human altruism or generosity. Supposedly good motives are often deemed untrustworthy, because self-interest is seen as inevitably lurking in the wings. This is enshrined in the famous statement by Michael Ghiselin (1974): 'scratch an altruist and watch a hypocrite bleed'. This belief was dubbed by Frans de Waal as 'veneer theory' (De Waal 2008), the idea that morality and care for others are but a superficial gloss and not to be trusted.

Some new research insightfully suggests that certain forms of altruism can be deemed pathological and help neither the helper nor the recipient (Oakley *et al.* 2012). This includes how some highly anxious people try to buy affection with gifts, while others force their help on unwilling recipients. It is argued that we *should* be primarily self-interested, and it is only from the strivings of untrammelled individuals that important developments occur. The novelist and supporter of libertarian market economic models, Ayn Rand, stated, 'If any civilization is to survive, it is the morality of altruism that men have to reject' (Rand 1984).

Such thinking fits neatly alongside some evolutionary ideas of which Thomas Huxley (1984) was maybe the first major exponent. He believed that morality can be cultivated and consciously chosen by humans but is not natural. His evolutionary theory was quite different to that of Darwin (1860), who in fact made more space for sympathetic emotions. Much evolutionary thinking has argued that we tend to look after 'number one', and also by extension, those who share our genes. Altruism in this way of thinking is at best 'reciprocal' (Trivers 2002). In reciprocal altruism I will help you but only because you might later help me in return, and most importantly, if it will increase the chance of my genes being passed on to another generation.

As we will see, much new research is suggesting that this is by no means the whole story. We do have selfish, base and competitive instincts, but also selfless, moral, altruistic and prosocial personality traits. These are not just a superficial gloss. I am not arguing for a naïve theory about human beings being 'sugar and spice and all things nice', but the contrary views underestimate our potential for *better* behaviour, whatever we mean by that. I think we can reframe the idea of an innate battle within the human soul between good and bad, selfishness and selflessness, by looking hard at what factors tilt any person, or indeed any organisation or society, in one or other direction. This means understanding what brings these potentials out, both at an individual and a social level.

Much exciting research casts new light on these subjects. This comes from a variety of academic fields, many of whose representatives would barely have communicated with each other until recently. These include brain science, evolutionary, social and developmental psychology, attachment theory, as well as psychoanalysis and systems theories and a host of social sciences.

Much evidence also comes from neuroscience, a field still very much in its infancy, and one for which too many grand claims are often prematurely made. It is important to be circumspect in discussing the claims of both neurobiological research, and much psychology experimentation. Brain scans only show us so much, such as the extent of blood flow in certain brain regions, and often use worryingly small samples (Button *et al.* 2013), claiming more certainty than is often justified. Psychology research is often done with atypical samples such as university students, and many findings are not convincingly replicated. Both often naïvely assume they are researching universal qualities rather than states of mind which might be specific to our culture, or indeed to a specific moment. None the less, while scepticism is needed, techniques for investigating how our brains function, as well as innovative psychology research protocols, have enabled us to develop genuinely helpful understandings, which I draw upon.

I start our research journey in the next chapter by showing how being kind and caring are a natural part of what most humans spontaneously do, and that being generous and altruistic fires reward circuits in our brains. We see at what a very young age infants and toddlers will actively offer help, distinguish between good and bad behaviour and empathically reach out to others.

Next we see how our early attachment relationships have a huge effect on how moral, altruistic and caring we become, and how abusive or neglectful experiences inhibit moral and empathic urges. This leads us, in Chapter 4, to examine how helping others depends on being able to empathise and understand other minds, which in turn depends on sensitive early parenting, without which generosity, caring and trust rarely develop. Here I unpick some of the different motivations behind actions that come under the heading of altruism.

I next look at important research about the stress system. We see how the most deprived and abused in our society too commonly struggle to find a place within it. New research shows how those receiving an onslaught of bad experiences can become psychobiologically programmed to live with huge levels of fear, tension and anxiety, while others can become cold and fearless in a cut-off way. Both kinds of states of mind inhibit the ability to care for others.

From here I look at impulsiveness and low levels of emotional regulation, and the effect of this on how people relate to others. This includes looking at what can give rise to the form of impulsive behaviour seen in people who display 'hot-headed' reactive aggression and cannot seem to control themselves. I also look in Chapter 7 at colder, more callous forms of aggression, such as in psychopaths. Some suggest (e.g. Stout 2007; Hare and Babiak 2007) that these are on the increase in contemporary life, alongside a serious decline in empathy (Konrath, O'Brien and Hsing 2011) and an increase in narcissism (Twenge and Campbell 2009). If so these are serious issues.

Psychopaths are an extreme example of people who do not empathise, and who rely on reason and logic more than feeling.

This pull between reason and emotion is described in Chapter 8 and is also a central thread throughout this book. Psychology for a long time had stressed the role of cognition and reason in morality (e.g. Kohlberg 1976; Turiel 2002; Piaget 1965), but in recent years the role of care (Gilligan 1977) and emotion (Haidt 2012) has been returned to the heart of moral understanding. There is a big difference between actions driven by emotional states such as compassion and empathy, and those motivated by abstract moral principles.

Neuroscience has entered this debate. We have learnt that those with different activity in brain areas central to emotional processing often have very different moral responses to most of us (Damasio 1999). Studies of stroke victims, brain scans of criminals, and much other research help unpick such matters. We also see that, while emotion is central to morality, a morality without reason and thought, and just based on gut reactions, is a diminished one, and can lead to all kinds of discrimination and prejudice.

We look in Chapter 9 at how neurobiology and hormonal systems are programmed not only by genes but also by experiences, and how this affects how generous, trusting and prosocial we are. Thus experiences of family life, and also cultural expectancies, are written into both our belief systems and our very body states. Next I look at the work of evolutionary anthropologists (e.g. Boehm 2012; Wilson 2012) who seek the origins of many of our more cooperative and moral behaviours in our hunter-gatherer pasts. There is recent evidence that altruistic traits and the ability to form close bonds within groups were extremely important for surviving in the environments in which much human evolution occurred.

In Chapter 11 I look at research using experimental game theory to illustrate how we are born wired for altruism. We see how acts of kindness and generosity are common even in one-off anonymous encounters (Delton et al. 2011). This is a challenge to the theories of human nature propounded by economists; if standard economic theory was right it would always make more sense to feather one's own nest.

Close, coherent and loyal groups seem to have the edge over less cohesive ones in which in-fighting is rife, and it is to group life I turn in Chapter 12. Our tendency to cooperate and fit in is extraordinary. We feel happier, and indeed have longer and healthier lives, when we are members of close communities and groups. Yet we should be wary of idealising groups and belonging.

To be 'like us' means that there are others who are 'not like us', and we have a huge propensity to be prejudiced against people whom we classify as different and 'other'.

In Chapter 13 I look at some of the ways in which social cohesion and cultural norms are enforced, through processes such as teasing, gossip and overt punishment. I ask what motivates us to act well, looking at drivers such as the importance of our reputations. Finally I spend a bit of time examining the impact of some contemporary social trends, such as the rise of more consumerist and materialistic values, on how moral and other-centred people act. I examine how social changes might be affecting values, belief systems and behaviours. I also look at how social changes might be affecting the very balance of our brains, particularly that between our two cerebral hemispheres. I question whether we are living in a culture in which left hemisphere, more rational functions are becoming increasingly dominant, at great human cost (McGilchrist 2010).

Certain terms crop up throughout the book which need defining, such as altruism and prosociality. I define altruism as an act that is done for another's welfare. Rather than engage in too much debate about whether 'pure' altruism exists, I define altruism to include acts which might bring inadvertent benefits to the altruistic person, such as the warm glow one feels, or the likelihood of being thought well of. However, the *primary* motivation of an altruistic act should be to help another, and so acts which seem mainly aimed, for example, at enhancing one's reputation, would not count. This is different from the stronger more self-sacrificing definitions of altruism derived from Auguste Comte (1966), who first coined the term. By prosocial I mean basically the opposite of antisocial, describing acts which aim to help another person or a community or society. Prosocial is an ungainly word, but I can find no alternative to describe that set of acts which encompasses behaviours such as generosity, cooperation, helping and sharing, for example.

I am all too aware that terms like altruism have a particular cultural and historical resonance. We increasingly live in a world in which understanding starts with the individual, in which society or groups are seen as collections of separate selves. This is a very culturally specific view, rooted in contemporary forms of social organisation. It risks underestimating both how formed we are by our social environments, and indeed how society and culture are written into the very fabric of our beings. Other, more sociocentric cultures, do not have quite the same distinctions. An overly individualistic conception also sidesteps the value many place on group and collective action, such as in political movements.

I do not dwell much on acts of extraordinary altruism and self-sacrifice, such as brave fire-fighters and soldiers risking their lives, German citizens hiding Jews from Nazis, or the saintly behaviours of the likes of Mother Theresa. These maybe speak for themselves but we will see how less grand yet very real acts of altruism tend to pervade social life, and we will look at where the roots of such behaviours might lie.

While many of the findings I describe are new, the old philosophical debates are as alive and hotly debated as ever, but with a new and growing knowledge base. Political differences are argued out on the basis of such ideas. Many on the right might distrust left-leaning tendencies to care for the weak and the needy. Those on the left often have little time for loyalty and tradition. Indeed the recent work of Jonathan Haidt (2012) adds another dimension in showing that left-leaning liberals and the conservative right not only disagree about moral values, but generally even conceptualise what is defined as morality differently.

This book aims to ask, and begin to answer, important questions about human nature, and how that nature is shaped by cultures and social practices, whether parenting, a society's belief systems or the kind of institutions it develops. I bring together a host of exciting new scientific discoveries, and also some older but still too little-known ideas, to help make sense of what leads humans to act antisocially or prosocially. By 'human' I mean to encompass both the narrower scientific meaning of us as a biological species, but also something slightly more nebulous, signifying what we mean by acting with humanity, indeed the opposite of what is often referred to as being 'inhuman'.

A central thesis running throughout this book is that feeling good and being good need not be in conflict. Indeed, to state this more strongly, generally the better loved and cared for one feels, and the more one feels safe, and part of a community, then the better one tends to feel both about oneself and others, and the more likely one is to be kind and generous. Feeling good and being good, we will see, in fact feed off each other. The opposite is also true, as my clinical practice with abused and traumatised children and young offenders too often teaches. Our prisons and psychiatric systems sadly house too many such people. Most have never been given the psychological building blocks to manage interpersonal relationships, rarely feel much psychological wellbeing, struggle to empathise, and can be seen as not 'very nice'. For those who have suffered in this way, not feeling good and not doing good often go come together.

The new research about morality has not made anything simpler. The complexity of human development remains undiminished, but we are finding that there are new answers to many ancient questions. Moral psychology, once a rather dull branch of psychology, seems to be transforming into one of its most vibrant and exciting fields. This book aims to tap into that excitement to present ground-breaking research about how we can reconceptualise moral life.

Chapter 2

Primed for goodness

Genuinely other-centred motives?

This chapter shows how propensities to be moral and kind are 'online' surprisingly early in life. This is not to deny that we are all born with tendencies to be selfish, aggressive and competitive, nor that human nature has been shown in nearly every known culture to have a capacity for deception, selfishness, ruthlessness, violence, cold-blooded warfare and worse. The conflict between our self-interest and the interests of others is only too real, and there is often good reason to distrust seemingly altruistic motives. I am not proud to say that research shows consistently that we males often become considerably more generous in the presence of attractive females, a generosity not born simply of being bigger hearted (e.g. Van Vugt and Iredale 2012). The sceptics have a point, which I return to later. For now though I will show that, as well as such unsavoury character traits, humans have an inbuilt propensity to be generous, helpful and moral. Later we will see how bad experiences and stressful environments turn off these capacities and exaggerate antisocial traits.

I began writing this on holiday, after driving back with friends from a beach, along a sandy rutted route where I managed to get our car stuck in a nasty ditch. One driver came near, peered at us and drove on. Next a group of cyclists came by, who at first nervously slowed, then stopped and offered to help. Soon there was a whole crowd of helpers, and a range of views and complex advice was being offered, angles assessed and soon sand was being dug, stones and boulders placed strategically until the car was pushed, lifted and liberated, with much mutual pleasure and great camaraderie. None of us knew each other, nor were any of us likely to meet again. It was not obviously in any of their *self*-interest to do this. However, I think we all felt better in ourselves and about the world afterwards. There might have been a range of motives here, but they included a wish to help, and an enjoyment of the process. We have, perhaps surprisingly, found that such an urge to help is present from a really young age. In one of a range of ingeniously simple but very rigorous experiments by Michael Tomasello and his colleagues at the Max Planck Institute in Leipzig (Warneken and Tomasello 2008) an adult is walking across a room and pretends to drop an object. Fifteen-month-old toddlers consistently come over and pick up the object and pass it to the adult. In another variant an adult places a pile of books into a cupboard, goes back for more but has seemingly inadvertently closed the cupboard door, and on returning does not have a hand free with which to open it. Once again these toddlers cannot help but get up to open the cupboard. Such toddlers demonstrate a clear wish to help, and for no obvious ulterior reason.

Such sympathy for those in distress and reaching out to them is seen in infants as young as ten months old (Kanakogi *et al.* 2013). After watching one animated figure hurt another, infants spontaneously reached out for the victim rather than the aggressor or a neutral figure. Here and in Tomasello's experiments we witness an intrinsic tendency for what Daniel Batson calls 'empathy-induced altruism' (Batson 2011). Here the act of helping is spontaneous, genuine and indeed pleasurable and provides its own reward. For this to happen a few conditions must be in place. Most notably the infant or toddler needs to be in a sufficiently relaxed and safe state of mind and, I think also, to have had enough attuned parenting early on for a basic capacity for empathy to develop.

When Tomasello and his fellow experimenters split toddlers into two groups and rewarded, with toys and smiles, just one of the two groups of children who had helped an adult, those who received no reward (and had no idea other children were offered rewards) next time spontaneously and generously helped the most (Warneken and Tomasello 2008). The rewarded ones lost interest in helping. When mentioning this research, people have queried whether the unrewarded children keep trying 'selfishly' in order to get a reward. In fact, as Michael Tomasello told me, 'The kids in the No Reward never got any reward for 14 trials. Only the most resilient children would keep trying more than a few times.' The reward was in the act of helping.

We know from many studies that being *extrinsically* rewarded for being good, such as with money or valued objects, is not as rewarding as the *intrinsic* rewards gained from undertaking an altruistic and generous act. Helping others fires reward circuits in our brains (Moll *et al.* 2005); it makes us feel good. On the other hand, doing something for an ulterior motive, such as a financial reward for an adult or a toy for a child, is just not as intrinsically rewarding. Indeed recent studies of toddlers under two years old showed that they even felt happier when giving treats to others than when receiving them themselves. Not only that, they were happier if the gift was costly and they gave up some of their own resources for another person rather than giving a treat at no cost to themselves (Aknin *et al.* 2012). Altruism and happiness are surprisingly interlinked.

We also know this from research with adults. Blood donations often decrease when donors begin to be paid for them, for example (Costa-Font *et al.* 2012). When we actively choose to donate money voluntarily, then reward circuits fire up in the brain similar to when we get a reward for ourselves (Harbaugh *et al.* 2007).

Ori Brafman, an organisational consultant from San Francisco, and his brother Rom, a psychologist, have helped us to see that few of us are motivated only by extrinsic rewards, but we often are motivated by doing what we feel is right (Brafman and Brafman 2008). They described how Swiss authorities tried to tempt some of its citizens to accept a nuclear waste dump situated near their town, by offering financial compensation. The good citizens refused and their refusals became more steadfast as the financial offers increased.

The Brafmans have also found that specific brain-based reward centres fired (such as the posterior superior temporal sulcus) when high scores were achieved in games and high scores meant more money going to charity as opposed to their own pockets. However, when the same game was played but this time the financial rewards were kept by the players instead of going to charity, then the nucleus accumbens was fired up. This is a very different part of the brain and its activation can feel rather like taking a small dose of cocaine, and is linked to the release of the hormone dopamine and potentially addictive behaviours. The nucleus accumbens is a more primitive brain area, related to a 'wilder' side, such as in exuberant triumph, very different from the warm glow that altruism brings.

There is often a conflict for any of us between the warm glow of giving and the buzz of personal reward. Pleasure-seeking can often win out, and our seeking systems (Panksepp 2004), for which dopamine is central, drive us to acquire things such as the latest gadget, car, handbag or kitchen. However, research suggests that acquiring such goods does not generally bestow a sense of wellbeing, whereas being generous and altruistic actually does. Despite often trying to make ourselves feel better by buying new outfits or gadgets, research suggests that better feelings come with spending more on *others*. Indeed, international studies have found that happiness levels across countries are firmly linked with how much people value prosocial giving and helping others (Aknin *et al.* 2013). Being helpful even increases our health and prolongs our lives, especially in older people (Brown, Smith *et al.* 2009). Helping others feels so good that it is even used as a treatment for some people with Obsessive Compulsive Disorder, who live richer lives after being encouraged to help others (Keltner 2009).

Innate morality

We are born with inbuilt inclinations to be helpful and indeed also for being moral, findings that are a counterweight to our equally innate selfish potentials. Infancy researcher Robert Emde suggested that we need a concept of a *we-go* alongside that of the infant *ego* (Emde 2009). It was not so long ago that most psychologists believed that children did not develop any kind of moral capacity until quite late in childhood, and that we were born egocentric, as the great Swiss psychologist Jean Piaget had suggested. Not for the first time psychology underrated the extraordinary capacities of infants.

Babies between three and five months can tell the difference between nice and nasty behaviour, as the research by Kiley Hamlin and Karen Wynn (2010) at Yale University showed in a series of fascinating studies. Using video animations and puppets, they presented stories to babies. The protagonists were goodies and baddies. In one story someone was trying really hard to open a box, but annoyingly the partially opened lid automatically closed of its own accord. Babies were then later shown two alternative scenarios. In one a goody came along and helped the box stay open, while in the other, when after a great struggle the puppet opened the lid, a nasty character arrived and slammed it firmly shut again. Babies as young as five months old, when given the choice after the experiment, nearly always chose the good puppet over the bad one. The same results have been found using lots of other stories and characters, and carefully controlling for a range of factors. Amazingly babies as young as three months also prefer the kind characters; at that age they cannot reach out for their preferred character but they look longer at it. This is a striking finding. It seems that we are born endowed with some clear pull towards good behaviour and even a rudimentary moral value system.

Babies look longer, in surprise, if sympathetic and friendly characters make friendly moves towards nasty ones; it seems that infants are aghast that anyone would approach someone who had done them harm. They do not look so long if the approach is towards the friendly figure; they seem to understand that it does not make sense to approach a scary person. Thus babies of only a few months have some understanding of what we might call good and bad behaviour.

It would be interesting to know what babies who have already suffered cruelty or abuse do in such situations. In one of the few studies linking parenting styles and helping behaviour, children watched as a mother and baby climbed some steps. The baby could not keep up, got upset and started to cry. In one version the mother returned for the baby, and in the other the baby was just left. Securely attached children, who have had more attuned parenting, showed evident surprise when the baby was left, but the insecure children had the opposite reaction, showing surprise when the mother returned to her children (Johnson *et al.* 2007). Clearly the expectation of helpful behaviour is built on previous experiences. Good experiences are maybe necessary for our innate altruistic tendencies to come alive.

Thus children and even babies can clearly distinguish between antisocial and prosocial behaviours. This is about preferring *good* rather than nice behaviour. Eight-month-olds prefer puppets that are horrible to nasty characters over the puppets that are nice to them. Babies like nice behaviour, but not if being nice is to a bad person (Bloom 2010).

Understanding another's intentions, as the babies in these experiments did, is essential for making moral decisions or judgements. Deliberately pushing someone, as opposed to unintentionally knocking them over, will be judged differently by most of us. A court of law wants to know if the accused intended to hurt the victim or did so accidentally. The babies in these experiments clearly made sense of the intentions of the characters, and acted on this understanding. This sophisticated skill of reading intentions and other minds, which I delve further into in the next chapter, is the bedrock of being a social person, enabling fitting into whatever social group one happens to find oneself in.

We even see a sense of fairness at such young ages (Sloane *et al.* 2012). In a typical experiment, some animated giraffes were placed in front of 15-month-olds and along came a character with some toys, and the giraffes showed excitement. When the toys were shared equally the babies barely reacted, seemingly because they expected fairness. However, if one giraffe got much more than the other, then the babies stared for longer and tended to look perturbed. These same researchers found that when two people were equally rewarded for a task, but one of them was not pulling their weight, then 21-month-olds stared for longer, presumably in surprise or bemusement, protesting that this was not right. Indeed, verbal three-year-olds actively state that rewarding shirkers is unfair (Kanngiesser and Warneken 2012).

Fairness, and anger at unfairness, runs deep. Eighteen-month-olds watched an unknown adult draw a picture. When the person who did the drawing left the room another adult snatched and tore up the picture (Vaish *et al.* 2009). All the children showed expressions of concern but showed none when a blank piece of paper was torn up. This was empathy and concern about mistreatment.

Not all babies respond in exactly the same way and some are more perplexed by unfairness than others, looking for longer at such unexpected behaviour (Schmidt and Sommerville 2011). These are babies who are more altruistic and generous and, for example, willingly give up their favourite toy if someone else asks for it. A million-dollar question is whether some babies are just born more altruistic or whether parenting makes the difference. We will look at these issues later.

Summary

We have seen how very young infants and toddlers act from what seem to be moral urges, whether preferring good characters or being impelled to help adults in need. This is maybe what the psychoanalyst Donald Winnicott meant by 'the innate morality of babies' (Winnicott 1996), whereby infants are not rule-bound but are driven by deep and indeed authentic feelings, such as we saw in Tomasello's toddlers who could not stop themselves helping. Infants of just a few months have an emergent sense of morality and justice, a capacity for empathy, for punishment, for making sense of other minds and for working out what is wanted and expected by others. These are all needed to become a moral being and function optimally as a member of a social group.

We noted how this human wish to help, cooperate and contribute to the welfare of others is such a strong feature of adult life, something that I come back to often in this book. We are a group species, primed from birth to imbibe and fit into cultural and social rules. Understanding other people's expectations and intentions is fundamental to such fitting in, and to altruistic moral tendencies. We see later how those who suffer neglect and abuse generally have much less ability to understand their own and other minds. Neither legal systems, nor most people's personal morality, support the principle of punishing unintentional or accidental acts, and we decide whether an act is intentional through our mind-reading skills, which we now know even relatively young infants can manage (Vaish et al. 2010).

Maybe it is not surprising that we humans are so sensitive to issues of fairness from such a young age, given that we are such a hyper-social group species, and have evolved to be adept at working out who we can and cannot trust, who to make alliances with and who to avoid. We also feel greatly rewarded when cooperating and being helpful. One can only assume that such reward systems have evolved because there has been an evolutionary advantage to working well with others in close-knit groups and relying on our fellow group members.

A major question for this book though is what conditions give rise to the expression of such altruistic, empathic and moral capacities, as opposed to the more nasty potential character traits we know exist in all of us. One of the central factors in determining how empathic, altruistic and prosocial people become is the quality of early relationships and the kind of attachment patterns that people develop. It is to this that I turn next. People with the most worrying attachment styles tend to show less empathy and spontaneous helpfulness. When we feel loved, safe and trusting then kindness and helpfulness tend to increase, and they tend to decrease when we are stressed or angry or frightened.

Chapter 3

Attachments and helping others

Relationship patterns as adaptations

We are an extraordinarily adaptive species. We can adapt to life in Saharan heat, the freezing Arctic and high altitudes. We can make social and family lives in as diverse environments as small hunter-gatherer bands, peasant societies, whether born to wealth and privilege or inner-city deprivation, in each using very different traits to get by. We similarly have a range of strategies to cope with the variety of emotional climates that we might find ourselves in. If we are born into a loving, kind and sensitive family we will develop different interpersonal strategies, emotional beliefs and biological responsiveness to those born into a household where anger and aggression are rife. The kinds of templates we develop for relating to others, including how trusting, empathic or altruistic we are, develop initially within our first environments, normally our families, while family relational patterns in turn are in part determined by cultural and socioeconomic influences. Our attachment patterns and our very neurobiology get laid down alongside cultural and social expectations.

Like many species, we humans need to fit into our environment or risk not surviving, and attachment patterns, our ingrained templates for relating to others, are basically adaptations to such early settings. In humans and other mammals early experiences give rise to a form of programming. Any mammal born into a frightening environment will be more stressed, anxious and jumpy, and their brains and hormonal systems will form accordingly. Being wary and vigilant, and not too relaxed, will likely aid the chances of survival in a violent environment in which being too relaxed and chilled out will probably end badly. Rats or monkeys raised in threatening circumstances have higher levels of stress hormones, an easily aroused sympathetic nervous system, and they also play less, groom each other less, are less exploratory and as adults become less attentive parents (Parker and Maestripieri 2011). These are profound effects.

I have spent much of my professional life working with both children and adults who have suffered difficult early experiences. What has struck me for a long time, and what the research is starting to explain, is that many who had emotionally depriving or abusive early relationships do not develop high levels of empathy and are often not the most popular of children or adults. Too many end up in prisons, psychiatric systems and outside the mainstream of society. Their ways of behaving might be seen as maladaptive by mental health and other professionals, but in fact their behaviours can be viewed as adaptive for their particular early environments.

Take 24-year-old Nicholas as an example. He was quite a loner, and came to see me for therapy at the behest of his girlfriend, in fact his first ever girlfriend, who insisted he came or the relationship would end. She complained that he was distant, ungiving, cold and unresponsive. Nicholas indeed seemed cut-off and out of touch with his own and other people's feelings. Although details of his early life are sketchy, he reported an isolated and very asocial life. His parents were lower-middle-class English people, to whom the world of emotions was rather alien. He reported having few friends at school, and spent a lot of time in his room alone, playing games. His emotional world was flat, his skin colour pallid and he lacked liveliness and vigour. He reported incidents that most people would find upsetting but which he described as if mundane affairs, or with comments like 'well, you just have to get on with it'. These included, for example, the death of his younger sister.

Nicholas seems very like other children with similar presentations who tend to be described as *avoidant* in terms of their predominant attachment style. Attachment theory was developed at the Tavistock Clinic in London, by John Bowlby in the 1950s (Holmes 1993), and is now maybe the world's foremost body of research about child development. In an attachment experiment that has been replicated countless times, the Strange Situation Test (Ainsworth 1978), infants of about a year are observed when their mothers leave the room, then when they interact with a stranger who comes in, and also when their mother returns. Those with secure attachments, who most of us see as the most emotionally healthy, cry and protest and are disturbed when their mothers leave, but they quickly calm down on their mothers' return. Children with primarily avoidant relationships, and one might hypothesise that Nicholas was one of these, barely react when their mothers leave, or when the mother returns. They seem extraordinarily self-contained.

As a therapist I have seen many adults and children with similar presentations (Music 2009). Many sit in the back of classrooms unnoticed and have few friends. They have often suffered emotional neglect and then in turn are neglected later by both other children and adults, in part due to their cut-off quality. Nicholas certainly did not evoke a warm response in many around him, or even an interested one.

What is most predictive of attachment patterns is not inborn temperament or genetic inheritance, but rather the kind of parenting a child receives (Prior and Glaser 2006). Some adults, maybe like Nicholas' parents, find strong emotions like crying too difficult to bear. If their baby cries, this cry might be ignored, or worse, the child might be admonished or rejected. Any baby or child wants to be emotionally understood, but what an infant needs even more than this is to ensure that they are not rejected. Without this their chances of surviving, let alone thriving, are greatly reduced. Thus such babies learn to quell any urge to express strong emotions in order to be accepted by the people they depend on.

When we observe such avoidant babies in these experiments it is hard to believe that they are at all worried by their mother's absence; they look like they do not care. However, if we take measures of stress, such as heart rate, we see that they are showing the same physiological reactivity as the babies who actively protest. They have seemingly already learnt to cut off from the signals that their body is giving them. In such children the capacity for empathy and generosity is quite curtailed and as adults they tend to be held in and less big hearted or helpful. This style of emotional presentation is sometimes called *deactivated* (Holmes 2009). As adults they tend to think of themselves as self-sufficient, and to approve of that trait in others too.

Such attachment styles link to how caring of others people become. For example, avoidant adults rely on others less and engage in less voluntary and community activities. This is almost definitely an extremely sensible adaptation to their first environment, their family of origin. However, unless they have lots of contact with alternative more emotionally attuned adults, such patterns are likely to stick, and their neurobiology will become programmed by these early experiences. Thus sometimes it is adaptive to be cold and unempathic, as presumably it was for Nicholas in his family of origin, even if not with his new girlfriend.

Measuring attachment

The avoidant attachment that Nicholas demonstrated is just one attachment style. The best known and researched versions of attachment theory tend to differentiate attachment styles into four main kinds, often called avoidant, ambivalent, secure and disorganised. These styles are measured at about a year old via the Strange Situation Test mentioned earlier. This test is so illuminating because it builds on the fact that infants experience stranger anxiety at eight or nine months, and that a baby's response to this anxiety is hugely revealing of what they already expect from relationships. It predicts how they are likely to interact with other adults and children in nursery or school, and to what extent they believe that the world is a safe and reliable place. It is predictive of how cooperative, prosocial and empathic they will be and how they respond to distress in others.

Children who at a year have a securely attached style with their primary caregiver will cry when their mother leaves the room, will not feel comforted by a stranger, but when Mother returns they will quickly calm, and return to playing in a trice, the signs of the painful separation no longer being visible. Such children are more likely to have had sensitive and attuned parenting of a kind that is often described as mind-minded (Meins *et al.* 2002), in which their feelings are empathised with and they have been helped to make sense of their psychological states. They also tend to become kinder and more generous children and adults, and get on better with others.

The securely attached child's sense of trust in the world comes from learning that they will be responded to when they are distressed or fearful. When the securely attached toddler toddles off and then suddenly gets anxious there will be the secure base of the mother or another trusted person to return to. Because they trust that their secure base is there when needed, they can explore with confidence. Through having their minds and emotions understood, they tend to become more self-aware and in touch with their own thoughts and feelings, and also become more empathic of other people's feelings.

Some parents, though, are inconsistent and unpredictable, loving one minute and maybe angry the next. Their children do not develop the same sense of safety and security as securely attached children, but nor are they cut-off like avoidant children. If our parent has an extremely volatile or changeable personality, and if we do not know when they will be in a happy or furious mood, and cannot predict whether they will be there when we need them, then we are likely to become watchful, wary, and less confident that things will work out well.

In the Strange Situation test, when the parent leaves, a one-year-old child with such an ambivalent attachment will show upset, but they would already have been vigilant before the parent left and would not easily calm on their parent's return. They remain anxious, clingy and on the alert, lacking confidence that their needs will be met. We tend to call them *hyperactivating* in contrast to more dampened-down *deactivated* avoidant children. Hyperactivating children can be quite good at picking up emotional cues, such as whether a parent or partner is in a friendly or aggressive mood. This mind-reading is not the same as empathy or genuinely putting themselves in the other's shoes. They might be overly concerned with other people's feelings and, as children, often develop beliefs that they are responsible for their parent's moods. As adults they might be kind to a friend or their boss to curry favour, to keep the other person on their side or to avoid confrontation. However, they reach out less to others in distress and their seemingly kind acts often have more self-interested motives.

Neither those with avoidant nor ambivalent attachment styles manage as much genuine empathy as a securely attached person. Our attachment styles describe our dominant modes of relating, although different environments will also draw out different propensities in us. It is possible, maybe with the help of a therapist, new relationships or other major life-changes, that we can shift into other modes of relating. Despite this, attachment styles are reasonably stable and measureable character traits. If Nicholas had had a fun-loving and emotionally attuned father alongside a cut-off mother he might have been more able to access an empathic and playful side. Our attachment patterns are not life-sentences but are normally quite constant. They also profoundly influence the extent to which we show empathy and compassion or are likely to be helpful or kind.

Some children who have suffered even worse trauma can develop an attachment style which is generally called disorganised (Main and Solomon 1990). Often their parents are both frightened and frightening, show little mind-mindedness and are more inconsistent than even parents of ambivalently attached children. In fact they are often downright abusive, sometimes inflicting quite shocking experiences on their children. The real tragedy is that these children are not only brought up with no sense of safety or consistency, but worse, the person who they are designed to turn to for help when danger looms, the secure base we need when in trouble, is the very person who is perpetrating the abusive and traumatic experiences. This is an awful predicament as there is nowhere safe to turn. Such children have the worst prognosis of all (Prior and Glaser 2006), and often end up, for example, in the criminal justice or psychiatric systems.

Very typical was Bernie. His mother was a prostitute, his father a violent pimp; he witnessed a huge amount of inappropriate sexual behaviour as well as terrible violence. By the time I saw him, at six years old, he had already been thrown out of two schools, his foster placement was at risk of breaking down, he was constantly getting into fights, had no friends and professionals were very worried. As the psychoanalyst and infancy researcher Beatrice Beebe has shown, such patterns can start to develop in children as young as four months of age (Beebe and Lachmann 2013). They are attempts by children to adapt to their environment, however awful. If your parents are angry and very intrusive, it is neither sensible nor safe to be too open and trusting. These children have highly charged stress systems, often cannot even look in their mothers' eyes, and are wary and vigilant, watching but not trusting. For them the world is certainly not a safe place and all too often they become unpredictable and aggressive, lacking compassion, empathy and cooperativeness.

Attachment and patterns of helping

Mario Mikulincer has shown in a series of studies that one's attachment style is very predictive of how prosocial, generous or altruistic one will be (Mikulincer *et al.* 2005; Erez *et al.* 2008; Mikulincer and Shaver 2010). Adults with secure styles, for example, are more likely to donate to charity, volunteer, spontaneously help others in distress, look after the elderly, give blood and they are generally more 'other-focused'. Yet their focus on others is not of an anxious kind; they do not feel the need to keep others happy to gain approval but rather genuinely care for people's plight. They are also more sensitive and responsive as romantic partners. The attachment styles we form are predictive of how we act morally.

On the other hand, when people with primarily anxious ambivalent attachment styles help, they often do this for ulterior motives, such as self-enhancement or to gain approval (Erez *et al.* 2008). They tend to be extremely sensitive to social disapproval and their sense of self-worth depends disproportionately on others' opinions. Their cooperativeness is often not driven by a real commitment to a group but more by a wish to be accepted. Such character traits form in childhood due to inconsistent and unpredictable parenting styles. Julie was like this, a woman in her forties who came to therapy after a painful series of rejections. She was almost entirely unaware of her own needs but constantly looking out for how she could help others; if others were happy then she too felt safe. The help she gave had an edge to it. She was overly solicitous to me, constantly checking out how I felt, but I never felt that she cared as much about the other person as about how much she was appreciated.

Of course we can all shift between different states of mind, and are not confined to just one style of relating, but we tend to have predominant styles. A more anxious and needy style might for example be triggered by a work environment where disapproval and rewards are inconsistently meted out and where one has to stay on one's toes to survive. Attachment styles can be triggered artificially and Mikulincer found that this has quite an effect on compassionate and altruistic tendencies. When some people were encouraged to remember an experience of being kindly looked after as a child, and others were asked to remember either more neutral experiences, or ordinarily positive ones, it was those *primed* with positive attachment stories who became more compassionate to outsiders. Indeed, just triggering a memory of such a figure increased the likelihood of someone taking the place of another person who was evidently in distress. Similarly in another experiment Israeli Jews became kinder to Israeli Arabs in a food-sharing experiment when they had been primed with memories of a secure attachment figure. Secure attachment enhances empathy, compassion and altruism and is likely to lead to generosity and kindness (Mikulincer and Shaver 2007).

There is very little evidence that one's temperament or genetic inheritance affects one's attachment style. Most of the evidence points in the opposite direction, that a parent's capacity for mind-mindedness, empathy and emotional sensitivity predicts this (Prior and Glaser 2006). However, there have been some suggestions from recent research that genes in combination with parenting influence how attachment styles manifest themselves (Bakermans-Kranenburg *et al.* 2011), and that genes will be found to be more influential than had previously been thought (Fearon 2013). Attachment styles at a year alone do not predict adult ways of relating and much change can take place between childhood and adulthood. This is often explained by what are sometimes called 'lawful discontinuities' (Sroufe 2005), whereby new experiences, such as a very good adoption of an abused child, or the opposite, reasonably sensitive parents becoming highly stressed, might lead to a child adapting to such new parenting styles. Indeed a Dutch study found with an adoptive sample that there was continuity of attachment from infancy to adolescence only when parenting remained sensitive throughout childhood (Beijersbergen *et al.* 2012). Interestingly, as this was a sample of adopted people, genes would have played a negligible role.

Different temperaments do have some effect, but the most important factor is the degree of sensitivity a parent shows. A recent long-term study looked very carefully at infant temperament at birth and at six months old, and also examined the way in which mothers interacted with these children when they had become toddlers. To their surprise the inborn temperament of the children did not predict later behaviours. However, what did predict aggressive behaviours was the level of conflict at home and the degree of hostility and aggression observed in mothers towards their toddlers (Lorber and Egeland 2011). The children subjected to harsh and critical parenting by the time they were at school were becoming unmanageable, had few friends, showed little empathy and were already a disruptive influence. Such antisocial children would not have been securely attached, nor would they have been likely to feel very good about themselves.

Secure attachment relationships on the other hand are characterised by mutual enjoyment, sensitivity and reciprocity. Grazyna Kochanska from the University of Iowa studied the development of conscience in over 3,000 toddlers. She found that those who had more security-enhancing experiences were more likely to embrace the values of their family and immediate culture, were more responsive to those around them and more cooperative as they got older (Kochanska et al. 2010).

She also found (Kochanska and Kim 2012) that insecure mother–child pairs were marked by high levels of mutual anger and coercion, with the parents more likely to assert power and control over unwilling children. Such children were assessed by both teachers and parents to be more anger-prone, more likely to break rules, more antisocial, and more callous and oppositional; none of this was true of secure mother–infant dyads. Children who have more difficult temperaments are likely to be more oppositional, but with responsive parenting they become self-regulated and their potential oppositional personalities are reined in (Kim and Kochanska 2012).

Life-history adaptations

We are all the time adapting to our environments, and such adaptations trigger neurobiological patterns that have a profound effect on the rest of our lives (Belsky et al. 2012). Those born into highly stressed worlds tend to have a speeded-up metabolism, faster heart rates, more activated stress response systems and develop what some call a fast as opposed to a slow life-course strategy. We see this in a range of other mammals as well as humans, and it is a strategy that aids survival. We all have this in our evolutionary back-pocket, as otherwise any too trusting and complacent ancestors might well have met a violent end before they had time to reproduce. In some circumstances the best response is to be wary, vigilant and untrusting.

Life-history programming is so powerful that girls with insecure attachments tend to reach puberty earlier (Belsky et al. 2010), as do those born into highly stressed families, or adopted from poor-quality orphanages, or without fathers, and they are more likely to get involved in sexual activity younger, and reproduce earlier and more often (Ellis and Essex 2007). There is an evolutionary explanation for this which can only be speculative but which I think is plausible. In a dangerous world those who wait too long to reproduce might not survive long enough to do so, therefore starting early might aid passing on one's genes (Tither and Ellis 2008). Perhaps this is why animals, including humans, tend to take more risks when their environments are unstable, becoming more involved in violence or promiscuity for example, and living a more highly stressed life. The evidence is absolutely clear that the more adverse early experiences a child has, then the faster the life-course, which includes the more likelihood of physical and mental illness, less-stable relationships and work lives and on average dying younger (Felitti *et al.* 1998). Children with secure attachment styles, living in safe, relaxed environments, will non-consciously pick up very different messages, such as that it is sensible to wait longer to reproduce, it is safe to relax and trust the world, it is fine to have less children but to invest more in each one, and that one can rely on long-term stable relationships.

When people are given cues that suggest a dangerous situation, those brought up in poorer socioeconomic circumstances tend to take more risks, while those brought up economically advantaged tend to take the slower, more risk-averse strategy (Griskevicius *et al.* 2011). Similarly, boys living in areas high in violence and crime, or neighbourhoods with many boarded-up buildings, seem to pick up environmental clues non-consciously which induce a psycho-biological disposition for risk-taking. Indeed in such environments boys develop higher testosterone levels (Tarter *et al.* 2009). The logic of this is maybe that if there is a piece of fruit on the tree which is not quite ripe, if you feel fairly sure that it will be there in a few days, you wait till it will taste really good, but if the likelihood is that it will disappear then it is better to grab it now.

Such research is not about blaming mothers. The capacity to parent is profoundly affected by factors such as poverty, inequality, living in a deprived neighbourhood or having unsupportive or abusive partners (Music 2010). It is also affected by a parent's own childhood experiences. Parenting requires good social support, as the primatologist and evolutionary thinker, Sarah Blaffer Hrdy, showed, because humans are unlike most primates in being a 'cooperative breeding species' which has always reared its young in groups.

However, as Hrdy shows, when help is not at hand then mothers are more likely to withdraw from, or even abandon, their infants, a trait that has long been part of human mothers' repertoire. Secure loving mothering has by no means always been universal. A main determinant of whether to invest emotionally in a child is whether there is sufficient social support, and enough food. Mothers after all can only have so many children in a lifetime. It is foolhardy to invest huge amounts of love and attention, as well as energy and calories acquired with great difficulty, if a new baby is unlikely to survive and there might be better opportunities later on for a baby to thrive. Hrdy reports many such dilemmas in the anthropological literature which help make sense of why disinvesting in an infant might have been rather a sensible strategy in many societies. Many mothers in stressful environments or violent relationships in the modern world might well be making similar non-conscious choices by withdrawing from their children.

Summary

I have introduced the idea that different kinds of parenting give rise to different attachment styles which in turn have a profound effect on how we relate to others. People with secure attachment styles tend to be more prosocial, moral and altruistic than those with any of the insecure attachment styles, as well as being more cooperative and better at relationships. We have seen how a stressful environment can give rise to what is called a fast life-course, with speeded-up metabolisms and more risk-taking, alongside more aggression, less empathy, and generally less prosocial behaviours. I have stressed that all of these traits should be seen as adaptive rather than in any way *unnatural*, as strategies that make sense but can have unfortunate long-term effects.

There is a danger of being overly moralistic about parenting and indeed many early interpreters of attachment theory did get a few things wrong. In particular, the view that babies *should* be with mothers as much as possible left out the importance of alternative parental figures who have been so important in most previous societies. This has led to a huge burden of guilt being placed on mothers. We know that children fare better with sensitive care from a range of adults. Having several good attachment relationships predicts better self-control, behaviour and relationships (Belsky *et al.* 2007). It has been a mistake to assume that secure attachment is *natural*, an idea that casts other attachment styles as unnatural. In fact each strategy is a sensible adaptation to specific environmental pressures.

While our attachment styles are sensible responses, they certainly hugely influence character traits such as how moral, prosocial and altruistic we become. If we have good relationships with our parents or other primary caregivers we generally become more open, trusting, caring and interested in others. We also develop a good sense of agency and self-control, and become confident and appropriately assertive.

However, writers such as Hrdy have been arguing that we might be living in a time when such character traits are less adaptive than they once were. Babies can be reared without as much empathy now, and abused and traumatised children are more likely to survive than in our evolutionary past. Similarly the kind of character traits we see in securely attached people might be less advantageous in a competitive business and work climate where loyalty and continued relationships count for less, and indeed ruthlessness and rudeness might pay off more.

The origins of feeling safe and confident are in the families of our childhoods. In addition, to maintain traits like empathy and trust we need to inhabit safe and caring environments in our adulthood, whether in our relationships, neighbourhoods or workplaces. Early experiences deeply influence but do not completely determine us. Different contexts can trigger different predispositions. Furthermore, experiences such as therapy, mentoring, better parenting, and more benign neighbourhoods and workplaces can lead to more empathy, trust and compassion for both self and others (Jazaieri *et al.* 2012; Neff and Germer 2013). Change later in life is certainly possible, but the most profound influences are earlier in life.

Influential thinkers such as Sue Gerhardt (2010), a psycho-analytic psychotherapist who draws on neuroscience, child development and social theory, have argued forcefully for the importance of more attuned, empathic parenting as an antidote to selfish, individualistic social values. Some think that empathy and compassion might be under threat. Hrdy rather chillingly warns us:

> If empathy and understanding develop only under particular rearing conditions, and if an ever-increasing proportion of the species fails to encounter those conditions but nevertheless survives to reproduce, it won't matter how valuable the underpinnings for collaboration were in the past. Compassion

and the quest for emotional connection will fade away as surely as sight in cave-dwelling fish.

(Hrdy 2009, p. 293)

Next we will see just what life experiences are necessary to enable empathy and caring for others to develop, and we will look in more detail at what we mean by altruism, and in particular an altruism fuelled by empathy.

Chapter 4

How empathy and altruism grow

Empathy

Some people show little empathy. Sean, a nine-year-old adopted boy, was referred to the clinic where I work. He had been aggressive and was at risk of being thrown out of his school. His adoptive parents were very worried about him. I asked two trainee psychologists to observe him in school. In their detailed description they noted an incident in the playground. A younger boy had a packet of crisps and dropped them. Sean saw this, walked up to the crisps, looked long and hard at the boy and then stamped on the crisps. Here Sean did not lack the ability to understand the younger child's feelings, and in fact he knew only too well what feelings his malicious act was likely to evoke. Maybe he knew such feelings all too well from his abusive pre-adoption life.

Later, back in the classroom, another child was nervously trying to carry some books to his teacher and tripped, and they went flying. Two children were up like a shot to help; the psychology trainees glanced at Sean and they noted him smirking. He knew what the child was feeling but had no sympathy for him.

Empathy is a complex process. To empathise with the boy whose crisps were smashed, as I suspect most readers did, one needs to imagine what he is feeling. This though is not enough for empathy, and as we noted Sean knew reasonably well what his victim's feelings were. Here the psychology trainees' empathy, and that of the boys who leapt up to help, were immediate, gut-level responses. Sean though had a blind-spot, a lack of sympathy, presumably because he had rarely had his own distress empathised with. One might assume that his abusive biological parents had many blind spots of their own about feelings, whether his, their own, anyone's.

Families, and indeed cultures, vary hugely in what feelings have an allowable place, whether, for example, anger or sadness are tolerated, or even exuberance or passion.

Some struggle to recognise one feeling from another, not knowing, for example, what we mean when we talk about sadness, hopelessness, anxiety or excitement. This might particularly apply to people on the autistic spectrum. For them the world of feelings, their own and those of others, can be an alien, incomprehensible universe. Autistic people might still follow the rules of good behaviour, and indeed many are desperate to understand rules and work them out. We do not necessarily need empathy to act morally on the basis of rules, ethical codes, religious principles or even the logic of courts of law. However, we most certainly need it to respond to another person out of the 'goodness of our hearts'.

Recognising another person's feelings is not sufficient for empathy. In addition one must be able to tolerate whatever is stirred up in ourselves by that feeling, and also to feel some sympathy for them. In a therapy group for adults one member, Mick, divulged that his relationship had just broken up. His lip began to quiver and tears rolled down his face. Another group member, Anthony, jumped in to try to reassure him that it would all work out fine and that he was sure they would get back together. Here Anthony's attempt to reassure Mick is very different to showing empathy. In fact Anthony was himself too distressed to bear what Mick was feeling, which was not surprising as his own relationship was on a knife-edge. What Mick in fact yearned for was someone who could understand and show sympathy for his plight.

Anthony wanted to 'help' but partly because he could not bear Mick's feeling. This is a kind of altruism that is not primarily motivated by empathy.

Most of us have the potential for empathy, a potential which is realised if we are lucky enough to be raised in 'good enough' emotional environments. Empathy often withers in the face of stress, anxiety or threat, and also in social systems and situations which are very competitive, violent or aggressive. In some people empathy does not ever develop, for purely biological reasons, as in some forms of autism or brain damage.

Forms of altruism

I now look at different forms of altruism, before examining what needs to happen for someone to become an empathic person.

In some forms of altruism, empathy plays only a minimal role, such as in reciprocal altruism, the 'I'll scratch your back if you scratch mine' kind, originally theorised by the evolutionary scientist, Robert Trivers (2002). I might help my neighbour not because I really care for them, but because I expect similar favours to be returned when needed. A friend described taking a bottle of wine round to welcome a new neighbour. On discovering that the neighbour was only renting the home for a few months, my friend shamefully admitted that he wished he had not taken the wine round; after all, the newcomers were not going to become part of the fabric of their lives. His gesture was not an act of empathic altruism, and maybe at best was altruism with a hope of reciprocity.

Many evolutionary psychologists, as well as libertarian free-market thinkers, have questioned whether there can ever be something we might call *genuine* altruism. This belief fits with the idea that humans are basically self-seeking individuals whose good deeds are either *really* self-interested, like helping because I expect something in return, or dissembling to make a good impression, while in fact a ruthless selfishness lurks just beneath the surface.

Daniel Batson (2011), Professor of Psychology at Kansas University, probably has done more than anyone to help us understand that this more cynical view of altruism is not the whole story. Batson has spent the major part of his professional life investigating what he has called 'empathy-induced altruism', something that depends on an ability to understand and sympathise with another's feelings, not be overwhelmed by such feelings, and to care about the person's plight.

I earlier elected to use a similar definition of altruism to Batson's, an altruistic act being one whose *ultimate* aim is to further another's wellbeing. An egoistic act has the opposite aim, to further one's own interests. Of course there are many grey areas in between. However, as I define it, if I happen to derive personal benefits from an altruistic act, but that is not my main motive, then the act is still altruistic. Of course, if another person incidentally derives benefits from my egoistic act, that does not make my act altruistic either. For example if I soothe a crying child because I hope to be seen in a good light, or because I cannot stand the noise, that is different from really feeling empathy for the child's plight and genuinely wanting them to feel better.

Batson has meticulously researched and I think proven the existence of empathy-induced altruism, distinguishing it from altruism driven by a host of different motivations. For example, imagine watching someone experience some electric shocks. This would be unpleasant for most of us. Batson found that those low in empathy, and overwhelmed by watching, were unlikely to help a person receiving shocks if they were given the chance to beat a hasty retreat from the scene. In fact they grabbed the chance to escape after watching just a few shocks. Those high in empathy were more likely to stay for up to ten shocks, and also to offer to take some of the shocks themselves, given the chance. They did not help in order to lessen their own distress, as they could have done this by leaving, just as the low empathisers did.

Many critics point out that we often act helpfully because it enhances our reputations and not because we really care about another's welfare. This of course is true, but not necessarily all the time. To look at this, Batson undertook a series of experiments in which people were told about a young woman, Katie, who badly needed some help. For example, her child was suddenly diagnosed with a life-threatening illness, and she needed support to get to college. A tape of Katie talking about her plight was played. Some but not all the participants were informed that on no account would anyone ever find out if they offered help or not. Maybe not surprisingly, those low in empathy for Katie were less likely to help when they believed that no one would find out if they helped. However, those high in empathy tended to offer help irrespective of whether they thought anyone would find out. In other words, the motive for helping, for some at least, was empathy rather than preserving their reputation.

But, cynical critics might continue, what if such altruistic acts are undertaken to get rewards from helping: that warm glow inside, that firing of the brain's reward circuits that neuroscientists have shown occurs when we give help (Moll *et al.* 2006)? Are the helpers really helping themselves, not the person in trouble, by enhancing their own good feelings? In fact by the definition I am using, gaining such a personal emotional reward from helping does not stop the act being altruistic. None the less Batson found that those high in empathy were more relieved if the person's problems improved or went away, even if the help was provided by someone else. The reward was that the condition improved. This finding is even seen with children as young as two years old. Their sympathetic arousal, measured by signs such as pupil dilation, was altered both when they helped someone who needed it but also when they saw another person offer this help. Even tiny children genuinely want people to be helped, and do not just want to take credit for helping (Hepach *et al.* 2012a).

Another common criticism is that we help because we feel merged with the other, and so are really helping a projected version of ourselves. In fact neuroscience and other research shows that people high in empathy are actually less merged, and have increased self–other differentiation. Imagine the excruciating experience of watching a film of a finger being trapped in a door. Not surprisingly, whether we think of the finger as our own or another person's, pain regions in the brain tend to be activated. However, those asked to imagine it was another person's finger also had activation in different brain areas, those linked to distinguishing self and other. Empathy requires knowing we are separate from the person experiencing pain (Jackson *et al.* 2006).

This is an important distinction, as without some emotional separation we can become overwhelmed by another's distress. Nancy Eisenberg (Eisenberg *et al.* 1996) of the University of Arizona asked school children to watch a video of children injured in a violent accident. Some winced and were overwhelmed by what they saw, whereas others showed definite compassion. Given the opportunity to later take homework to help these child victims, the ones who offered help were those who had previously shown compassion. They also showed heart rate deceleration, a classic signature for compassion and empathy. Those who had been overwhelmed by the distressed children did not later offer help.

Daniel Batson tested well over 30 hypotheses that challenged his empathy-altruism hypothesis but it has withstood all investigations. The fact is that we help sometimes because we empathise with another's plight. Even though we can also be altruistic for any number of more selfish motives, altruism primarily motivated by empathy does exist. This is what those toddlers were doing in Tomasello's experiments when they helped adults who dropped objects, and that is what the children in the classroom were doing when they unthinkingly leapt to help the boy who stumbled.

Those who score higher on tests for empathy are also likely to yawn contagiously when others do, and are more likely to help people they empathise with. However, to empathise we need certain psychological skills, which some of us have more of than others. In addition, our empathic capacities will increase or decrease depending on who we are with, what mood we are in and what immediate external influences there are.

Indeed, we can deliberately reduce our levels of empathy, such as by actively suppressing feelings of compassion, and if we do this, for example when walking past a beggar on the street or not helping a friend in need, it has a cost (Cameron and Payne 2012). Those induced in experiments to override their compassion were later more likely to believe that moral rules do not always need to be followed, or that it is fine to be flexible about ethical codes. Compassion and empathy are profoundly linked with being moral.

How empathy develops

Now I turn to the roots of empathy, how it comes 'online'. People's interest in other minds, in their thoughts and feelings, in fact begins at the very start of life. An infant only 20 minutes old will imitate many of the gestures of adults in front of them, most famously the sticking out of tongues (Meltzoff 2007). This is not simply copying but shows a definite awareness of another's feeling states and intentions. Infants do not imitate non-intentional gestures such as sneezing. We have all probably seen how infants resonate with those around them, smiling broadly in response to laughter, or looking sad when others are upset, as if barometers of people's moods. These responses do not constitute conscious awareness of other people's feelings but do demonstrate sensitivity to them.

When a baby makes a gesture, such as a startled judder or a sad cry, then if a parent responds to this by for example saying 'oh what a huge shock that was, that big door slamming', then not only has the infant's emotional state been regulated, but he or she has been pulled into a world of meaning by another person. Parents who act in such a sensitive way have been labelled mind-minded (Meins *et al.* 2003), and they tend to have children who develop empathy and understanding of other minds sooner.

Such attuned parenting provides what Colwyn Trevarthen (Trevarthen and Aitken 2001) calls 'a companion in meaning making' for infants. If a crying or excited infant's state is understood, then not only has their emotional state been regulated, but the infant gains an understanding of their own feelings from the other person's viewpoint. This is what the British paediatrician and psychoanalyst Donald Winnicott described as an infant gaining their first sense of themselves via the vision of themselves as reflected back through their parent's eyes (Winnicott 1971). Some babies and children, such as many of the abused ones I have worked with, have feelings which are ignored, contradicted or even ridiculed. Their experience is more akin to seeing themselves reflected back in a fairground's distorting mirror, giving rise to warped self-understandings. Such children then also struggle to be sympathetic to such feelings in others. It takes being empathised with to become empathic.

It is no coincidence that we say that eyes are windows into the soul. We humans are unique in having that expanse of white sclera around our irises and pupils, making it so much easier to work out where someone is looking and what they are preoccupied with. Even very young babies know when they are the object of another's attention (Reddy 2008); one four-month-old might smile with pleasure knowing that an adoring adult is looking at them, while another might be uncomfortable and turn away in the face of an adult gaze, but either way they fully know the difference between an attentive adult mind being on them as opposed to being with an adult who is not attending.

This is how psychological and emotional understanding about oneself develops. By three months, many can lead their 'companion in meaning making' to attend to something specific. By eight months, many infants can clown, show off and even tease a parent. Professor Vasu Reddy describes an eight-month-old playing with her dad. They were passing an object back and forth, having fun. Then after several goes the daughter made as if to pass the object, looked at her dad, whisked the object away, looked back at him and smiled, to which the tricked dad smiled too (Reddy 2008).

This is a sophisticated set of skills, including knowing what was in her dad's mind, knowing they were thinking about the same thing, understanding how to confound her dad's expectations, and being able to predict and then enjoy her dad's reaction, knowing he would enjoy this with her too. Not every eight-month-old can do this, but many who have received attuned, empathic attention can (especially if they also have parents who can have fun!).

By about nine months, infants can check out whether their caregiver thinks a situation is safe by reading their facial expressions, which we call *social referencing*. It might be unclear whether it is safe to approach a person and most nine-month-olds will 'reference' a parent to find out. The world is being interpreted through the eyes of the mother, and an infant's world literally becomes different depending on their mother's perspective.

Autistic children tend not to manage this, and it is also true of some from abusive or neglectful backgrounds. Many abused or neglected children already rarely look to parents, who they have often tragically learnt not to trust. Most children, though, who have had good-enough parenting have learnt to read such signals.

Children, with luck, become adept at recognising states of mind like happiness or worry, and also understand what the state of mind is *about*. They need to know if a parent's anxious expression refers to a snake nearby or some food that is not safe. Infants generally can manage such shared attention by about nine months. Shared attention also includes sharing pleasure in something, maybe a funny picture, with both parties knowing what is in the other's mind. Such critical developmental milestones depend on the kind of mind-understanding skills which are also needed in empathy.

As already discussed, we are different from most primates in that we are a cooperative breeding species and rear our children in groups (Hrdy 1999). This has endowed human infants with the ability to read other minds sufficiently well to communicate, respond to needs and work out who they can rely on. Adults respond with feeling and extremely rapidly to infant faces, in fact within a seventh of a second to unfamiliar infant faces, according to scientists at the University of Oxford (Kringelbach *et al.* 2008). The brain areas triggered are linked to feeling rewarded, and this does not happen with adult faces. We seem wired to react empathically and dotingly to baby faces generally, not just to our own babies.

Many toddlers already show empathy for another's distress at just over a year old, and altruistically help others in need. Slowly and surely most children gain even more sophisticated skills. Eighteen-month-olds can work out what someone intended by watching them *fail* to achieve a task, but inferring what they wanted to do (Meltzoff 1988).

By three years old, many even make clear decisions about whether an adult's display of distress was appropriate or an over-reaction (Hepach *et al.* 2012b). They show concern for an adult who has been upset for a seemingly good reason, and only when the upset seems justified do they intervene on the adult's behalf and check up on them later. This shows sophisticated understandings of intentionality.

However, many neglected children who receive little empathic attention are barely able to understand mental states in others, and indeed in themselves, and show little interest in them. Children who rarely receive attuned attention become deadened to emotional nuances. This is partly why so many maltreated children too often get misdiagnosed as on the autistic spectrum when in fact they have not had the right experiences for their empathy circuits to grow (DeJong 2010).

Many who experience abusive rather than neglectful parenting develop a skewed understanding of others. They have often learnt that for self-protection they need to pick up the intentions of frightening or unpredictable adults. Such mental-state understanding tends to be more superficial, a fearful watchfulness for clues about untrustworthy adults' moods. Many children I work with worry constantly about whether their mother is about to 'fly off the handle' or their dad has been drinking alcohol again, signs they become extraordinarily adept at picking up. Sadly they also see even benign caring adults in the same untrustworthy light.

Sean, who cruelly stamped on his classmate's crisps, had in fact been the victim of violence, and he picked up signs of aggression far quicker than most other children I have worked with; he probably had to in order to feel safe. In such hypervigilant children and adults, their brains show much stronger reactions in fear regions, such as the amygdala, than most people (Killgore and Yurgelun-Todd 2005). Such vigilance is very different to empathic understanding of another, as empathy requires also being able to put ourselves in another's shoes and have fellow-feeling with them. Such genuine empathy is central to what philosopher Martin Buber described as I–Thou relationships rather than I–It ones (Buber 2002).

Mind-reading

The making sense of another's intentions depends on our mirror-neuron system, something scientists discovered just a few years ago (Rizzolatti *et al.* 2006). Similar neurons fire in my brain as in yours when I see you do something deliberately. If I see you struggling to reach a high object, I might be willing you on, and here corresponding neurons will be firing in my brain too. Mirror neurons respond to intentions, which are how children learn, by reading another's intentions and then later replicating the actions. Mirror neurons provide evidence of the human capacity to form powerful connections between people, allowing one person to understand another from the inside in a bodily as well as mental way (Gallese 2009).

Not surprisingly, scientists (Oberman *et al.* 2005) have found that autistic people who tend to lack empathy also often have a deficit in their mirror-neuron functioning. We might speculate about the impact of severe institutional neglect on a developing mirror-neuron system, given that so many children adopted from emotionally depriving situations lack a capacity to be in touch with their own and other people's minds and emotions. The jury is out on whether mirror neurons are one of the most important discoveries of recent decades (Ramachandran 2000), or if the claims for them are somewhat over-hyped (Hickok 2009), but few doubt that they have cast light on how we pick up the intentions as well as the feeling states of others.

As researchers have shown (De Waal 2012), empathy starts in this very immediate way. Show people pictures of powerful facial expressions and they react well before higher-order cognitive processes get a look-in. Moral feelings are seemingly quickest of all. We detect in a split second whether a hurtful act is intentional or not. New high-density neuro-imaging found that as adults watched images of people being harmed, when the harm was deliberate then brain responses were considerably faster (Decety and Cacioppo 2012). Within just 60 milliseconds an area called the right posterior superior temporal sulcus was activated, quickly followed by the amygdala, central for emotionality, and slightly later the 'thinking' cortical areas. These latter areas did not even react when the harm was accidental, presumably because we are most powerfully primed to speedily spot immoral behaviour.

Both morality and empathy-induced altruism depend on knowing what someone intends. I will judge you differently if I think you accidently knocked over that child as opposed to doing it deliberately. One fascinating study (Dunfield and Kuhlmeier 2010) beautifully illustrated how the wish to help is linked with understanding intentions. Twenty-one-month-old infants had seen an exciting new toy and were confronted by two actresses, neither of whom in fact gave this toy to them. One seemed at least to try, placing the toy on a sloping table and looking on in feigned surprise as it rolled out of reach. The second actress showed the toy to the child but was blatantly unwilling to hand it over. Later both actresses were sitting opposite this infant and someone placed another toy on the edge of the table but in such a way that it fell off the edge. Both actresses stretched unsuccessfully for the toy. The infants were far more likely to pick up and give the toy to the actress who had at least *tried* to pass the toy to them. It was the *intention* that was understood, paid attention to and acted upon, even at this tender age.

Such an ability to make sense of other people's thoughts or emotions from the earliest months are precursors of what is often rather clumsily called Theory of Mind. This describes stepping outside of ourselves, understanding the intentions and beliefs of others, and distinguishing these from our own. If I watch a child about to grab what he thinks is a full packet of cookies, but I know that the packet is really full of paper clips, I assume that the child has a different belief and sense of anticipation from mine, and that when he finds the box he might be disappointed. If I had previously shown another child that the packet contained paper clips, I could ask what he thinks the first child would expect to find in the packet. Up until about four years old children tend to answer incorrectly, assuming that because they know the packet contains paper clips that others will think the same. They are unable yet to take the other's point of view as fully.

These skills do not just automatically come online at a certain age. Having siblings close in age speeds it up (Dunn and Brophy 2005), and particularly having parents who are more mind-minded (Meins *et al.* 2003). In older children, empathy and secure attachment together predict prosocial, kind behaviours (Thompson and Gullone 2008; Carlo, Mestre *et al.* 2012). It is no coincidence that parents who are mind-minded tend to have securely attached children, and that these are the children who get on best with other children in nursery and are most likely to show empathy when another child shows upset (Lieberman, Padrón, Van Horn and Harris 2005).

On the other hand, parents with very troubled lives and insecure attachment styles, who struggle to empathise, tend to have children with diminished understanding of other minds. For example, mothers with borderline personality disorder are often less in tune with their children's emotional states, and might ascribe all kinds of thoughts and feelings to their child that reveal more about them than the child (Hobson 2002). I will later think about the lack of empathy in psychopaths or children with callous-unemotional traits. Low empathy can lead to children and adults who cannot manage relationships, nor keep friends, who are socially isolated, and in serious cases can find themselves outside the mainstream of society.

Altruism, compassion and minds

Altruistic tendencies and empathy normally emerge alongside being able to conceptualise oneself as part of a story with a past, present and a future. Such autobiographical skills develop quickly once children start to recognise themselves in mirrors, normally between about 18 and 24 months. We see this in the classic 'mirror-recognition' test in which someone discreetly places a blob of rouge on an infant's face and children are said to have *passed* this test if they recognise in the mirror that it is *their* face with rouge on, such as by trying to rub the mark off. Interestingly, research in Holland has shown that toddlers who responded empathically and helpfully to another child's sadness were the same ones who had passed the rouge–mirror self-recognition test (Bischof-Köhler 1994; 2012), whereas those who offered no support or empathy failed the rouge test. Self-understanding grows simultaneously with increased understanding of other minds and feelings, and is a big step on the path to participating in a moral community. People whose empathic brain areas are working hardest seem to be more altruistic and helpful (Tankersley *et al.* 2007).

Those with more grey matter at the junction between the parietal and temporal lobes are seemingly not only better able to see things from another's perspective but are also more altruistic (Morishima *et al.* 2012). This is about higher levels of empathy but also working hard to minimise selfish impulses. In games in which people had to choose between being generous or keeping money for themselves, the more generous players had higher activation in this brain area, which was firing up most when the conflict between being selfish and selfless was at its height. In altruism we need both to enhance empathic traits but also inhibit selfish ones.

There can be a shift with maturity from a spontaneous, almost unthinking empathy which leads to altruistic gestures, to what some see as deeper feelings of compassion for others. Compassion describes a feeling for someone else's suffering or distress. The 'feeling for' here is important, maybe rather like the German word from which empathy derives, *Einfühlung*, which literally means 'feel into'. This might be contrasted with pity, which suggests a somewhat condescending if benign response. Compassion I think suggests a deeper form of empathy, and here, given the lack of rigorous psychological formulations, I am thrown back on philosophy, maybe again on Buber's I–Thou relationships. I also rely on the work of that other great philosopher Emmanuel Levinas (Levinas and Hand 1989), whose ethical thinking presupposed a movement towards really appreciating the other in face-to-face encounters, in a way that precluded selfishness and entailed a profound wish to act in the best interests of the other. Such ideas are at the heart of much psychotherapeutic practice (cf. Gordon 1999).

There is much writing within the mindfulness tradition that illuminates the role of compassion, how this can be cultivated and its transformative effects (e.g. Germer 2009; Germer and Siegel 2012). In psychotherapy the movement towards what Melanie Klein (1998) called the depressive position also describes a powerful recognition of the other as other. These issues risk slipping into sentimentality but the concept of compassion is maybe an under-used and under-theorised one. Compassion entails empathy, but describes also a deep feeling for the other's suffering and an urge to help them. It is maybe best contrasted with its opposite, treating the other as an 'It' in Buber's sense, as less than oneself, that dehumanisation of the other which is present in so many off-hand everyday interactions, let alone many atrocities.

Empathy and compassion are hard to differentiate completely, but compassion perhaps suggests a deeper feeling for another's plight. Empathy, and presumably compassion, is beneficial on many levels. We feel less pain, and illnesses heal more quickly, when cared for by empathic nurses, while a recent study of over 20,000 diabetic patients found that those with empathic doctors had significantly lower metabolic complications (Del Canale *et al.* 2012). A study of children undergoing cancer treatment found that those whose parents were overwhelmed by their children's plight felt more pain than those whose parents showed high levels of concerned empathy (Penner *et al.* 2008).

Summary

I have stressed the importance of the development of empathy for altruism, and looked at different forms of altruism. Empathy, as Batson has helped us see, is at the root of genuine concern for others.

No other species is empathic in the way we humans are, and our empathy is at the very root of our moral selves. We have seen how the child's mind literally grows and develops through being attuned to and empathised with. Real empathy and understanding of others' thoughts and feelings, what Homer (Pope *et al.* 1867, Book XVIII line 269) described as how 'taught by time, my heart has learned to glow for other's good, and melt at other's woe', this ability not just to understand another's mind but to feel with them, is not one that everyone is lucky enough to develop, but it is essential for humane care for others. Our best hope for being good to others in an empathic way comes from being given plenty of love, mind-minded attention and empathy, preferably early in life, and living and working in a safe and supportive community or society. Without these there is little empathy, and without empathy lives are less caring and prosocial. Empathy is the bedrock of being a genuinely moral person.

Empathy as a moral force certainly has its limits, as many critics such as Jesse Prinz (2011) have argued. Empathy can lead to favouring those we know, such as people from our own social group, culture or ethnicity, and maybe not being so moved to help complete strangers from another culture who need help at least as much. We expect from good government and courts of law judgements based less on personal empathy but more on fairness and what is in the best interests of all. However, we also worry if people make decisions too unemotionally. If too driven by empathy we can help the cute child but not the ugly one, respond to people in an accident in *our* road but not people in more need on the other side of town, and judges driven by empathy would give harsher sentences to people who are 'not like them'. Emotions can get in the way of what many of us think is right, but few want moral decision-making based purely on 'cold' utilitarian reasoning.

Of course empathy and reading such cues are not only crucial for social relationships but our survival can even depend on them. We react and respond constantly, often out of consciousness, to the messages we receive from other people. Next we see how powerfully our very bodies and particularly our nervous systems are affected by messages about whether the world feels safe and benevolent or frightening and dangerous. When the world feels dangerous and untrustworthy then we do not so easily act kindly or generously, but when it feels beneficent and bountiful, we are more likely to reach out to others. We will now see how frightening experiences can diminish empathy, and lead to more primitive modes of being and relating, such as fight, flight or freeze responses.

Chapter 5

Why stress can make us nasty

Feel good, do good

A client described walking down the road on a balmy summer's afternoon. She noted how others were scurrying back to work. She, though, was now on holiday and after seeing me she was going to meet her best friend and they were going away for the weekend. She told me how she felt an excited tingle, how her breathing had deepened and she was experiencing a warm glow inside. She described her mind returning to childhood memories, particularly of her mother, of how safe and enjoyable life felt when her mother would take her away, how she remembered those times as if the sun was always shining. These are newly refound memories; in fact her mother had died tragically when she was just nine, casting a dark shadow over her life from which she was only just recovering. Today she found herself smiling at people and was surprised that they smiled back at her. She realised that she had given money to a beggar almost without thinking. In her session she recalled her mother's quietly kind gestures to a neighbour in need. The world felt good at this moment, imbued with love, hope and wellbeing. It is in moods like this that we are far more likely to be open to other people, sympathetic, compassionate and also generous and helpful. Our own wellbeing generally does not run counter to that of others.

In a famous experiment from the 1970s (Isen and Levin 1972) a dime was sometimes left in a phone booth and at other times no money was left. Random people were observed using these phone booths, and as they came out an actress pretended to drop a sheaf of paper. Fascinatingly, over 80 per cent of the people who had unexpectedly found a dime helped the person who supposedly had dropped the papers, while less than 10 per cent of those who did not find a dime offered to help. Of course a dime was a very insignificant amount of money even in 1972, but when the world feels like a more beneficent place we tend to respond more kindly.

Both adults and children are generally more generous when they are in better moods. Toddlers become more helpful after they have been shown pictures of people who are nice, such as dolls cuddling (Over and Carpenter 2009). In another 1970s experiment children were induced into either happy or sad moods, by getting them to reminisce about either upsetting or enjoyable times and then talking in detail about what they remembered (Rosenhan *et al.* 1974). Those who were feeling happier grabbed just as many sweets as the unhappy children, but were far more generous in giving sweets away than those in sad moods. Similar findings have been seen in adults. Care of others tends to increase when we feel good (Rosenthal and Rosnow 1975).

Happy people tend to be more generous, but in turn being generous also makes people feel happier, as many studies have shown (Anik *et al.* 2009). Indeed we seem to positively like giving things away, and even toddlers of less than two have a higher level of happiness after giving treats to others than when receiving them (Aknin *et al.* 2012). Feeling good and being kind and altruistic seems to constitute some kind of virtuous circle, good acts fuelling good feelings which fuel good acts.

Trauma and stress

However, the opposite, a vicious rather than virtuous circle, can be all too common.

Often those who have had the worst lives, such as many of the abused and traumatised children and adults I have worked with, can be ungenerous and aggressive. Such people demonstrate something true of us all. When we are highly stressed and anxious we become less nice and less compassionate to ourselves and others. A lifetime of chronically bad experiences builds deep beliefs about relationships that are hard to shift, typically that others are not to be trusted and will not treat us well. Such bad experiences also lead to bodies and nervous systems programmed in expectation of a scary, unpleasant world, which in turn has a dramatic effect on levels of empathy, helpfulness and aggression.

Take Micky. He was another child with a distressing history of trauma and abuse. He was raised in a violent home, his feelings were ignored or laughed at, his mother preoccupied and too often drunk. Overwhelming experiences such as doors slamming, screaming, and much worse, were what he knew. He was always in trouble at school, reacting in microseconds to events that others took in their stride, such as disappointment or some mild teasing. In his therapy any mention of things still too painful to tolerate led him to shift instantaneously into aggressive fight-flight responses: his eyes flashed, his body tensed and his sympathetic nervous system shot into action. He was a bully at school, and had no real friends, only a few followers. His social worker reported that in his previous placement he would, though, sometimes become extremely still, his eyes glazed over and he would look like he wasn't breathing. This would particularly occur when an adult male raised his voice. His teacher noted this too, and found it hard to put together with the angry, aggressive child who was such a handful the rest of the time.

In recent years we have learnt a huge amount about such responses, and in particular the role that our nervous systems play in generosity, kindness and morality. We use very different parts of our brains when in different moods, or in different contexts, such as when in a loving environment or under threat. When in danger we tend to become very aroused, tense up and resort to primitive survival responses such as fight or flight, or even freeze. Then our physiology becomes geared to surviving the threat in front of us, while other bodily functions such as digestion or immune responses temporarily go into abeyance, as do higher-order thought processes. Compassion and empathy are low on the agenda when we feel fearful or endangered. The majority of species, apart from extremely primitive vertebrates, have such a fight-flight response.

Stephen Porges (2011), Professor of Psychiatry in Illinois, has helped to make sense of why people are less kind and helpful when stressed, anxious or angry, and in particular how these effects are magnified after chronically bad childhood experiences. He shows that we have three very different responses to stress, each rooted in a different stage of our evolutionary history. Our most basic reaction is one we share with the least developed of species and depends on a primitive branch of a nerve called the vagus nerve, in fact the so-called dorsal vagal branch, which is shared with vertebrates, reptiles and amphibians. When it is activated it leads to complete immobilisation, freezing and the closing down of our systems. This is maybe what we saw in Micky when he went very still, and was probably the coping mechanism he resorted to when experiencing literally mind-numbing violence before he was old enough to flee or fight back. Dissociation and metabolic shutdown are typical of a 'rabbit in headlights' coping strategy, and we know that predators are not attracted to seemingly lifeless creatures. For example cats often stop playing with mice they have caught when the mice go limp in their mouths. Such 'playing possum' is a successful strategy, as it often allows creatures to escape and live another day, and thus breed and pass on this trait. We only resort to this in the most extreme life or death situations.

An evolutionarily more advanced stress response comes from our sympathetic nervous system, which includes the fight-flight response. This might kick in when we feel stressed, terrified, or furious. This is how Micky reacted all too often. When this fires up we experience increased heart rates, sweating, and quicker breathing, dilation of pupils, cold feelings and inhibited digestion. When either this or our more primitive freeze responses are active we are not predisposed to be nice, kind or generous. We all need this arousal system and all experience times when we resort to it, such as when frightened or angry. Some people like Micky go into highly aroused sympathetic nervous system responses far more easily and often than others, though.

Polyvagal

The third element of our autonomic nervous system is seen in mammals, and in an increasingly complex form in humans, and is central to both feeling good and being open to others. It depends on a sophisticated (ventral) branch of our vagus nerve, sometimes called the 'smart vagus', which connects our brain stem, heart, stomach and our facial muscles. This myelinated branch of the vagus nerve is active in processes like bonding, social communication, recognising faces and emotions. It will be firing when we get that warm glow in our chests when we are with someone we love or when we are showing appreciation. This system stops working when we feel anxious or threatened.

Even low levels of anxiety can lead to this system being turned off, and most of us will admit that we are not very nice when we are in a rush or anxious. Another classic experiment showed this (Darley and Batson 1973). Theology students were instructed that they had to give a talk in a nearby hall. Some were then told they had to hurry as the talk was very soon, others were told that they had plenty of time. Also some were instructed to give their talk about the parable of the Good Samaritan while others talked about a non-helping topic. An actor told to look like he was in trouble was positioned en route to the talk. Normally, being primed with the Good Samaritan story would increase the likelihood of any of us offering help to someone in distress, and presumably theology students even more so. Interestingly though, of those in a hurry, only 10 per cent stopped, as opposed to 63 per cent who had more time, irrespective of the talk they were to give. Stress, busyness and anxiety, even in small doses, make us less caring and other-minded. Chronic levels have an even worse effect.

When feeling calm and open to others, the system involving our 'smart' vagus nerve will be active. It is interesting that faces give so much away about our moods, given how the smart vagus connects our facial muscles, heart, guts and brain stem. This system has an opposite effect to the sympathetic nervous system's arousing mechanisms, and is part of the parasympathetic nervous system which calms us down. Its thousands of nerve endings communicate with many internal organs, like the gut. Indeed the gut is termed by some the enteric nervous system, or our second brain (Gershon 1999), containing about 100 million neurons, and releasing all kinds of mood-altering hormones. The smart vagus is implicated in bonding, love, team-work and cooperation. When it is to the fore we feel relaxed, loving, and we are more likely to show empathy and help others in need. Physiologically it leads to lower heart rate and blood pressure, better digestion, more relaxed states, deeper breathing and enhanced digestive and immune systems.

A well-functioning smart vagus nerve is a distinct advantage. This is an easily measured trait linked to what is called heart-rate variability, the variation in intervals between heartbeats. Heart-rate variability is often seen as the central driver of our autonomic nervous system responses. People with more variation have what is called high vagal tone, a sign of many hopeful psychological and physiological aptitudes, such as being relaxed and open. Premature babies with low vagal tone are more stressed and less likely to survive. Adults with borderline personality disorder have lower vagal tone, and less variable heart rates (Austin *et al.* 2007), and it is no coincidence that so many people with this diagnosis have suffered childhood trauma. Ideally our heart rates go up when anxiety is triggered, and come down when we relax (Goetz et al. 2010). At our most healthy we move easily between these states, and clinicians worry about children and adults who can only respond within a very narrow range, something we see in many traumatised people.

People with high vagal tone experience more emotional well-being on many measures, and are more able to take life as it comes. There are even people described by Dacher Keltner (2009) as vagal superstars, who have very high resting vagal tone. They react to stressful situations very calmly, are more resilient, tend to have wide networks of friends, seem better able to defuse conflict, are more cooperative and handle adverse situations better. Five-year-olds with higher vagal tone are more popular, open and have more facial flexibility (Graziano et al. 2007). Children with good vagal tone are the ones who are friendly, generous and helpful in class whereas those with low vagal tone are more likely to have behavioural problems and be unhappy (Eisenberg et al. 1996). Adolescents with secure attachment relationships with their parents tend to show more empathy, are better able to regulate their own emotions, and also have higher vagal tone (Diamond et al. 2012).

Of course, on hearing such accounts we all want to have high vagal tone, but how does this happen? Our vagal tone is powerfully affected by our experiences and although some practices such as mindfulness also improve it, early life experiences appear to be particularly crucial. Human infants and children have a nervous system which initially requires considerable emotional and physiological regulation by a parent, and without this they develop out-of-kilter systems, respond atypically to many experiences and often become unable to participate in the richness of human social life. We now know the extent to which each infant's brain is sculpted in response to the child's specific experiences, our brains being far from self-assembly. Rather, an infant's brain architecture, neuronal pathways, glial cells and hormonal systems are developing in response to its environment, preparing for the kind of world it already knows and expects to continue. An infant's heart rate, temperature and other body rhythms become entrained to the mother's in skin-to-skin contact, for example, and infants who are soothed and emotionally regulated, contrary to many people's beliefs, become best able to regulate their own emotions.

Yet children who suffer ongoing maltreatment grow up to have chronically lower vagal tone (Miskovic *et al.* 2009), as well as having a much more highly activated sympathetic nervous system; generally they are easily aroused, often in a dramatic way, and find it hard to calm down, concentrate or feel at ease. Similarly infants whose parents have conflict-ridden relationships have lower vagal tone and also are more unnerved by stressful situations (Moore 2010). Such aroused states are healthy for any of us in moments of threat, such as when we need to escape an attacking lion, but are not so healthy when, for children like Micky, this becomes their default way of being. While we are designed to resort to sympathetic arousal states when danger looms, we are also designed to calm down quickly afterwards, which is what we see in people with high vagal tone. Chronic bad experiences can lead to an inability to quieten.

Children exposed to violence will pick up the slightest hint of anger or aggression in someone's face much more quickly than the average child, and might speedily move into a defensive or offensive posture. Both researchers and psychotherapists who work with criminals (e.g. Gilligan 1997) have consistently found that the most violent ones generally have histories of terrible abuse in childhood. Many violent offenders are extremely sensitive to any hint of threat or humiliation. Feeling disrespected stirs up aggression, firing sympathetic nervous systems into overdrive incredibly fast.

Children can be primed for such aggression, and an accompanying lack of empathy, from a very young age. In fact, even six- to twelve-month-old infants from families where there is more marital conflict showed, compared to those from calmer homes, heightened reactivity to very angry voice tones in brain areas linked to stress and emotional regulation while sleeping (Graham *et al.* 2013). In a striking early experiment, when toddlers in a nursery heard another child in distress they were likely to offer support or sympathy. However, abused children showed no empathy or concern for other children's distress, and in fact could be quite aggressive to them (Main and George 1985). We saw earlier that securely attached children tend to play well with other children in preschool, whereas there are more fights and conflicts between insecurely attached children (Sroufe 2005). We have long known (Feshbach 1989) that abused children tend to show less compassion, and are less likely to be able to take the perspective of another person. Such children not surprisingly often have unsatisfactory and short-lived relationships with peers, partly due to their poor abilities to understand other people's feelings.

It is not that popular children are not aggressive, and indeed they generally know how to 'dish out' aggression, but less reactively, and they also have finely honed social skills, and know how to be empathic, generous and make friends (Cillessen and Rose 2005). Chronically maltreated and neglected children and adults, too, often do not have the social skills to find a place in social groups, and can over-react, seeing threat where there might be none.

Porges' ideas can be demonstrated in the diagram in Figure 5.1. We all have what the body psychotherapist Pat Ogden has described as a *window of tolerance*, represented by the middle section in the diagram. This is where the 'smart vagus' is firing and we feel relaxed and at ease. In times of stress we are likely to be pushed out of this comfort zone into the *hyper*-aroused sympathetic arousal system, or when things are really dire, into the *hypo*-aroused, numbed-down place represented below. We all have different comfort zones, and

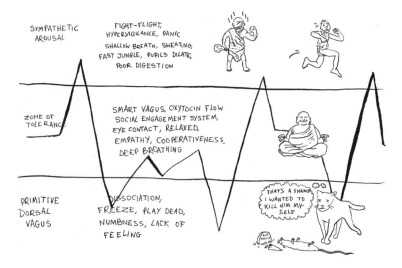

Figure 5.1 The autonomic nervous system

Sources: Porges, S.W., 2011. *The Polyvagal Theory: Neurophysiological Foundations of Emotions, Attachment, Communication, and Self-regulation*. New York: Norton.

Ogden, P. 2006. *Trauma and the Body: A Sensorimotor Approach to Psychotherapy*. 1st edition. London: W.W. Norton & Co.

Illustration © Lawrence Dodgson

maybe we worry most about people who are easily pushed out of theirs. Some of us, those with higher vagal tone, such as Keltner's vagal superstars, have broader, more capacious windows of tolerance. Others have a very narrow window of comfort and are easily pushed over the edge into more defensive states of mind. The work of therapy and parenting can be to try to help people find a way back to this zone, and indeed to try to widen its boundaries so people can spend more time in at-ease states.

Most mothers tend to show stress reactivity (fast heart rate, high blood pressure, sweaty palms) when their children cry or exhibit strong emotions (Frodi and Lamb 1980). Yet attuned, non-abused mothers, while still being aroused by their babies' distress, can look after their own feelings, calm down and offer empathy and loving care. Parents who were abused as children often cannot manage this, and struggle to empathise with their own children's distress. Mothers are similarly less responsive to their toddlers when they are themselves depressed, and also if they live in very poor or violent neighbourhoods (Sturge-Apple *et al.* 2011). The heart-rate patterns of depressed mothers living in violent areas spike when their toddlers are upset and these mothers also struggle to calm down. This is what we see in people with low vagal tone, both higher reactivity and less emotional flexibility.

Again we see just how crucial empathy and tolerating emotional states are. We process the pain, distress and upset of others in the same brain regions as we represent these feelings in ourselves (Shirtcliff *et al.* 2009). It is not easy to bear or tolerate feelings of hurt and upset in others if similar feelings in oneself have never been recognised and given sympathetic understanding. This might be why so many psychotherapy trainings insist that therapists have their own psychological help.

Adaptation again

We see similar processes in larger-scale studies. One looked at over 1,500 young people in Spain (Carlo, Mestre *et al.* 2012) and found that those who were emotionally more reactive, in other words with more activated sympathetic nervous systems, were not only more aggressive, but also less empathic, and that self-regulation came with empathy and altruistic behaviours. It is no coincidence that prisons and the criminal justice system are so packed with people whose lives have been mired by too many bad experiences and too few good ones. A hugely disproportionate number of prisoners have, for example, been in public care and suffered trauma and abuse.

Culture and social contexts also make a difference. Males in the Deep South of America are much more reactive to any hint of aggression than their Northern counterparts, for example (Nisbett and Cohen 1996). Stressful work experiences also affect people's nervous systems, such as very aggressive and competitive organisations where there is massive pressure to succeed or huge uncertainty about one's future. This has been demonstrated all too clearly in studies of people working in the financial sectors, whose lives are marked by high levels of adrenaline, the stress hormone cortisol and raised levels of testosterone (Coates 2012). That very primitive part of the brain central to the fear response, the amygdala, is very active in such processes (see Figure 5.2). In children exposed to violence it fires away dramatically when they see aggressive or frightening images. Such children will struggle to

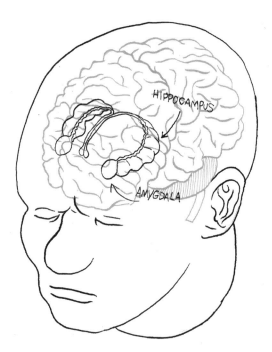

Figure 5.2 The amygdala

Illustration © Lawrence Dodgson

show empathy for others in distress. This makes sense. When we are stressed or scared then survival comes first, rather than opening ourselves up to being vulnerable or interested in others' feelings.

Thus, experiences programme our hormonal systems, as well as our nervous systems, and as we grow older these patterns can become biological templates that are hard to shift. We might become predisposed, for example, to swiftly become sympathetically aroused, releasing large amounts of adrenaline and the stress hormone cortisol in response to the slightest stimulus, such as a loud noise down the road, and we might not have the buffer of the protective hormones such as oxytocin that can lower fear and increase feelings of ease. Indeed, the smart vagus seems to be a kind of oxytocin super highway, and when vagal tone is high, we become calmer, more at ease and open, and release protective hormones. Yet to achieve these states we need attuned, sensitive early care, the more and earlier the better. We also need to be living and working in reasonably stress-free, emotionally calm and friendly environments.

It is important to point out that some forms of stress, rather than leading people to be unhelpful, can make them overly, even pathologically helpful (Oakley *et al.* 2012), responses that are also adaptive. For example, we know that parents who threaten to withdraw their love often have children who are overly concerned to please important adults in their life, and such children often develop internalising problems such as depression (Rakow *et al.* 2009). We saw in the chapter on attachment that children with inconsistent parents often resort to what are often called *tend-and-befriend* behaviours, being overly responsive to other people's needs. This is also a pattern that can be seen in children whose parents are often in conflict. These children can become overly solicitous and try very hard to make things better, a pattern more often seen in girls than boys (Zahn-Waxler *et al.* 2008).

Rather like our attachment patterns, responses such as pathologically caring for others, or high emotional and stress reactivity, can be viewed as a sensible and adaptive response to the environment one finds oneself in (Simpson and Belsky 2008). Hypervigilance and alertness to potential danger would aid the chances of survival in frightening and uncertain environments, as might trying to cheer up a depressed mother or reduce conflict between warring parents. We might need the same hyper-alertness to survive in aggressive and unsafe work situations. In tough, ruthless situations, it does not pay to be kind and trusting, whereas being aggressive, selfish and ruthless might be more successful. A 'fast' life history, with increased risk-taking, less self-regulation and more stress, enhances the chances of reproductive success in such environments. Christopher Boehm, using an evolutionary frame (Boehm 2012), points out that when faced with serious dangers our archaic aggressive and individualistic tendencies trump our cooperative and altruistic ones. Ruthless selfishness was probably essential for survival in very extreme circumstances, and when the going gets tough, such as when water or food is very short, then scruples and morals are set aside, as survival at all costs is prioritised. A version of such responses is probably what we see in children growing up in traumatised, violent and stressful environments where emotional resources such as love, safety and reliability are scarce. People find it much easier to be kind and cooperative when the world seems safe and abundant.

There is, of course, a difference between people with a chronic ingrained pattern of heightened reactivity and those who can normally be at ease and empathic to others but whose prosocial capacities are turned off in the face of short-term threats or stressors. One client, Suzanna, was upset that she was being less patient with her children, and she also found that her relationship had become more tumultuous. She could not make sense of why this shift had occurred, but further exploration revealed that the change coincided with a huge culture shift in her work. A supportive and encouraging manager had left, replaced by a seemingly controlling and bullying regime. She did not feel understood or appreciated. She had become stressed and unhappy, feelings which fed into her other relationships, becoming a less supportive partner and a less sensitive mother.

Interestingly, recent research has been suggesting that even brief stressful experiences in adults, such as a 90-minute mock job interview including difficult arithmetical questions, causes an epigenetic effect whereby the stressful experience actually alters the DNA and the action of a gene central to oxytocin production (Unternaehrer et al. 2012). We know now that adverse experiences such as abuse and trauma have a big effect on gene expression (Lesch 2011). Such epigenetic effects alongside the psycho-biological aftermath of stress, trauma and anxiety, help explain how empathic and altruistic tendencies can shrivel in the face of bad experiences.

A huge longitudinal study in America (Felitti and Anda 2010) found that people with the most adverse early experiences, such as of trauma, abuse or loss, end up suffering the worse health as they age, and indeed tend to die younger, often from diseases linked to metabolic syndrome (Tamayo *et al.* 2010). Such diseases, such as heart attacks, strokes and diabetes, are very linked with our stress responses. Such experiences also tend to lead to high levels of psychiatric issues and more likelihood of criminality.

The kind of care received early in life has profound and often long-lasting effects. However, many social trends also increase levels of stress and anxiety, leading to less open, caring, socially minded ways of being. These include highly pressured work environments, less-secure employment, financial worries, a faster pace of life, the loss of stable careers, and rising levels of inequality. Stressful work environments have been shown to be detrimental to many aspects of health and wellbeing (Pandey *et al.* 2010). In addition, other social developments have led to reduced access to the kind of support systems that can mitigate some of the worst effects, such as the social glue provided by community and family life (Putnam 2000).

Mental health outcomes have got worse in recent years for both adults and children, and those in Britain and the USA are some of worst in the Western world. Most mental health disorders, whether depression or borderline personality disorder, also come with a lessening of empathy and an increase in what we often call narcissistic disorders, a turning away from the other, heightened self-preoccupation and less capacity to mentalise (Baron-Cohen 2011). For example, parents with mental health problems such as borderline personality disorder are often more intrusive and inconsistent and do not easily empathise with their children (Hobson *et al.* 2005), while many with depression can be cut-off from children, who then in turn develop a dampened-down emotional system and less interpersonal skills (Marwick and Murray 2010).

Summary and remedies

I have emphasised how our stress responses are powerfully bio-logically programmed by good and bad experiences, leading to different branches of our autonomic nervous system playing central roles in our lives. Stress, abuse and trauma, we have seen, have an ongoing effect, on vagal tone, stress levels and our ability to be calm, empathic and altruistic, as well as on our long-term life trajectories.

Fortunately, good experiences later on can help modify early stress responses, even if the traces of bad early experiences always remain. Meditation, for example, can lead to lower stress, and interestingly also lower levels of the kinds of inflammation that are linked to health issues such as heart problems (Pace *et al.* 2009). Mindfulness also leads to better vagal tone, alongside increased social connectedness and empathy (Kok *et al.* 2013) and has been shown to help people regulate their stress reactivity (Davis and Hayes 2011). It has even been found to change many areas of the brain in the process, particularly prefrontal areas central to self-regulation and empathy.

In one recent study, people were asked to wait in a room for some psychological tests. There were three chairs and on the other two were a couple of actors. Then another person (also an actor) came in on crutches, seemingly in terrible pain and needing help. The actors sitting down were instructed to look away, read their newspaper and not get up to help. This would put many of us off helping. However, those who had recently undertaken an eight-week mindfulness course were nearly four times more likely to get up and help than those who had not done such a course (Condon *et al.* 2013). In another study, people were trained in an age-old mindfulness technique designed to enhance compassion. Brain changes were noted, particularly in cortical areas, after just seven weeks, and the practices increased the likelihood of participants giving away money to help someone in need (Weng *et al.* 2013). Psychotherapists also tend to see changes in the same direction: more self- and other compassion, better empathy and relationships and more relaxed states of mind (Music 2012). Much of my work as a therapist is in trying to shift people into states in which the smart vagus is dominant, where calmness, openness, empathic and loving feelings are possible.

The effects of bad experiences can be countered at a variety of levels. Being able to take oneself out of both stressful and anxious situations in adult life, whether uncertain and pressured work environments, poor relationships or frightening and violent neighbourhoods, will decrease the powerful spiral of autonomic arousal. Supporting parents, developing more emotionally literate schools and closer communities, would all have an effect, as would changes in the cultures of organisations and workplaces, and of course bigger structural social changes. Mentalisation and empathy flourish with the possibility of feeling safe, trusting and curious but not with too much stress, threat or anxiety.

Having one's feelings understood and empathised with in a way that makes us feel safe leads to higher vagal tone, more emotional flexibility, a better-functioning oxytocin system and more openness. It also increases the likelihood of wanting to help others in distress. A task of mental health and other professionals, parents and policy-makers is to enable the conditions in which we see the development of the sophisticated social, biological and psychological systems linked to feeling more at ease, happier, healthier and more caring, spending more time in parasympathetically calmed states, hopefully with our smart vagus nerve firing nicely, leading to more self- and other compassion. Ultimately feeling safe, loved and cared for, and not feeling too threatened, opens up all kinds of possibilities for rich interaction and both empathic and altruistic acts. This happens both inside secure attachment relationships and in safe social situations, in caring work environments, families or communities.

However, too many children and adults are living in less than safe psychological and real-life worlds, are hypervigilant and perpetually on high alert and flip easily into primitive fight-flight responses; they can scarcely reach out to others, or indeed be reached by others. For many, even neutral or friendly signals can be interpreted by their stress response systems as threats. This often leads to acting impulsively and it is to impulsiveness that I now turn, and the factors that give rise to traits such as impetuousness, thoughtlessness, recklessness and also violence; all may be the opposite of a mindful life.

Chapter 6

Impulsiveness, self-regulation and aggression

Temptation

Anecdotally many suggest that we are living in a time when concentration spans are shorter, people flick around from activity to activity more, particularly on the web, and have less capacity to be still, concentrate, ignore temptation and focus. In this chapter I look at the relationship between impulsivity and prosocial behaviours, both in terms of what might be happening across society, as well as after particular experiences.

The myth of Faust, who sells his soul to the devil for immediate gain, is a compelling tale, given that temptation is something most of us face regularly, perhaps more so in consumerist cultures with sophisticated marketing techniques. We often struggle with dilemmas such as whether to stick to the diet or have that one piece of chocolate cake, pour one more whisky, or splash out on the glamorous shoes or gadget. Some of us are less able to control our impulses than others. Impulsiveness, short attention spans and the inability to self-regulate are often poor prognostic signs, tending to come with worse relationships, less altruism, and in some cases also increased aggression. We will see how impulsivity can be caused by a range of factors, such as poor parenting, degraded neighbourhoods, poverty as well as wider social trends.

In the USA and UK we know that diagnoses of Attention Deficit Hyperactivity Disorder (ADHD) have been increasing dramatically. Short attention spans and an inability to defer gratification tend to go hand-in-hand with poorer relationships, less empathy and less prosocial behaviours. These character traits seem to have increased in a contemporary world where instant gratification is on the increase, whether in the form of fast food, sophisticated sales techniques, easy credit, immediate downloads or instantaneous communications. For example, apparently almost 6 per cent of Americans suffer from 'compulsive buying' (Koran *et al.* 2006), a disorder commonly occurring alongside a host of other symptoms, such as mood and anxiety disorders, and issues connected with impulse control.

A 'must have now' mind-set is, by many people's definitions, an immature one, but it can also be seen as adaptive. If life is short, chaotic or unpredictable, if resources, whether emotional or material, are limited, the best policy can be to grab what is there now rather than delay for a future one cannot rely on. Psychology research has consistently demonstrated that capacities for self-regulation, executive functioning and deferred gratification improve with age, but are also crucially dependent on having received reasonably attuned parenting and safe environments.

In the famous marshmallow test devised by Walter Mischel in the 1970s, children are placed in front of an enticing sweet and told that if they can resist the temptation to eat the marshmallow for ten minutes, they can then have two rather than just one. The children resort to agonising contortions to avoid taking a bite.

It is with emotional maturity and the development of executive areas in the prefrontal cortex that we become less impulsive and more strategic (Steinbeis *et al.* 2012; see Figure 6.1). We generally see such good prefrontal brain development in children who receive attuned and sensitive parenting, which in turn leads to better emotional regulation and less reactive behaviour. Professor Nancy Eisenberg from Arizona, who has trail-blazed research about parenting, empathy and prosocial behaviours, has consistently found that those who best regulate their emotions are also less likely to be overwhelmed by other people's feelings, and as a consequence are also more able to show empathy (Eisenberg *et al.* 2010).

Poor self-regulation is linked to behavioural problems, seen more in children who have not been well attuned to, or who have been traumatised. Emotionally sensitive attachment figures can empathise with their children and help them manage an array of difficult experiences such as frustration or anxiety, thus promoting self-regulatory skills, empathy and emotional regulation, all more common in securely attached children. Secure children also are better at internalising parental rules and negotiating peer relation-ships and group expectations. Stress, frightening environments and a lack of safety will be detrimental to these capacities.

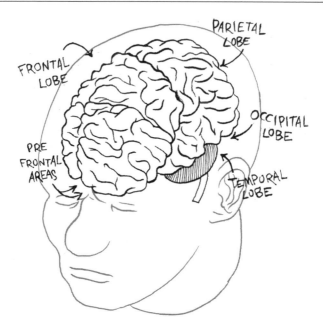

Figure 6.1 Frontal lobes

Illustration © Lawrence Dodgson

Studies show that having a traumatic childhood is highly predictive of being impulsive, dysregulated, having poor executive functioning and even of later drug dependence (Ersche *et al.* 2012). In families displaying high levels of negativity, anger or aggression, not surprisingly children tend to struggle much more with emotional regulation (Morris *et al.* 2007). Indeed where there is violence and aggression we see extreme sympathetic nervous-system arousal alongside the externalising behaviours (El-Sheikh *et al.* 2009). Many abused children I have worked with cannot tolerate waiting, are easily frustrated, and quickly feel provoked, seeing aggression and threat where others do not.

From the perspectives of Life Course Theory (Belsky *et al.* 2012), a speeded-up metabolism, less trust, less relaxation, more suspicion and risk-taking might be adaptive for abusive homes or violent neighbourhoods. Here there is little emotional security or expectation that things will work out well. It is a strategy, though, that is not good for health or relationships. Being able to defer gratification depends on feeling sufficiently relaxed (high vagal tone) and being able to bear and regulate one's emotions (Moore and Macgillivray 2004). Deferred gratification and altruism are linked and use many of the same brain areas.

Mischel found that children from low-income families in violent parts of the Bronx tended to have below-average ability to self-regulate compared to more privileged children. Other studies found a link between low socioeconomic status and the growth of executive parts of the brain (Noble *et al.* 2005), even linking poverty with chronic stress and neurocognitive outcomes right up into adulthood (Evans and Schamberg 2009). By just six months, infants from socioeconomically deprived environments are less able to pay attention (Clearfield and Jedd 2013).

Colleagues of Mischel (Casey *et al.* 2011) followed up 55 of his original marshmallow test subjects 40 years later, looking at similar numbers of those who were originally low and high delayers on the marshmallow test. Their capacity for delaying gratification was tested. For example, they were asked to do a go-stop task, in which they had to press a computer's space bar only when they saw a smiling as opposed to a frowning face on a screen. They were then told to switch and only press when seeing frowning faces. Switching tasks was challenging both because it is not easy to alter previously learnt behaviour, and also because smiles rather than frowns stimulate approach. They found that the original high delayers did quite a lot better. The subjects were also placed in an fMRI scanner and the results were as we might expect: areas in the prefrontal cortex central to tasks like working memory, self-control and directed attention were much more active in the high delayers.

Similarly in a recent study (Slutske *et al.* 2012) of over 1,000 children followed up right into adulthood, the three-years-olds who were most restless, inattentive, oppositional and moody were over twice as likely to be addicted to gambling as grown-ups. Interestingly, neither IQ nor even socioeconomic status was anywhere near as predictive. These are powerful indicators of the long-term effects of early impulsive traits.

Self-regulation

Self-control in children also predicts scores in maths, reading, vocabulary and SATS tests (Sektnan *et al.* 2010). Of students having to choose between having a dollar immediately or two next week, delaying was far more predictive of later exam results than IQ

(Duckworth *et al.* 2011). In fact, as researchers such as Metcalfe and Mischel show (1999), self-regulation in early childhood worryingly predicts a huge swathe of outcomes right into adulthood, such as the likelihood of holding down a job, managing a stable relationship or negotiating good friendships. In a recent study, over 1,000 children were followed up until the age of 32 (Moffitt *et al.* 2011). Early self-control predicted physical health, substance dependence, financial success and criminal offending, again irrespective of IQ and social class.

Grazyna Kochanska (Kochanska and Kim 2012) has shown how effortful control, moral development and the ability to feel guilt are closely linked. Children who can defer gratification are also more likely to stick to rules set by parents and teachers. Although temperament also plays a role, effortful control depends on feeling sufficiently safe and at ease, which for children means being protected by parents and being helped to regulate their feelings. In empathy we learn to tone down more self-preoccupied perspectives (Kirman and Teschl 2010) in order to reach out to another's state of mind. Children and adults who have rarely been empathised with often struggle to regulate their emotions or inhibit socially inappropriate responses. They are also more likely to have poor executive functioning and are more likely to show antisocial personality problems (Morgan and Lilienfeld 2000).

Thus several personality variables are linked. Children who can self-regulate tend to also be more trusting, prosocial and moral, achieve better academically and have better relationships, as well as having secure attachments and more sensitive parents (Carlo, Crockett *et al.* 2012). As explained in the last chapter, to feel at ease, with our smart vagus firing, to be open to other people and to new experiences, we need both to have had good-enough early parenting, and also be relatively free of immediate influences that stir up anxiety, defensiveness or aggression.

Those able to delay gratification have more activity in prefrontal brain regions, central to both abstract thinking, planning, working memory and emotional regulation, all aspects of what is called executive functioning (Barkley 2012). Those with more impulsive character traits tend to lack these prefrontal 'brakes' on their impulsivity (McClure *et al.* 2004). Instead, more primitive subcortical brain areas are active.

Samuel was typical of many children who have suffered abuse. He was beaten by his step-father and not protected by an alcoholic mother. At six he was described as over-active and restless. He could not wait for anything. If he saw something he wanted, he would just grab it, irrespective of whose it was. If he was not picked for the football team he would have a tantrum. He could not wait like other kids as he did not believe good things would come, for him it felt like now or never. He similarly could not concentrate for long. If a task felt too difficult, such as a puzzle or spelling, he would destroy what he had done, often hurtling pieces across the room. He felt bad afterwards but could not bear to keep trying. Not surprisingly Samuel had few friends and often got into fights.

Children like Samuel, and most of us when feeling stressed, anxious and uneasy, tend to have higher levels of stress hormones, such as cortisol, and lower levels of feel-good hormones like serotonin, both of which lessen ability to interact well (Kiser *et al.* 2012). Males with lower serotonin levels are more aggressive and less likely to find a place in their group.

Change

The good news is that, despite the predictive nature of Mischel's long-term studies, it is possible to learn some of the skills of self-control as we get older. Indeed, Mischel's team recently taught children skills to aid resisting temptation, such as pretending sweets were really just play dough, and he found that real gains can be made through practice and training. We know, for example, that praising a toddler appropriately for a particular behaviour, as opposed to praising them whatever they do, predicts the level of effort they tend to make five years later (Gunderson *et al.* 2013). Such interventions are in effect growing regulatory neurobiological systems.

Other studies are similarly giving hope. Some have used simple procedures such as variants of the well-known 'Simon Says' games, for example the Head–Toes–Knees–Shoulders task. How well children managed such tasks, which include tricks such as being told to touch your head when the teacher is touching their knees, is very predictive of exam results in a range of subjects in an international four-nation study (Sektnan *et al.* 2010). Those of us working therapeutically know this from our clinical experience. Children, as they begin to feel better, learn to trust themselves and others, become calmer, more at ease and adaptable, and then do not give up so easily, which is what I saw in Samuel in the course of his therapy.

Thomas Denson in New South Wales (Denson *et al.* 2011) managed to get a cohort of adults to use only their non-dominant hand for a whole range of tasks, such as writing, using a computer mouse, stirring tea or opening doors. This required a lot of effort. Interestingly after two weeks both those who had practised this as well as a control group were subjected to provocative behaviours from strangers. Those who had undertaken the self-control task managed their aggression better, were less easily aroused and less reactive. This is a very encouraging finding.

As already stated, there is a substantial and ever-growing body of research showing that mindfulness meditation practices help hugely, and they actively affect the structure of our prefrontal cortex, leading for example to increased grey matter (Hölzel *et al.* 2011), more cortical folds as well as hugely enhanced brain connectivity (Luders *et al.* 2012), working particularly on the areas involved in executive tasks and self-regulation. Indeed, much of what we see developing in people who practise mindfulness meditation is just what we see in those who can delay gratification.

The high-delaying children in the marshmallow task, as Mischel pointed out, were those who could find a way to think about something else, to distract themselves and not get obsessed. They found a distance from their thoughts and impulses and shifted attention elsewhere, just as those who meditate do. David Eagleman (2011) has suggested that we can give people what he has called *prefrontal workouts* that will train the 'muscles' of the regulatory and reflective areas of the brain. He has described a method which includes putting people into fMRI scanners and watching their own brain responses as particular cravings are triggered. The subjects learn which brain areas are firing up when temptation looms, and work out how to bring these under control with 'real-time' scanning feedback, a technology being pioneered by his neuroscience colleagues (LaConte 2011). These are just a few of many interventions, from biofeedback to psychotherapy, which can enhance both feelings of ease and also capacities for emotional regulation. Early intervention is best, but there is hope for change throughout the life course.

Digital worlds

Some argue that there are many countervailing trends in society, one of which is the exponential rise in screen use. The research in this area is contested and controversial. Some evidence at least shows that both watching TV and playing video games are linked to children having shorter attention spans (Swing *et al.* 2010), that the more TV preschoolers watch, the less capable they are of concentrating by school age (Christakis 2009), also having more behavioural and cognitive deficits (Cox *et al.* 2013). Another study of over 1,000 young people in New Zealand found that, even when allowing for a host of other factors, those watching the most TV were significantly more likely to have criminal convictions, diagnoses of antisocial personality disorder and aggressive personality traits (Robertson *et al.* 2013). Chicken and egg are hard to unpick here, as self-regulation and emotional ease come with good relationships and attuned parenting, and presumably children left alone in front of the TV or other screens get less of this. Indeed, by definition much screen use is either solitary or at best a more distal form of communication, without the usual relationship signals of eye-contact, smell, touch and body language.

Even using mobile phones, which are there to aid communication, apparently can diminish prosocial behaviours. In one study, after just a short period of cell phone use, compared to a control group, those using the phones were less likely to volunteer for community or charitable activities. They were also less persistent at problem solving when success would have triggered donations to charity, and generally they showed less interest in other people (Abraham *et al.* 2012). Another study found links between addictive mobile phone use and other compulsive behaviours such as shopping and credit card over-use (Roberts and Pirog 2013). They found that materialism and impulsiveness drive a dependence on both cell phones and instant messaging. Email use also increases distractedness, and raises heart rate and blood pressure, all of which improve when we have an email holiday, even while remaining at work (Mark *et al.* 2012). Using social networking sites such as Facebook can also lead to lessening self-control; for example, users are more likely to snack afterwards or use credit cards (Wilcox and Stephen 2013).

Much of the web is designed to provide instant rewards. Google earns more money the more sites that are looked at, for example.

Regular internet users develop specific behaviour patterns. For example, web pages are rarely read from left to right, but are skimmed and flicked through (Tapscott 2009). These behaviours become habitual. Flicking around multiple web pages is very different to immersing oneself in a book, which requires screening out distractions and focusing carefully. The tethered 'always on' world, with constant promptings from email, Facebook, Twitter, RSS feeds and the rest is having a profound effect.

As Turkle (2012), Carr (2011) and others have found, such technology promotes more cursory reading, lower concentration and increased distractedness. Turkle in her aptly named book, *Alone Together*, found in her research that students often sit in lectures skipping around multiple websites, some relevant to a lecture, but also doing email, shopping, and watching videos. Research shows that such multi-tasking lowers performance in studies compared to those who do not have access to the internet during lectures (Hembrooke and Gay 2003).

Not only young people do this. Turkle found that senior academics did the same too. Electronic media use has increased, and indeed even TV viewing has not suffered much in recent years, but reading print is certainly on the decline (Carr 2011). Unlike reading printed books, internet use is more strenuous in many ways, depleting working memory but also leading to an increased propensity for distraction.

Our brains are plastic and change in response to our habitual actions. London black-cab drivers develop different shaped and sized hippocampi, the brain area so central to memory (Maguire *et al.* 2000); the brains of people who play the violin are different to those who do not (Elbert *et al.* 1996), and research is suggesting that internet use, like the use of any tool, also changes our brains (Carr 2011). However, the paradox is that the plasticity of the brain then leads to habitual behaviour patterns that are hard to shift. Using the internet and other digital media will develop new habits. Carr suggests that the skimming, scanning, more superficial form of consciousness used with electronic media is leading to a change of habits which is also increasingly taken into relationships.

Multi-tasking leads to extreme alertness to any incoming stimuli, which is a great skill, but one which can also lead to an inability to concentrate on a task, or a person (Ophir *et al.* 2009). These are the skills designers from Google and elsewhere actively aim to increase; they encourage speedy, superficial scanning, aiming for users to click as many links as possible, all leading to increased advertising revenue. As Carr suggests, companies like Google aim to constantly tempt us with exciting information, with the new, with what is immediately of interest, enhancing our speedy, jumping-around mental skills. Such overload of information inhibits not only working memory but also the kind of frontal-lobe activity necessary for concentrating, for relating in depth to others, and indeed for empathy. Carr, building on research by Damasio and others (Immordino-Yang *et al.* 2009), argues that speedy, skimming mentalities will impede empathy, compassion and the brain areas needed for intimate, empathic relationships.

Research is suggesting warnings about electronic media, but the jury is certainly still out on this, and will be for some years. What is clear is that spending time with an attuned parent is good for a child's development and that screens are no substitute for this. A mother and young child watching TV together is far better than a child watching TV alone, but it leads to less social development than when mother and child read a book together (Nathanson and Rasmussen 2011).

Video nasties

Bigger controversies centre around the ever-increasing use of video games. Douglas Gentile and his colleagues from Iowa University have studied thousands of cases, finding that the more time spent playing such games, the more impulsivity and the poorer the concentration, and maybe surprisingly factors such as socioeconomic status have no bearing on the result (Gentile *et al.* 2012). Again, though, there are chicken-and-egg issues here, as impulsive children seem to play more video games, and kids who play more video games become more impulsive.

Many argue that violent video games are even more worrying. There is some controversy about how damaging they are but much research suggests bad effects. In one study, some children were exposed to media violence early in the school year and were both physically and verbally more aggressive to other children later in that year (Gentile *et al.* 2011). Other studies suggest that exposure to violent media, whether games or film, leads to more emotional reactivity and less prosocial behaviour (Coyne *et al.* 2011), priming young people to respond swiftly to any hints of aggression. Not surprisingly this has a detrimental effect on school work, but perhaps most importantly, on peer relationships, and the more violent video games people play then the worse these kinds of effects are (Hassan *et al.* 2013).

One study of violent video games (Montag *et al.* 2012) found that participants had heightened activity in the amygdala, that brain area central to fear and strong emotions, and lower activation in prefrontal regions needed for emotional regulation and empathy. The players were becoming desensitised to powerful negative emotional images, which leads to lower empathy, less prosocial behaviour and probably more aggression. Not surprisingly many argue that use of such media leads to shorter attention spans, and less empathic human contact and more likelihood of impulsivity (Kronenberger *et al.* 2005).

Even more worrying than violent videos are pornography and other sex-based internet sites. Once again, cause and effect are hard to unpick, as people who struggle with relationships are more likely to be drawn to the use of the internet for pornography and other forms of sexual arousal. Not surprisingly those who suffered harsh parenting indulge more in internet pornography, and are also more likely to get involved in coercive sexual relationships (Simons *et al.* 2012). There is a clear link emerging between male pornography use and increased likelihood of being excited by sexual aggression towards women (Malamuth *et al.* 2012). Males who use more pornography are not only more likely to be aroused by violence generally, but also in a range of tests were shown to be less likely to help another person who is in trouble (Foubert *et al.* 2011). Indeed, the same is true for women: those who view a lot of pornography are less likely to come to the rescue of those needing help (Brosi *et al.* 2011). Almost by definition pornography treats people as sexual objects rather than as human beings to relate to and many of us working clinically with such cases find that internet pornography and sex sites, as well as other electronic media, are used as substitutes for relationships (Wood 2011). A common clinical finding is that internet sex becomes compulsive and can escalate, leading to profound deterioration in the capacity to manage ordinary real relationships.

However, others argue strongly that such views smack of a Luddite fear of the new and that there is much to gain from such technology use. It is true, of course, that when mass-produced books became available many worried that this could destroy society (Carr 2011). Indeed, with regard to pornography, a powerful finding is that in most countries where adult (not child) pornography is made more freely available, then sex-crimes have in fact reduced (Diamond 2009), presumably because powerful gratifications can be achieved in privacy.

Also on the positive side, video games can increase forms of concentration (Oei and Patterson 2013), improve certain kinds of logical thinking, and less surprisingly, increase reaction speed (Graf *et al.* 2009). Screen-based games certainly have their hopeful sides. Games which require group-work and have moral and prosocial values can increase empathy, caring for others, helping behaviours and reduce aggression (Greitemeyer 2011). Studies in Singapore, Japan and the USA all showed that students who played such games later behaved more prosocially, some even showing improvements years later (Gentile *et al.* 2009). Even violent video games, when played cooperatively rather than competitively, lead to more cooperative behaviour afterwards (Ewoldsen *et al.* 2012).

Thus, good use of screens and new technologies might do some good, but what we know of course is that nothing does as much good as attuned, interested human relationships. Yet maybe even more important than the time children are spending in front of screens, is what they are not doing instead, particularly old-fashioned playing. Neuroscientist Jaak Panksepp (2012) has shown what many of us know intuitively, that play is vital for all kinds of development, including of frontal-lobe brain regions involved in self-regulation. He suggests that reinstating play as a central component of what children do, especially preschool children, rather than subjecting them prematurely to academic curricula, would lead to better frontal-lobe development, less impulsivity and more prosocial behaviours. Being able to play, whether rough and tumble games or symbolic imaginative ones, depends on feeling reasonably safe, at ease and unhurried. Children are increasingly deprived of the emotional states needed to be able to play properly due to busy parenting, the temptation of screens and the pressure of academic and other timetabled activities.

It is no coincidence that stressed or traumatised young primates or rats, as well as humans, often cannot play and struggle to fit into groups as they grow up. Many of the children I have worked with, especially those who come from compromised emotional backgrounds, are too tense, angry or anxious to be imaginative or use symbolism. As described, only with emotionally attuned parenting do children build capacities for mind-mindedness necessary both for good social interaction and also for play. Interestingly, Panksepp discovered that in rats bred for generations to be very hyperactive, those given play opportunities showed decreased hyperactivity and better self-regulation. He argues that the same applies to children. Interestingly, most therapeutic work with children is undertaken through the medium of play, and the first stage in most evidence-based parenting programmes is to teach parents to follow a child's lead and to play alongside them (e.g. Webster-Stratton *et al.* 2004). Those delightful make-believe games we sometimes see young children indulge in depend on sophisticated understanding of other minds. To really play in an imaginary creative way children need to be able to put themselves in the shoes of both their play partner and the make-believe character being enacted, and negotiate the to-and-fro of complex imaginative interactions. Children from traumatised or stressed backgrounds often cannot do this. Even children who have been sensitively attuned to can nowadays lead such timetabled lives that there is little time to just play.

Sherry Turkle has interviewed many people while researching the effects of technology (2012). Most strikingly, she found that what is underestimated is the very powerful effect of parental screen use on their children. For example, children bemoaned being picked up at school by parents looking at their cell phones rather than showing interest in them, or emailing at meal times. There is much yet to find out but Turkle's accounts and most readers' personal experiences suggest that screen technology is powerfully affecting how we relate to other humans.

Aggression: the impulsive, hot-blooded kind

Impulsivity and an inability to tolerate frustration can also be fuelled by early abuse and trauma, leading to aggression and violence. One kind of aggression is very often linked with impulsivity: a 'hotter', *reactive* kind, as opposed to a 'colder', *proactive* form (Dodge *et al.* 1997). Reactive aggression is often seen in those with poor social skills who misread social cues, for example, seeing anger and aggression where others would not.

One child whom I worked with, Harry, was accidentally hit by a soft toy and was furious, clear that this was done by another child 'deliberately'. Harry was quick to assume that people were being unfair to him, and he got into many fights. Such reactions are typical of reactive aggression and are also more likely in any of us when feeling tense or frustrated. Harry's reactive aggression was of an explosive kind. I discuss the 'colder', more proactive kind of aggression in the next chapter, in which children and adults show more calculation, actively enjoying the gains made from aggression. Proactive aggressors do not feel guilty about their anger, whereas impulsive reactive types often do (Arsenio et al. 2009).

Self-control and impulsivity are very much linked to this hot form of aggression. When people's self-control is depleted then they tend to be more reactive (Denson et al. 2012), while those trained in self-control skills become less so when provoked (Denson et al. 2011). Such self-control training also decreases aggression to intimate partners. Interestingly, neuroscience research shows that when we are provoked our brains are pulled in opposite directions. Part of us wants to retaliate, seen in reactivity in primitive brain areas, such as the insula, which is very involved in disgust; however, another part of us wants to stay calm, as seen in activity of prefrontal areas involved in self-regulation and self-control.

We have already seen how children with secure attachments tend to be less impulsive and more emotionally regulated. William Arsenio has helpfully made the link between attachment styles and forms of aggression (Arsenio and Gold 2006). Children with insecure attachments have lacked the attuned mutual reciprocity experienced by those with secure attachment styles, all the more so when there is violence and trauma. As a result they suffer from a profound lack of empathy and mentalising capacity. Such children come to believe that life is not fair or just, let alone safe and consistent. Indeed, few of us would find fairness in the violence, poverty, inequality and degraded environments that so many of these children grow up in, let alone the inconsistent and un-attuned parenting.

Interestingly, children with reactive aggressive styles seem generally to have clear moral beliefs, often bemoaning the *unfairness* of situations, reacting strongly to what they perceive as injustice. This is different from more proactive aggression where the victimisers see the benefits of aggression in order to get what they want. For reactive children and adults, the motivation (fairness or justice) is there but they misperceive the motivations of others and can very easily feel that they are 'victims'. Their physiological arousal, such as heart rate, shallow breathing or sweating, tends to be greater too (Hubbard *et al.* 2010); these are the people whose amygdalae fire away in response to pictures containing violence in a way that is not seen in the average person (Qiao *et al.* 2012). Reactive forms of aggression are associated with lower attention spans and also lower verbal ability, which is not the case for the colder, proactive aggressive children who also are better at making and keeping friends.

What is clear is that the worse the early experiences, such as physical aggression from parents, the more likelihood of reactive, impulsive forms of aggressive behaviour towards others (Lansford *et al.* 2012). There are, of course, other factors, including temperament. For example, there is a slightly increased likelihood of externalising behaviour with some genes such as *GABRA2* (Dick *et al.* 2009) or low *MAOA* (Dodge 2009), but the main 'pathogen' is always the maltreatment in the home. Those with certain genetic inheritances might be somewhat protected from, but never unaffected by, terrible experiences. A tendency towards impulsivity, indeed as measured via activity in the brains of current prisoners, even predicts re-arrest rates up to four years later (Aharoni *et al.* 2013).

Much impulsive behaviour starts for defensive reasons, maybe as attempts to manage stress or feelings of inadequacy. However, it then too often becomes addictive in its own right. We know both from research and clinical experience the dangers of addictions such as gambling, pornography or compulsive shopping. Even more worryingly, aggression and violence can also become addictive and pleasurable, even when they start for more defensive reasons. Researchers have found how many soldiers in war-torn areas speak of the excitement and pleasures of killing. This is often called appetitive violence (Weierstall *et al.* 2013), with many perpetrators stating how their pleasure increases when they see spilled blood. Indeed many such soldiers report returning to a warzone because they miss the power and thrills. Research with child soldiers in the Congo suggested that such a return to fighting actually warded off post-traumatic stress symptoms (Weierstall *et al.* 2012). This might make sense of atrocities such as those in Guantanamo or Abu Ghraib, which can be dismissed as the work of evil people but might well be an expression of a potential for violence and its enjoyment that is part of humankind's evolved predispositions.

Summary

Reactive aggression is one of several forms of impulsiveness I have discussed. I have focused on the powerful long-term effects of the inability to defer gratification. I have also emphasised how the triggers for aggression, violence and other forms of impulsivity often lie in early experiences, as well as particular social configurations, and that they are thus often preventable. I have also discussed how we are finding that there are many hopeful possibilities for change and for enhancing self-regulatory skills, whether by attuned parenting, prefrontal workouts, mindfulness, psychotherapy and creating calmer environments generally. However, it might also be the case that many developments in society are working in the opposite direction. These include an increasingly materialistic and consumerist ethos, less attuned parenting, deprived and violent neighbourhoods, poverty, powerful advertising techniques, faster change, less predictable futures, worsening mental health, insecure work environments and a culture which values immediate gratification. It is maybe not surprising that impulsivity, addictions and ADHD are on the rise.

With regard to violence, I have distinguished the more hot-headed reactive kind from colder proactive aggression. These are similar to forms of aggression seen in most mammals. Angry reactive aggression, such as a cat either bristling and snarling when under attack, is different to colder aggression, maybe seen in the same cat when stalking a bird to kill. Humans too are capable of both the cold aggression of the hunter and hotter reactive angry aggression. Many with the more deliberate and calculated aggressive style often also show reactive anger, but often more reactive children and adults do not display proactive aggression. I will now think in more detail about these colder forms of aggression and violence, including their more extreme variants as seen in adult psychopaths and children with callous and unemotional traits.

Chapter 7

Cold aggression, callousness and psychopaths

Cold aggressors

Some people have a propensity for colder, more proactive forms of aggression. Unlike those who are more hot headed, these cold aggressors are more likely to have better verbal and cognitive skills, better abilities to read social cues, have more friends, and indeed are often leaders of their groups. They tend to use aggression in deliberate targeted ways in order to achieve definite goals for themselves. They might read minds and intentions very well but have little fellow-feeling, and so their empathy is limited. Many who display proactive aggression are more than capable of also responding reactively when they feel angry (Thornton *et al.* 2012). Proactive aggressive acts, though, do not occur due to feeling affronted or wronged; they are more calculated. In fact such people often feel very positive about their violence, as it serves clear purposes, and they are even sometimes called 'happy victimisers' (Smith *et al.* 2010).

Unlike the reactive children and adults who might cry out against unfairness, these cold-headed aggressors seem to lack much moral sense, caring little about those they harm and lacking remorse about their actions (Arsenio and Lemerise 2010). The aggression perpetrated by such characters includes non-physical forms of aggression such as taunting, gossiping and excluding others (Marsee and Frick 2010). Colder forms of aggression are harder to treat, partly presumably because perpetrators have less desire to change, they do not feel bad about their acts and indeed are often motivated by the gains from them. Proactive 'happy' aggressors, for example, are barely touched by anger-management interventions, unlike more reactive types (Walters 2009).

As William Arsenio suggests (Arsenio and Gold 2006), many children who come from backgrounds where love, support and empathy were not available, are liable to develop deep beliefs that relationships do not revolve around mutual care or genuine interest in others. Rather they come to believe that relationships are about power, control, domination and getting what one wants. This is a more cynical take on life, arising from toxic adverse experiences which were not compensated for by sufficient good ones. This is certainly also what I have seen in several decades of working with abused and traumatised children, some of whom become very hardened.

Callousness

There is a group of children and adults, though, who are much further along this cold-hearted spectrum, who are said to lack any moral sense, who are callous, have no empathy, do not show either remorse or guilt, and often display severe antisocial tendencies. Many show impulsivity and behavioural problems. The worst crimes tend to be committed by this group, who also are often the most intransigent offenders. These are the people described as having psychopathic personalities, and children and young people with similar traits are labelled *callous-unemotional* (Viding *et al.* 2008). As the term implies, these exhibit a lack of care for others, as well as little emotion and a high degree of callousness. For adults the term sociopath is also used, sometimes interchangeably, and more often in relation to those with a personality disorder marked by antisocial behaviour. Cold proactive aggression is a much more central part of their personalities.

One boy I saw, Jo, filled me with dread before each session. He displayed a calculating coldness and could engage in chilling violence. His pictures were of mutilated bodies, death, gore and torture. He showed evident enjoyment in this, and in real life had been seen torturing school pets. At school pupils and staff felt uneasy around him. Jo, in fact, came from a home where there was both terrible neglect, and quite shocking abuse. In his infancy he was reported to have been left on his own on a sodden mattress, probably for days, but also sexually and physically abused in nasty ways. I am not sure if my therapy with Jo would have been successful, but his foster placement soon broke down and he was placed in a residential unit far from my clinic. I hope people found a way of reaching him but I had to admit feeling some relief when our work ended.

Often such children show signs of similar behaviours from an early age and researchers have found a lot of continuity into adult life (Frick and White 2008). Many adult psychopaths when they were children were reported to have been antisocial, started fires, tortured pets and shown cruelty. The presence of callous-unemotional traits in children, alongside conduct disorders, hugely increases the likelihood of serious offending, violent crime and shorter periods between reoffending (Brandt et al. 1997). Not surprisingly, those designated as psychopaths have frequently become notorious, their crimes making news headlines. Often they are extremely manipulative, charismatic, skilled at drawing people into their web and exploiting them. The question of what leads someone to become a callous-unemotional child or a psychopath is riddled with controversy, and there seems to be a variety of routes. Key questions are whether people are born psychopaths, whether it is due to genes or other aspects of their biology, or to environmental triggers such as serious early deprivation and abuse. Some experts have argued that people simply are or are not psychopaths, and are almost beyond help, not treatable, and all society can do is closely watch them. Others have suggested a significant genetic loading for psychopathy (Viding et al. 2008), arguing that it is primarily caused by inherited factors.

Kevin Dutton (2012), of the University of Cambridge, suggests that we think of psychopathy as a spectrum, rather like the autistic spectrum, on which we might all situate ourselves somewhere. The view that psychopaths cannot change has recently been challenged by some experts in the field. Aina Gullhaugen (2012), a Norwegian researcher and clinician, has suggested that we need to rethink how we describe psychopaths. She found in her examination of 30 years of studies, in addition to her clinical work with high-security prisoners, that most psychopaths have had childhoods marked by abuse, trauma and neglect. She and other researchers and clinicians argue that certain forms of treatment for them can be successful (Salekin et al. 2010; Polaschek 2011).

Martin, referred by the courts for a therapy he barely attended, was typical of many psychopaths in the literature. In his heyday he was CEO of an international corporation, powerful, respected, feared and extremely charismatic. He was assertive, decisive and could charmingly win over influential people. He always looked immaculate, bedecked in designer clothes, driving expensive cars, with a beautiful trophy wife. What was less obvious was Martin's ruthlessness, lack of compassion, and power-hunger. Scratching below the surface it became clear that he was cold, callous and calculating, his charm and persuasiveness superficial and manipulative. He made people feel important but in reality he heartlessly left a trail of victims in his wake. Martin in fact eventually became a victim of his own omnipotence as he was caught defrauding the company, stealing and lying, and was guilty of sexual voracity. As is typical in psychopaths, he denied any wrongdoing to the end, blamed everyone else and showed no remorse.

Many notorious psychopaths, from serial killers to powerful businessmen, have had people fooled. It is hard for most of us to accept that someone who is charming and friendly really could have no conscience. Anne Rule worked one suicide-hotline desk away from one of the most infamous serial killers ever, Ted Bundy, whom she saw as a friend. Unbeknown to her, Bundy would lure women in cunningly and manipulatively, sexually abuse and kill them. A classic Bundy ploy was to use crutches, which he did not need, and deliberately drop something, acting helpless just as a potential female victim came into his vicinity. When they offered help, he entrapped them.

For much of this chapter I concentrate on those at this extreme end of the spectrum of proactive aggressive, like Martin and Jo, although of course many proactively aggressive children and adults are nowhere near as callous as this.

Powerful psychopaths

Boehm (2012) and others argue that psychopathic traits would not have thrived in the stable small-scale cooperative hunter-gatherer societies in which humans lived for over 25,000 years. Anthropological evidence suggests that in such communities psychopaths were ostracised, even killed, and people had to tone down such traits in order to remain in the group. We also know from such evolutionary accounts that such cold, asocial ruthlessness was almost certainly an advantage in rare times of environmental disaster, such as when food was extremely short and the usual optimal survival units of cooperative groups would not work.

In fact, Kevin Dutton suggests that psychopathic traits have survived because they can be both effective and useful. He has investigated people, perhaps not surprisingly mostly men, who work, for example, as surgeons, as Special Forces Soldiers, stockbrokers and CEOs of large companies. He found that their ability to be calm under pressure, not to feel anxiety or be frightened by danger, is vital to their success. We, of course, need people who can hold their nerve and, for example, land a full plane with only one disintegrating engine, or dispose of a bomb in a built-up area when time is short. Dutton also found that many who score high on psychopathic traits are uncannily adept at sniffing out vulnerability and anxiety accurately. This is what makes so many good at grooming victims, alongside a lack of fear and anxiety in themselves.

Describing such people as cold, inhuman or callous suggests what we colloquially tend to think of as a lack of humanity. Of course, we all have some of these traits, even if this is hard to acknowledge, and we are all capable of being callous and self-interestedly aggressive. Such traits might come to the fore more in the face of danger or threat, amidst violence, competition or survive-or-die environments. The traits associated with psychopaths, of being cold blooded, reptilian and ruthless, are those we share with many animals. In psychopaths and callous-unemotional children we see the cold, emotionless aggression of predators as they stalk their prey. While such traits exist for good reasons, and can be the difference between life and death in extreme situations, most of us can also be empathic, sensitive and compassionate, despite having darker sides to our natures; psychopaths lack these redeeming character traits.

Yet even if there are clear evolutionary explanations for the survival of such traits, the downsides for society are clear. Many psychopaths have little or no ethical core. They can understand the feelings of others but do not 'feel with' them and so cannot show altruism motivated by real empathy. Although many can 'pass' for normal, they lack compassion and for them other people are definitely 'It' rather than 'Thou' in Buber's terms. It is unclear how many psychopaths exist, if there is such a thing as a pure form, but estimates range from between 1 and 4 per cent of the population, and those using the upper estimates, such as Martha Stout, author of *The Sociopath Next Door* (2007), suggest that we might expect to meet one daily on our streets or in our workplaces.

As stated, in an extreme or pure form psychopaths are callous, manipulative, deceitful, grandiose, secretive, untrustworthy, irresponsible and lacking in empathy. The words I use, like callous, deceitful or manipulative, have a judgemental ring to them, and it is hard to find pure descriptive labels for such behaviours. Bob Hare, maybe the best-known researcher in this field, has developed a psychopathic check-list (Hare 1999b), and this includes all these traits as well as shallow affect, a lack of remorse, refusal to take responsibility, glibness, superficial charm and pathological lying. Promiscuity and short-term relationships are also common. Many are easily bored, unable to control their behaviour or make long-term goals. They also have often had behavioural problems as children or were in trouble as adolescents.

As we saw in earlier chapters, understanding another's intentions is necessary for empathy but by no means sufficient, as to care about another we also need to feel *with* them. Beneath the ordinary presentation of a psychopath one often sees a cold superiority and lack of compassion. This is what Kent Kiehl of the University of New Mexico (Kiehl 2006) found in his studies of examples like Brian Dugan, who raped and killed many children. Dugan described his acts in as mundane a way as others talk about their journey to work.

Psychopathic brains?

We are beginning to learn that the workings of the brains of psychopaths like Dugan or Bundy are different, and that something has gone awry with their emotional circuitry. One of the first to explore the neuroscience was Antonio Damasio. In his famous Iowa gambling task (Bechara *et al.* 2005), people are presented with four decks of cards. Some yield huge winnings but also big losses, others do not perform so spectacularly but eventually pay out profitably. Participants learn non-consciously and intuitively whether a deck is trustworthy or not. The physiological signs of this are seen in sweaty palms and shallow breathing. As ever, bodily intuition is well ahead of the rational mind. Patients with damage to their ventromedial prefrontal cortex do not read such signs, going after the immediate big rewards and unable to resist temptation. They might be able to debate moral issues from an intellectual perspective, but their moral decision-making is not allied to their emotional brain circuitry.

Damasio's patients were not born like this but had suffered brain damage leading to serious personality changes. Many seemed superficially like their pre-accident selves but in fact became impossible to live with, uncaring, amoral, impulsive, and unempathic. Psychopaths perform similarly to Damasio's brain-damaged patients in these tests and they too have deficient functioning in their ventromedial prefrontal cortex, so central for empathy and self-regulation. Shamay-Tsoory and colleagues (2010) found similar deficits in empathy and in the orbital prefrontal cortex of a group of psychopathic criminals as well as in adults who had had accidents which had damaged that brain area. Both the psychopaths and those with frontal-lobe damage had poor connectivity between prefrontal brain areas and the amygdala, something that other researchers have also found (Motzkin *et al.* 2011). One study of three-year-olds with damage in similar brain areas showed that they were prone to impulsivity, lying, stealing and cheating, and displayed many psychopathic traits as they grew up (Anderson *et al.* 2000).

Unlike impulsively aggressive children and young people, those with callous-unemotional traits barely react to negative emotional words, or to distressing pictures, such as of children in distress (Kimonis *et al.* 2006). Interestingly they also tend to look at other people's eye regions less (Dadds *et al.* 2006). Callous-unemotional children have minimal amygdala response in the face of fear, compared to most of us (Jones *et al.* 2009), seem barely affected by another's pain (Lockwood *et al.* 2013), and struggle to recognise sadness, but not other emotions such as happiness, disgust or anger.

The lack of connection with the amygdala, that primitive brain region central to fear and other emotional responses, seems important; many adult psychopaths show severely reduced amygdala volume (Raine 2011; see Figure 7.1). Children profoundly lacking in fear are at risk of criminal and psychopathic behaviour as they get older. Indeed, low autonomic arousal and lack of fear in infancy is predictive of later behavioural problems (Baker *et al.* 2013).

The idea of not feeling much anxiety might seem attractive to those of us who easily feel stressed, but it would in fact make life very difficult. Anxiety is an important signal, even if some of us feel too much of it. If I get a shock from an electric fence one day, I need my fear response to warn me about being careful next time,

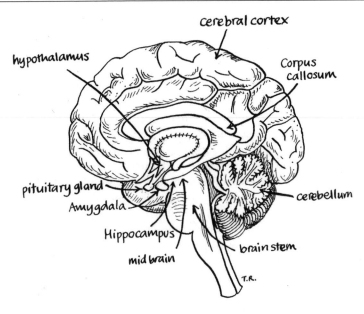

Figure 7.1 Cross-section of the brain

Illustration © Teresa Robertson

otherwise no learning takes place. It is no coincidence that fearful children generally tend to display greater moral understanding. Many psychopaths, and others who get into trouble with the law, are extremely impulsive. Many abused children I work with show high levels of fearlessness alongside impulsive traits, maybe stealing or hurting others on a whim. We know, of course, that amygdala abnormalities are a common effect of being abused and traumatised.

When they are posed with moral dilemmas, psychopaths and those with damage to prefrontal areas make logical calculations only (Greene and Haidt 2002). Kevin Dutton describes a classic experiment. After hitting an iceberg, a boat disintegrates. The 30 survivors cram into a lifeboat that can only stay afloat with seven people aboard. The captain must decide whether to throw 23 people off. Using logic, one could state that if they were not thrown over they would die anyway. When asked whether they would throw 23 people over board, most struggle and take about nine minutes to decide. Psychopaths have no such qualms. For them it was a 'no brainer', obviously they must be thrown off, and their decisions were made in about nine seconds, not the nine minutes of most of us. Incidentally Dutton's psychopaths were not serial killers, but surgeons, stockbrokers, Special Forces soldiers and CEOs. These all need to make very tough decisions under pressure, their psychopathy presumably being an advantage in their professions. As already suggested, the brains of psychopaths react more slowly to words such as *anguish, upset, terror* or *rape* than non-psychopaths. In psychopaths such words are processed not in emotional brain areas but more in left-hemisphere cognitively dominant ones, alongside non-emotional words like tree or car. They can have conversations *as if* they understand emotional language but in the core of their beings they simply do not. When shown pictures of violence or horrific injuries they have less physiological arousal than most of us, for example less sweating, or fast breathing. Not surprisingly, the lower the reactivity in brain areas that register another's pain, such as the amygdala, the worse the psychopathic traits (Marsh, Finger *et al.* 2013). Their prefrontal areas necessary for empathy are also less activated (Decety 2013). They also seem not to understand the distinction between conventional and moral rules that Kohlberg (1964) and Turiel (2002) both saw as a crucial sign of moral development, maybe assuming, for example, that not wearing school uniform is on a par with hitting another child for pleasure.

Most societies have examples of people with psychopathic qualities. If even a part of these qualities is genetically inherited, then psychopaths' ability to be sexually predatory and spawn many offspring would lead to the reproduction of such traits. Interestingly *kunlangeta* is a Yupik Inuit term that Jane Murphy (1976) in her fieldwork found meant 'a man who … repeatedly lies and cheats and steals things and … takes sexual advantage of many women— someone who does not pay attention to reprimands and who is always being brought to the elders for punishment'. When asked, one local Yupik person said that they would happily throw such a person off the ice when no one was watching. As Boehm suggested, such antisocial people would be unlikely to survive and thrive in smaller cultural settings with strong moral codes. It is perhaps different in our rather anonymous competitive late-capitalist world.

Where are they?

There are disproportionate numbers of psychopaths not only in prisons but also in positions of power, such as political leaders,

CEOs, heads of cults, senior soldiers, conmen and unscrupulous salespeople. We might be living in a world which values charismatic individual leadership over cooperative action, logic over emotional connection, in which it is easier for people with sociopathic tendencies to flourish. As Martha Stout points out, there are higher numbers of sociopaths in the Western world than in most other cultures and societies. Eastern cultures seemingly have between 0.03 per cent and 0.14 per cent, which is very different to the 4 per cent and increasing in America. Cultural factors have a huge effect on downplaying psychopathic and callous behaviours. Gary Olson argues that if positions of power and leadership in so many walks of life suit psychopathic tendencies so well, then people who find themselves in such roles might need to act more psychopathically to be successful (Olson 2013).

People with psychopathic traits are not all serial killers or paedophiles or criminal extortionists, and most have normal lives. Many seem to have the qualities the modern world seems to want: fearlessness, the ability to take risks, to confidently assert authority, to be cool headed under pressure, to be focused and determined to succeed. They certainly seem suited to the financial industry, so much so that Bob Hare stated that if he could not study psychopaths in prison, his next choice would be a Stock Exchange (Hare and Babiak 2007). Hare and others argue that some business models ape those of psychopaths, treating people coldly, as commodities, as units of labour or consumption, exploiting them, selling un-needed produce which can be genuinely harmful, all for personal and corporate profit. Tobacco companies hiding clear evidence of the serious health dangers of smoking, while actively advertising their products, might be such an example, as might pharmaceutical companies concealing poor long-term outcomes of drugs on which patients can develop a lifetime dependence (Whitaker 2011; Goldacre 2012).

Olson and others argue that a social system increasingly based on profit at all costs, on treating people as commodities, units of labour or as markets for goods might also tilt the balance towards such tendencies, especially alongside increased competition, job insecurity and anxiety levels. Non-psychopaths will be pushed into less prosocial behaviours while many with predominantly psycho-pathic tendencies will thrive. Bob Hare co-wrote a book called *Snakes in Suits* (2007) which described this phenomenon, and we are living in an era where what has been called 'situational psychopathy' can flourish, in part because ruthless practices are often financially rewarded. Hare estimated that there are four times more psychopaths who are heads of large corporations than in the general population, their ruthlessness being a huge advantage.

We all have such unempathic tendencies but they are more likely to be turned on in some environments, such as very competitive and ruthless ones. Changes at a societal level might be linked to this, such as levels of empathy dropping over several decades, as evidenced by large studies in America (Konrath, O'Brien and Hsing 2011), and higher-than-ever rates of narcissistic character traits (Twenge and Campbell 2009). High inequality levels are also likely to contribute (Wilkinson 2005).

One study (Piff *et al.* 2012) found that people from more privileged backgrounds were three times more likely to cut off a pedestrian about to cross a road. In another test in a school, when offered the chance to take some sweets from a jar which was later to be given to children, richer subjects took twice as many as anyone else, were more ruthless and dishonest when interviewing job applicants and more likely to cheat in games, reporting higher scores in a dice game than were possible (the dice being loaded). Valuing greed was the best predictor of such poor behaviour. Whether it was their position of power that reduced their empathy, or the lack of empathy that propelled them to power, was not researched and remains a moot point. However, we do know that certain contexts and social positions are likely to seriously reduce empathy and compassion.

Causes

While ruthless, stressful or competitive environments, as well as abuse and trauma, can diminish empathic capacities, it is less clear why people become full-blown psychopaths, as opposed to being ordinarily decent people who are nudged by particular pressures into 'situational psychopathy'.

About 20 per cent of the prison population are measurably psychopaths, and even worse, that 20 per cent cause most of the violence and trouble there. The million-dollar question is whether they are born psychopaths or become so. We have seen from Damasio and others how brain damage can lead to such symptoms. David Eagleman (2011) reported many extraordinary cases such as

Alex, a normal man who suddenly was overtaken by paedophilic desires that he could not inhibit. A tumour was discovered in his frontal lobe, and on removal his paedophilic urges disappeared. Eagleman suggests that maybe he, and any of us, might have such desires lurking in us, desires which are usually inhibited by frontal-lobe brain areas so central to executive control.

Many serial killers like the infamous Gary Gilmore had truly horrendous childhoods, while others, like the British mass-murderer Dennis Nilsen who picked up men, killed them and cut up their bodies, have less obvious evidence of an abusive past. Questions remain about why only some and not others who experience terrible childhoods become psychopathic. Some genetic inheritances also influence how susceptible people are to developing psychopathic traits after abusive experiences. Some researchers using massive samples of twins, identical and non-identical, seem to have shown a strong genetic loading for callous-unemotional traits, for example (Viding and McCrory 2012).

Yet not everyone is convinced by research using twins (Joseph 2004; Richardson and Norgate 2005) and genes alone do not explain enough. Any trip into a high-security prison reveals consistent tales of early abuse, neglect, trauma and lack of basic parenting, tales that therapists and others who spend their professional lives working in these units attest to. It is almost unheard of to come across a violent or psychopathic criminal who has had a relatively ordinary childhood, and often the stories of abuse are unthinkably horrendous, something that Aina Gullhaugen's research backed up (Gullhaugen and Nøttestad 2011; 2012).

Whatever the genetic research turns up, there certainly are links between early trauma and both psychopathy and callous-unemotional traits. Poor early attachment has been linked to callous-unemotional traits (Pasalich et al. 2012), and trauma and abuse affect brain regions where we see abnormalities in psycho-paths, such as the amygdala, hippocampus and ventromedial prefrontal cortex. The lack of early maternal care and maltreatment have been clearly linked to callous-unemotional traits and aggressiveness (Kimonis et al. 2013). Very tellingly, longitudinal samples from orphanages have found high levels of callous-unemotional traits in children adopted into even very caring and loving families (Kumsta et al. 2012). In addition, good parenting can effectively reduce the risk of externalising behaviours in children with callous-unemotional presentations (Kochanska *et al.* 2013). Of course, trauma and poor attachments cannot be the whole story, and children with attachment issues do not always charm and manipulate seductively in the way some psychopaths can. None the less, trauma has a powerful predisposing effect.

Aina Gullhaugen's research showed that psychopaths tend to come from atypical backgrounds, a high proportion with parents who were uncaring and overtly neglectful, or else extremely rigid and controlling. This might explain some of the anomalies. Neglect, the absence of good experiences, might be more likely to lead to psychopathy but it is harder to spot and research than overt trauma and abuse (Music 2009). Gullhaugen, surprisingly, found far fewer differences than would be expected between her psychopathic sample of Norwegian prisoners and more 'normal' populations. While they tend, she says, to not feel guilt, they often experience high levels of irritability, hostility and, maybe surprisingly, shame. Possibly her sample was atypical, comprising more female prisoners than most. The high numbers with psychopathic traits in other walks of life, such as heads of corporations, in the military or in politics, might have quite different profiles. Gullhaugen (2012) is attempting to develop new tools to enable more sophisticated assessments of psychopathic tendencies and pick up more finely nuanced issues.

Christian Keysers, a neuroscientist who has examined many psychopaths in high-security settings, warned that despite their shocking crimes, if you took the questionnaires they filled out at face value, they would seem as empathic as soft-hearted lambs. It seems likely that it is the more impulsive and slightly less controlled ones who are most likely to be caught. In fact Adrian Raine reports differences in the size of hippocampus of successful and unsuccessful psychopaths, success being defined as committing criminal and callous acts and getting away with it (Gao and Raine 2010). It seems that unsuccessful psychopaths do not read warning signals so well.

Some studies make a distinction between primary and secondary psychopathy, the former being more genetic in origin and the latter more due to poor early experiences. While genetic inheritance clearly has an influence, this is likely to be only part of the story. Terrible experiences play a major role in turning on or off any genetic potential for psychopathy just as trauma has a powerful effect on empathic capacities. One large study of Swedish male prisoners found a clear correlation between the extent of early abuse and the degree of both violence and also psychopathy (Lang *et al.* 2002). Another German study found a clear correlation between early physical and emotional trauma and psychopathic traits in detained adolescents (Krischer and Sevecke 2008). Several recent studies have similarly found links between early trauma and psychopathy, although always as only part of the story (Poythress *et al.* 2006; Patrick *et al.* 2010). This fits with the sad fact that a high proportion of children who have been in public care following abuse end up in prison.

There is another group who struggle to process emotions and do not manage empathy ordinarily: those on the autistic spectrum. While some criminality exists in autistic people, it is rare and certainly of a very different order to that seen in psychopaths. Autistic people, it is true, can seem very left-hemisphere dominated and struggle with empathy, but they lack that capacity to be manipulative and mendacious seen in psychopaths. In fact, they are far more likely to become victims rather than perpetrators. Psychopaths are often able to read other minds and work out people's intentions, making them successful at manipulation. Autistic people cannot do this and despite not reading the meaning of people's emotional signals, they are often very sensitive to and overwhelmed by others' emotional responses. They are also nearly always very keen to learn rules and follow them. Psychopaths on the other hand might know (cognitively) what is going on in another person but they are not affected by these emotions, and will carry out their plans irrespective of any distress in their victims. Bob Hare reported one psychopath stating, 'When I rob a bank, I notice that the teller shakes or becomes tongue-tied. One barfed all over the money. She must have been pretty messed up inside, but I don't know why' (Hare 1999a).

Summary

I have focused in this chapter on colder, more proactive forms of aggression, and particularly the more extreme forms seen in psychopathy and callous-unemotional traits. We have learnt a lot recently about those who display such amoral behaviours. Research is suggesting that early experiences play an important role but so do genes. We are also learning that psychopathic traits exist on a spectrum, and that none of us is immune from such callous ruthlessness. Some of us might have a higher or lower predisposition for psychopathy but particular early experiences, such as extreme neglect, and some social conditions, such as fear-inducing environments, will play a large part in turning potentials on or off. Gene-environment issues still need further investigation. Some think that there is a *primary* form of psychopathy that is more biologically based, as opposed to more environmentally caused *secondary* forms. Even those who argue strongly for a high genetic loading agree that gene–environment interaction is always central. For example, it may be that those with the short rather than the long version of the serotonin transporter gene are more susceptible after severe environmental triggers such as terrible early abuse (Glenn 2011). No gene for psychopathy has been isolated nor is it likely to be: unpicking nature and nurture is not straightforward and we have much yet to discover.

One promising line of enquiry suggests that what some call primary psychopathy might be marked by low levels of anxiety while secondary psychopathy is accompanied by higher anxiety (Kimonis *et al.* 2012). There seems to be more genetic loading for more proactive, colder and less reactive forms of aggression. While a more anxious form of psychopathy is seen in abused youths who are more reactive to upsetting stimuli, less-anxious youths with psychopathic traits barely react to distress cues and are more cut-off, or in attachment terms, deactivated (Bezdjian *et al.* 2011). The jury remains out about the extent to which psychopathy is biologically rooted or the result of serious neglect that turns off empathic qualities.

It is possible that we are increasingly living in a world which suits non-moral psychopathic tendencies and less emotionally attuned and empathic ways of living. The research has implications for how to organise society and our institutions, the extent to which we value individualism or collectivism, and of course how we bring up our children. Psychopaths, and presumably psychopathic traits, thrive in particular environments, such as harsh, ruthless ones, or where there is little room for softer feelings such as vulnerability. They also do well under cover of the anonymity of cities and where people can work unseen. The dark arts practised in the financial services industry before the financial crash might be a case in point. We have perhaps moved into a world in which it can be an advantage to rely on a colder, calculating and rationally instru-mental way of acting and relating. Next I turn to look more at this balance between emotion and reason, logic and feeling.

Chapter 8

A battle between emotion and reason?

Cognition versus affect

A moral act driven by empathy is very different to one driven by reason. This is starkly apparent when examining the excruciating moral conflicts that psychologists are so adept at devising. In one classic test you are asked to imagine that you are hiding in a basement with your baby and 15 other people. Outside you are being hunted by an enemy determined to kill anyone from your ethnic background. The baby cries, and you know that you must smother it to save the lives of yourself and the others present. If you act from a utilitarian, rational position you would calculate that it is better to sacrifice one to save several, because a truly ethical decision is one that is best for most people, not only our friends and family.

For most of us utilitarian logic cannot rule, and smothering one's own baby would be unthinkably difficult. On the other hand, moral decisions made only via emotions would lead to all manner of problems, such as favouring friends and relatives, and not being fair to people who we do not understand, such as those from another culture (Prinz 2011). This distinction between acting primarily from either emotion or reason is drawn out in great detail by Iain McGilchrist (2010), whose work on our two cerebral hemispheres I will expand on in Chapter 14. A more left-hemisphere-dominant morality will be more utilitarian, follow more logical rules and be colder, but surprisingly can be somewhat fairer than a warm-hearted right-hemisphere-led morality based on fellow-feeling and deep personal care for others.

As a psychotherapist I am in the business of helping people with emotional problems, and that often means supporting them to be in touch with feelings that are hard to bear, staying with emotions without defensively resorting to rationality. Typical is George, whose best friend had cancer. He began a session by saying things like 'well, it is meant to be, nothing you can do about it, it is best to just get on with things'. His distress, though, showed in his body, his slightly twitchy movements, anxious darting eyes and inability to be still. Being still might mean taking in the full horror of what was going on. Maybe not surprisingly George did not come from a family where emotions had much of a place. In fact, when his father died, nine-year-old George did not even go to the funeral, was told not to cry and was made to go to school the next day. As George, in the course of several years of therapy, got more in touch with feelings I saw a softening, an ability to be kinder to himself and more compassionate to others. Not only was he more likely to reach out to others in distress, and be more open and loving with his own children, but he was less likely to rely on rules and logic. In the past, if one of his employees were slacking, he would be very judgemental, saying things like 'that is not good enough, she owes it to us to be more committed'. In time, while being no pushover, he became more likely to try to understand why an employee's behaviour had changed, such as that perhaps something had happened at home to precipitate the slacking. He became less rigidly rule-bound.

Psychopaths seem to make rational and not emotional choices, something we also see in people with damage to areas of their prefrontal cortex. Experiments using a new form of technology that temporarily disrupts activity in the right prefrontal cortex precipitates people to make utilitarian decisions, compared with a control group whose decisions were more influenced by emotions (Tassy et al. 2012). Other studies have shown similarly that patients with damage to prefrontal brain areas central to social and emotional understanding become more utilitarian (Bechara et al. 2005; Koenigs et al. 2007; Martins et al. 2012).

In perhaps the most famous of all moral tests, popularised by Joshua Greene (2014), you imagine you are at a railway station and see a runaway train fast approaching a fork in the track. On the right track, where the train is headed, are five workers unaware of the risk to their lives, while to the left is just a single worker. There is a lever nearby allowing you to alter the train's direction and in a flash you have to choose. In this scenario the vast majority, up to 90 per cent, choose to direct the trolley to the left, leading to the death of one rather than five workers. But there is another variant of this dilemma which tends to cause more unease. This time you are on a bridge watching the same train carriage hurtling towards the five workers. Next to you is a man who is very overweight. You know that if he was to fall in front of the train his weight would stop it, saving the lives of the five workers but killing the overweight man. Do you push him over? This time most people do not think it is acceptable, even though the same people thought it fine to change the tracks so that the train killed one rather than five.

The first train dilemma is much more likely to evoke activity in brain areas specialising in reasoning and cognition, such as in the inferior parietal lobe and the dorsolateral prefrontal cortex. However, the more excruciating dilemmas such as whether to suffocate one's infant or throw the person over the bridge, tend to evoke activity in emotionally dominant brain areas, such as the ventromedial prefrontal cortex and also the amygdala (Blair 2004). To feel the excruciating nature of these dilemmas we need to be emotionally affected by them and feel empathy for the crying infant or the obese man, something not seen in psychopaths and people with certain kinds of brain damage (Dolan and Fulham 2007). Of course, how we answer these moral questions can be influenced by other factors such as what mood we are in or how the question is asked (Pastötter *et al.* 2013), but none the less the capacity to empathise is central. We are learning that there is a trade-off and that those who make more rational, utilitarian choices in such experiments have less capacity for empathy (Gleichgerrcht and Young 2013).

Reason's important place

Until recent decades, moral psychology took little account of emotion or intuition, being dominated by a more cognitive framework. Piaget (1965) argued that moral reasoning depends on the development of reasoning skills. Perhaps the best known of moral psychologists, Laurence Kohlberg (1976), asserted that children went through clear stages of moral reasoning, similar to how Piaget saw cognitive development taking shape. Kohlberg also used a range of hypothetical moral dilemmas to work out children's stages of moral development. Probably most famous is the case of Heinz whose wife was desperately ill. She needed expensive medicine, and the pharmacist was charging an astronomically high price and making a massive profit on this. Heinz had unsuccessfully tried every way he could to raise money to pay for the treatment. Eventually out of desperation he robbed the drug store to help his dying wife.

Psychologists were interested in the kind of thought processes behind children's moral views. For example, younger children might say that Heinz should not steal the drug because he would be put into prison, which would *mean* he was bad. Their decision about whether such acts were right or wrong depended upon whether an adult gives a punishment on a fear of consequences (being jailed) rather than believing an act is right or wrong.

As children mature they might say that Heinz should not steal because he should conform to rules, or, because the law prohibits it and one should abide by laws. Children who can reason like this already have an idea of a 'we', maybe a group or wider society, who share norms. Slightly more mature forms of reasoning move outside of conventional beliefs and enable thinking about issues such as human rights, maybe that Heinz has the 'right' to medicine at a reasonable price. Later on, still more sophisticated reasoning might occur and complex issues might be wrestled with. For example, is it more important to save a life than to respect the chemist's property rights? It is when people manage such sophisticated reasoning that early moral psychologists believed people became *properly* moral. This meant using principles, such as justice or fairness, to debate whether human life should be placed above money or property laws, as in Heinz's case, for example.

These psychologists suggested that ideally people move towards increasingly rational moral debate. Sophisticated moral thinking here means accepting that people need to be treated as human beings with their own lives, feelings and wishes, and that working out what is right or wrong can require complex thinking. This is a model of humans as individual rational actors able to make personal decisions. For example, let us imagine that Jack is seriously ill; he has explicitly stated that he really wants to die. On the other hand, his doctors and nurses believe that their job is to keep him alive. Jack could possibly live for many months, even years, but with poor quality of life. If we walked past the room and noticed Jack unplugging the machine that keeps his breathing going, would we tell anyone?

This would be typical of the dilemmas posed by early moral psychologists. Such questions do not necessarily evoke knee-jerk emotional reactions, but rather dilemmas that require some unpicking. For this we do need cognitive capacities to decide what seems right or wrong. Of course, we also need to be able to trust our emotional reactions and link the two together. We need to be able to empathise with the person who is ill, and decide how far we think they *should* be allowed to have their way, and we might also want to empathise with the position of the hospital staff, and the person's family and friends, as well as thinking about various universal principles such as the sanctity of life or the right to control one's own destiny.

Sometimes we can resort to very rule-bound reasoning, such as that one should always preserve life. Rules can be used to avoid emotional discomfort and excruciating dilemmas. Very often I work with clients, more often men, who cannot bear the strong feelings aroused by a situation. In one couple I saw for therapy the husband, Simon, was not happy that Stella, his wife, had again gone out and left him alone. He tended to resort to rules ('wives should not go out so much' or 'that is bad behaviour') rather than being able to bear the feelings that might be being stirred up (maybe 'I am a bit embarrassed but I just felt lonely and abandoned when she went out'). A big part of the role of a therapist is to help clients bear difficult feelings, so they do not resort prematurely to the safety of left-hemisphere-dominant rule-based behaviours. On the other hand, sometimes an emotional pull to help those we know and love needs to be tempered by a more rationalistic stance. In fact, Simon and Stella had two children as well as a son from Simon's previous marriage who lived with them. Stella had to work very hard to be as fair to her foster-son as to her own biological children. When Simon bemoaned Stella favouring her own children he had a point: her emotional pull towards her own children was not 'fair' even if it was understandable.

I often see a more rational and unemotional stance in people who have received less attuned emotional input, but I have not found research evidence to show that these are linked. However, Kohlberg did find that the most sophisticated moral reasoning was seen in children and young people who could put themselves in other children's shoes and who could think subtly and debate. Empathy increases, as we have seen, when we are less stressed, and also when we have been well attuned to. Secure attachment and emotionally sympathetic parenting have a big effect on empathic capacity, prosocial behaviours and making moral decisions (Affonso *et al.* 1999).

Power of feeling

In recent years there has been a new set of arguments suggesting that the focus on reason and cognition has led to underestimating the role of emotion, intuition and gut reactions in moral decisions. Carol Gilligan (1982; 1988) mounted the earliest serious critique of Kohlberg's work, in asserting that his moral psychology was based on a 'male' psychology. She argued that girls, when debating moral issues, were more concerned with an ethic of *care*, whereas for males *justice* seemed most important. Even if we are reluctant to buy into such a starkly gendered division, one of many important issues that Gilligan raises is that the role of caring for others, with accompanying emotional responses, was underestimated by Piaget and Kohlberg.

Jonathan Haidt (2012) is a psychologist who has led the charge to bring emotion back into moral psychology, suggesting that emotionality and gut instinct are much more important than reason when it comes to moral choices. This is the territory of whether to smother the baby, or throw the obese person off the bridge. In a typical Haidt scenario, we learn of a brother and sister, Mark and Julie, travelling abroad on vacation. They are alone in a seaside cabin and decide it might be interesting to try having sex together. Mark uses a condom and Julie is on the Pill. They enjoy making love but decide never to do it again and to keep this a secret. Haidt asks us whether what they did was wrong? Most people say yes. However, when asked why, they are hard pushed to give *logical* reasons for their view. The usual ones, such as the risk of birth defects, do not apply due to careful contraception use. Often people resort to 'it's illegal', or 'it's disgusting', although as Haidt points out, it seemingly was not disgusting for Mark and Julie. Our antipathy to the act is a powerfully emotional one.

Another often quoted Haidt example is that a man goes to the supermarket and buys a chicken. But before cooking it, he has sexual intercourse with it. Then he thoroughly cooks the chicken so there is no health risk and eats it. Is this ok? Most of us feel at least disconcerted by this, some again shriek 'disgusting', and again it is our 'gut' and emotions reacting.

Our moral judgements are very influenced by our emotional states. For example, people exposed to a messy room, a fart spray, or asked to recall an experience deemed disgusting, tend to be more moralistic and judgemental afterwards about acts such as first cousins sleeping together (Schnall *et al.* 2008). We are influenced by surprising factors. After washing our hands we tend to be more puritanical and judgemental about drug use or prostitution than those who have not washed (Zhong, Strejcek *et al.* 2010). Rationality has little place in these judgements. The debate between emotional and rational bases for morality is, however, not one that either side can ever win. To function as a moral person we need to use both, to link emotion and thought, take seriously our immediate knee-jerk reactions and also sometimes unpack and question them. We can rely too much on emotionality, such as trying to push someone we like a lot unfairly up a housing list (cf. Prinz 2011). This is partly why we also rely on 'impartial' judgements such as from courts of law or government-appointed bodies. We want juries to debate carefully and rationally but with their heart in the right place. People often react immediately at an intuitive 'gut level' to moral issues, but when helped to reappraise and think about the issues, then reasoning can play an important role in dampening down the initial strong reactions (Feinberg, Willer, Antonenko *et al.* 2012). Ideally the rational and emotional parts of our brains are working in tandem.

Linked to this, the important moral psychologist Elliot Turiel (1983) has taken forward the distinction between conventional and moral rules. The classic example of breaking a conventional rule might be running along a school corridor, or not wearing the right uniform. Turiel showed that even five-year-olds know that these are conventional and not moral rules. For example, if asked if it is OK to break a school rule by running in order to help someone who has fallen, or if a teacher said they could, then that is seen as fine. Breaking a moral rule such as not stealing someone's pocket money or hurting them would not be thought OK, whether or not an adult said it was. For most of us this is a breach of morality not convention. We normally have particular feelings in relation to someone contravening moral rules, such as anger at victimisation, and less strong feelings when conventional rules are broken.

Some struggle to tell the difference between conventional and moral rules, such as some autistic children, some with damage to the prefrontal cortex, and indeed many psychopaths. For most children and adults, with access to both emotional and rational capacities, moral rules are seen as different, and indeed have a universal and absolute quality. Turiel has the backing of much neuroscience research in asserting that emotion and reason cannot be so easily separated, that in fact emotions are embedded in reasoning (Damasio 1994).

Culture

We now know that both emotion and reason are vitally important. Haidt suggests that the sophisticated rationality that early moral psychologists celebrated might be the historically and social-class-specific morality seen often in left-leaning liberals, biased towards valuing reasoning and individual moral choice, but paying too little heed to the morality of those following clear, often God-given, authority.

In his Moral Foundations Theory, Haidt (2012) suggests that one of the reasons those on the political left and right cannot see eye-to-eye is that they have fundamentally different versions of what we even mean by morality, let alone fairness. Those on the left, he argues, view morality mainly from the perspective of the Foundations he calls Care and Harm, both strongly linked to empathy and attachment, the importance of which I have been stressing in this book. Here, kindness and care of others is valued and people do not want to see others in pain or harmed. Left-leaning liberals espouse a version of fairness which values equality highly as well as a belief in the importance of helping those in need. Those on the political right often advocate another version of fairness, which is that people should deserve their rewards, and that it is not fair that people who work hard have to pay for the welfare payments of those they deem lazy. This is a very different version of fairness to arguing that it is stark inequality that is really unfair.

However, there are three Foundations, according to Haidt, that left-leaning liberals tend not to endorse. One is the Moral Foundation concerned with Loyalty and Betrayal. A typical test of this would be a woman looking for a cloth to clean her toilet with and finding an old national flag. She promptly cuts it up and uses it as a rag. For many this would not be seen as immoral, but for those with more nationalist tendencies this could be a huge moral affront. Another Moral Foundation more espoused by those on the conservative right would be obedience and respecting authority. Children not respecting their elders would be seen as contravening a moral code. In addition there is a fifth Foundation, to do with Purity. In this, those with religious beliefs would argue that certain acts are wrong, whether it is a Jew eating pork, or some Muslims' views about anything that hints of blasphemy.

Interestingly, drinking very bitter substances tends to induce disgust and make most of us more moralistic, but this seems to be even more true for those on the political right (Eskine *et al.* 2011). Indeed, several studies are beginning to suggest that the brains of those on the political left and right often respond differently to the same stimuli, maybe not surprisingly, as every psychological trait has a brain correlate (Kanai 2012). Those with stronger involuntary physiological responses to disgusting images, such as of a person eating a plateful of writhing worms, are more likely to be conservative and, for example, oppose gay marriage, than those whose responses to such images are more muted (Smith *et al.* 2011). Apparently those on the political right are more likely to be motivated by disgust and aversion than those on the left (Dodd *et al.* 2012).

Haidt has helped us see that for many who are not in the liberal middle classes, distinctions such as between conventional and moral rules might not be always be as clear-cut as they initially appear to be. In many cultures, beliefs about what food is pure, or whether women should wear veils, are not just conventions but are absolute rules. This position is a serious challenge to the ideals of a free-thinking, rational Western way of being.

Writers on cross-cultural approaches to morality have helpfully pointed out that in many cultures the distinction between individual moral choice and moral action does not make sense in the way that it does to many in the West. For example, it simply would not be acceptable in South Indian Hindu culture to make a personal moral decision about whether or not to look after an ageing, ailing parent or disabled sibling (Miller *et al.* 1990). One would be culturally expected to do this, and personal choice would not come into it. This is typical of differences often seen between the values of people living in more sociocentric as opposed to more egocentric cultures, as I outline in Chapter 14. In more Westernised and individualistic cultures, personal choice, individualism and the sanctity of choice are much more highly valued, as opposed to more collectivist and socially embedded cultures in which there is more of a sense that one's first obligation is to the community.

This is complicated territory. We have seen in earlier chapters that it is a psychological and emotional achievement for children to grow into prosocial people who want to fit in and abide by the rules of their culture. We tend to see this more in securely attached children, for example, and less in insecurely attached ones, particularly those with disorganised attachments. However, abiding by the rules of one's community and culture might not always be viewed as moral. For example, what of those living in a country ruled by Nazis who unthinkingly accept the Nazi moral system and conventions? Partly for such reasons most readers probably have a version of morality that includes more than the acceptance of socially conventional beliefs.

Turiel (2002) in his later work addresses this issue head on, warning against the dangers of making simplistic distinctions. Even within a sociocentric culture there will always be some who oppose certain conventions because they think them wrong. He describes research with Bedouin women in Egypt, for example, who saw it as morally right to oppose the amount of power males have in marriages (Abu-Lughod 1999). Turiel does moral psychology a huge service in keeping alive the idea of resistance to hegemonic beliefs (Gramsci 1995), standing firm against the view that morality is only about conventions and social or cultural influences. He also importantly keeps alive the idea that different people within the same culture, including more sociocentric cultures, can have diverse beliefs. There are nearly always dominant and marginalised or subjugated discourses (Foucault 2002), some views carrying more weight, and people at times need to challenge hegemonic views.

Summary

The psychology of morality has changed dramatically in recent years, and our understanding of the balance between emotion and reason is central to this shift. I have looked at how moral decisions can be led by both more emotional drivers as well as more rationalistic utilitarian ones, each using different brain pathways. I have described how rationality and logic can often be used defensively as a way of warding off difficult emotions, and how as people become more emotionally aware they can become less utilitarian and reliant on reason. I have also stressed how an empathic and emotionally driven morality can at times lead to unfair preferential treatment. It has become clear that we need both our cerebral hemispheres and a morality which uses both reason and emotion.

Moral psychology had initially underestimated the role of emotion, and maybe over-idealised a culturally specific model of individualistic rational moral actors. The debate is by no means played out, and more brain and other research will undoubtedly cast further light on these issues. It will hopefully shed light on how children with distinct emotional and cultural experiences respond to moral questions differently as a result of their experiences. We should also learn more about whether psychotherapy can shift people into more prosocial as well as emotionally aware states of mind, changes that I personally have seen with patients (Music 2012), even if there is not as yet any definite research evidence for therapy causing such changes.

The relationship between our different brain areas and our moral functioning has recently been interestingly captured by Darcia Narváez (2009) in her theory of Triune Ethics, which uses many similar ideas to those argued in this book. She argues that our approach to morality and prosociality will be formed in large part by early experiences. Some people will function excessively from more defensive, stress-induced systems, leading to a lack of empathy, and others from a more compassionate, empathic and prosocial position, each utilising different psychobiological systems. She suggests that the evolutionarily more recent pre-frontal brain regions are implicated in what she calls an Ethic of Imagination, being able, for example, to envision a range of possibilities and to debate issues in the sense that Kohlberg and Turiel suggest. These capacities, though, can be harnessed, she states, by either a more heartless, unempathic way of relating or a more compassionate one, depending on people's formative experiences.

We know from research that those traumatised in childhood struggle with emotional processing as well as cognition, develop a reliance on different, more subcortical brain pathways, and also tend not to be able to follow moral rules as well. We have also seen how people with certain forms of brain damage, including some with psychopathic tendencies, approach moral issues differently. What research does seem clear about is that to function well in society, to be empathic, prosocial and altruistic, we need to have had support or scaffolding to develop both the emotional and rational parts of our personality, and the links between them. We now turn again to neurobiology to see how the balance of hormones in our bodies is affected by our experiences, and is hugely telling of the extent to which we develop a caring, empathically and other-oriented moral sense, as opposed to a more utilitarian and less generous-hearted one.

Chapter 9

Hormones of cooperation and competition

Cuddle hormone

A very anxious and timid client recently surprised herself when a group of scary adolescents approached her and her new baby. Unthinkingly she ferociously screamed and threatened them, and they beat a hasty retreat. She was convinced this was down to my therapeutic skills but I suspect it was much more the action of various hormones, including prolactin, which is triggered with breast-feeding and increases protective behaviours, and oxytocin, which is released in huge quantities in most new mothers, and which scientists have found greatly reduces the fear response, quietening activity in the amygdala (Viviani *et al.* 2011). Possibly such fearlessness is an advantage in protecting our young. Oxytocin, in fact, has lots of powerful effects and is particularly strongly related to our moral selves, so much so that the scientist who pioneered much research about it, Paul Zak, has even published a book about oxytocin called *The Moral Molecule* (Zak 2012).

In this chapter I discuss the role of oxytocin plus a few other key hormones such as serotonin and testosterone, in prosocial states such as trust and empathy. Hormones are basically chemical messengers that can have quite an effect on how people act. I am certainly not suggesting that hormones drive behaviour, nor that chemically targeting human hormones is a way to transform generous or altruistic traits. Rather, our bodies, including our hormones, are one site through which the expectations developed from our childhood experiences, culture and current social environments take root in us. I focus on these few hormones to illustrate typical potent effects but I could equally have described others, such as dopamine or endogenous opioids. Oxytocin, though, is maybe most pertinent to the themes of this book and certainly serves as a striking exemplar of the powerful interplay between bodily states and psychological experiences. Oxytocin is known to induce tranquillity, increase empathy and also altruism. We release it when we have a massage, or are being lovingly touched, and with more oxytocin we become more generous (Morhenn *et al.* 2008). In couples who are encouraged in medical trials to touch each other kindly, the husbands' oxytocin levels increase and blood pressure lowers (Holt-Lunstad *et al.* 2008). Most humans are responsive to touch, and oxytocin seems implicated in this, and for example, waitresses get more tips when they lightly touch a customer's arm (Guéguen and Jacob, 2005). A wife's fear responses are quietened if she holds her husband's hand when threatened with an electric shock, and interestingly the better quality the marriage then the less threat-related neural activity (Coan *et al.* 2006).

Other mammals such as rats and chimpanzees become calmer, more sociable and closer physically when administered oxytocin. Chimpanzees who groom other chimpanzees, especially those they are more bonded with, have higher levels of oxytocin in their urine (Crockford *et al.* 2013). Most of the effects seen in other mammals are also seen in humans. When shown pictures of threatening and scary faces, those given oxytocin beforehand had much less activity in their amygdala, the brain area linked with stress and anger, compared to a control group, suggesting that oxytocin lowers social fear (Kirsch *et al.* 2005). One client remembered how his father took his hand and stroked his back, calming him when as a six-year-old he startled in fear at a huge scary dog. Oxytocin was almost definitely implicated in the calm he reported feeling, as it works directly against stress reactions, such as the release of adrenaline, quicker heart rates, higher blood pressure and tense bodies.

Unfortunately, artificially introducing oxytocin is unlikely to be a medical or psychiatric panacea, particularly as it has a very brief life in the body of only a few minutes. None the less experiments give some indication of its power. Fathers given oxytocin intranasally not only became more sensitive to their infants, but these infants became more responsive in return (Weisman *et al.* 2012). Giving oxytocin intranasally increases people's willingness to cooperate and heightens altruistic tendencies as well as the expectation that others will cooperate with them (Israel *et al.* 2012). I suspect that similar processes are in play in therapeutic work. When we feel better, we interact differently with those around us, who in turn act differently towards us.

In a classic trust experiment, popularised by Paul Zak, subjects were given either oxytocin or a placebo. All were given money and a choice about whether to give an amount to a stranger who might, but might not, give them up to four times as much back. The oxytocin group were more trusting and generous, gave more away and reaped the rewards as they received more back. A linked experiment (Zak *et al.* 2008) found that those who naturally had higher oxytocin levels in their bloodstreams were also more trusting, generous and gave away more.

There are exceptions, though, and in most samples a small number of 'free-riders' exist who do not respond to the oxytocin and who 'milk' the experiment for their personal benefit. We do not yet know if their ungenerous response is due to a genetic deficit or adverse early life events. However, we do know that difficult early experiences reduce the propensity to release oxytocin. This makes sense. There is no point being trusting, open and generous if the world is scary, aggressive and unpredictable; our body and its hormones adjust to the world we expect.

Oxytocin is maybe best known as the hormone central to the bonding process, whether between parents and infants or between members of a couple. We tend to be kinder and more generous to those we are bonded with. It is no coincidence that other species who 'pair bond' and show monogamous traits also have more oxytocin receptors.

Perhaps the most famous scientific analysis of pair bonding was the study of two different kinds of voles, which are mouse-like rodents. There is a meadow vole that is very promiscuous, and also tends to practically ignore its offspring, showing few nurturing behaviours. Contrastingly the monogamous prairie vole is much more nurturing. The major difference between these two species is the amount of oxytocin they release, as well as another hormone, vasopressin, which is molecularly almost identical (females have more oxytocin receptors while males release more vasopressin).

Indeed if feckless male meadow voles are artificially given vasopressin they become loyal and faithful to their sexual partners, while if one inhibits their release of oxytocin and vasopressin then prairie voles become as undependable as their meadow cousins. We see the same pattern in humans. Men in monogamous relationships, but not single men, if given oxytocin keep more of a distance from attractive women, and even approach pictures of attractive females more slowly (Scheele *et al.* 2012). Oxytocin seems to increase faithfulness in men!

Genes

Genes also play some role, and there is much as yet to understand about gene–environment interaction. A Swedish study seems to have isolated a genetic variation (allele 334) in men that affects the likelihood of successful relationships (Walum *et al.* 2008). Indeed, men with two copies of allele 334 were almost twice as likely to be unmarried, and also much more likely to have relationship difficulties. Having this allele even predicted how satisfied a wife said she was with her marriage! This is all the more surprising as in Sweden there is no tax incentive to marry, and all the men in the sample had been married or cohabiting for at least ten years. Interestingly the gene involved here is almost identical to the one so central to the research on voles.

There are other genetic predictors of how much oxytocin we will release. There are two versions, A or G, of the oxytocin receptor gene, *OOXTR*, and we inherit from both parents, thus any of us might be AA, GG or AG. Those with two Gs seem to be the most prosocial, so much so that when observers watched less than half a minute of 23 romantic couples in conversation, they consistently tended to say that the listeners with two Gs were kinder and more empathic (Kogan *et al.* 2011).

Another study found that on perceiving a threat, those with two Gs remained charitable and helpful while those having other combinations became less prosocial (Poulin *et al.* 2012). Something similar has even been found in children. For example, preschoolers with one variant (the RS3 variant of the arginine vasopressin receptor 1A gene) were consistently less altruistic (Avinun *et al.* 2011). However, we know experience will moderate such predispositions. For example, securely attached children have been found to be more generous when they have one of two versions of a dopamine receptor gene (Bakermans-Kranenburg and van IJzendoorn 2011), and similar research is likely to come through in forthcoming years.

Thus, this is by no means all about genes; experience and culture have a big say in whether genetic potentials get turned on or off.

One study found that Americans with either two Gs or an AG combination were more likely to seek social support when in trouble, but the same was not the case for Koreans with the same gene combinations, for whom such support seeking was less culturally common (Kim *et al.* 2010). Another study looked at mothering and found that it was the combination of both the form of oxytocin gene a mother had and the kind of parenting a new mother herself received which were predictive of the quality of their mothering (Mileva-Seitz *et al.* 2013).

Recent epigenetic research is revealing much about how different experiences trigger the ways in which our genes are expressed. Jeremy Holmes (2013) has put this nicely in terms of the formula $Phe = G \times E^2$. By this he means that our phenotype, or in other words the observable characteristics of an organism, is the result of the interaction between our genes (G) and our environment (squared). He suggests we think of the effect of the environment being squared, as not only does our current environment have an effect on gene expression, but early experiences have a definite longer-term effect on future gene expression, sometimes even into the next generation. What is clear though is that genes, although influential, only explain so much.

Experience really counts

Life events, including parenting and a variety of social forces, can programme our hormones. The oxytocin levels of both fathers and mothers rise considerably in the months after becoming a parent, and the higher the levels, the more affectionate play we see from mothers and the more stimulating play from fathers (Gordon *et al.* 2010a). In fact when mothers and infants are in tune and their movements are synchronised, then oxytocin levels spike, but not when the pair are less attuned (Feldman *et al.* 2011). Being in love is often seen as a kind of blindness in which we can see no fault in the other. Maybe not surprisingly, new lovers, compared to single people, tend to have twice the level of oxytocin in their blood (Schneiderman *et al.* 2012), presumably playing havoc with normal levels of wariness.

A lack of good early maternal care leads to lower oxytocin release in many animals (Francis *et al.* 2000), and deliberately engineering diminished oxytocin release in animals leads to worse mothering (Shahrokh *et al.* 2010). Research with humans is pointing firmly in this direction. Lane Strathearn (2011; *et al.* 2009) probably more than anyone has looked at the effects of early neglect. He found that adults with avoidant attachment styles have lower activation of the oxytocin system and other brain regions associated with rewards. An earlier study of neglected Romanian orphans found that the adopted children released less oxytocin when cuddled by their adoptive mothers than a control group of birth children (Fries *et al.* 2005), and also had lower levels of vasopressin, presumably due to poor early nurturing experiences.

Oxytocin, whether transmitted in the blood stream or via our nerve cells, needs to find a receptor to have any effect, rather like a key needs a lock to work. The more good, loving experiences we have early on in life then the more oxytocin receptors we are likely to develop. Early stressful life experiences lead to less oxytocin receptors, lower oxytocin levels in men (Opacka-Juffry and Mohiyeddini 2011), and also in women abused as girls (Heim *et al.* 2008).

Indeed, early experiences of abuse can play havoc with oxytocin systems. Paul Zak and colleagues found in trust games that sexually abused women, after being given oxytocin, were either considerably more trusting than the control group, or considerably less so, but they acted outside usual parameters (Terris *et al.* 2010). Similarly for very rejection-sensitive people, such as those with borderline personality disorder or attachment issues, oxytocin can in fact decrease cooperation and trust (Bartz *et al.* 2011). Bad early experiences can disrupt normal workings of the oxytocin system. We know anyway that in trust games those with borderline personality disorder struggle more with trust and cooperation than most (King-Casas *et al.* 2008) and in psychotherapy such patients can be notoriously untrusting. Such findings help make sense of why so many people from emotionally depriving backgrounds struggle with empathy, trust or altruism.

Oxytocin can also increase the pleasure in the misfortunes of others that Germans describe as *Schadenfreude* (Shamay-Tsoory *et al.* 2009). Thus oxytocin is neither a miracle cure nor always a force for good. When things go reasonably well in childhood one would expect oxytocin to have a prosocial and even pro-moral effect but people respond differently to it depending on their mental state and early experiences. When given oxytocin and asked to recall childhood experiences people with insecure attachments tend to remember bad experiences, unlike securely attached people who recall positive and loving moments (Bartz *et al.* 2010).

Breast-feeding mothers with the highest levels of oxytocin have less stress symptoms, for example, lower blood pressure (Light *et al.* 2000). Mothers with a secure attachment style are not only better at picking up infant cues, but also their oxytocin circuitry is more activated when observing their baby laughing or crying (Strathearn *et al.* 2009). Mothers with more insecure styles, on the other hand, have high activation of brain areas such as the insula, central to a more rejecting and aversive response.

This is partly why providing support for new parents is so crucial. We know that thoughtful, attuned help for pregnant women speeds up births and reduces pain (Klaus *et al.* 1993), a process seemingly aided by the oxytocin release from touch and emotional support (Uvnas-Moberg and Petersson 2005). When new mothers have partners who are supportive and in tune with them, we see not only synchronised interactions, but also mother, father and baby, all three, have higher oxytocin levels (Gordon *et al.* 2010b). All this helps make sense of the link between secure attachment, altruism and prosocial behaviour in both children and adults.

Higher oxytocin levels increase the ability to understand what other people are thinking and feeling (Domes *et al.* 2007). Indeed, giving doses of oxytocin artificially leads to adults paying more attention to people's eye-regions (Guastella *et al.* 2008), even increasing the ability of autistic people to read other people's minds and emotions (Guastella *et al.* 2010). Oxytocin oils the wheels of social life, enhancing trust, generosity, empathy and loyalty.

This might explain many of the feel-good and health-enhancing properties of cohesive groups and close personal ties. Heart patients on average live longer if they have better relationships and if they are members of social groups and clubs. Isolation, loneliness and the lack of intimate contact with other humans are all risk factors for health problems. For example, old people living alone experience more physical health problems, mental illness, alcohol use and earlier death (Kharicha *et al.* 2007).

Living in a caring community has exponential effects on good feelings and increases our wish to help others. Going back to rats, if a single one in a cage is given oxytocin then not only does that rat become more at ease and trusting, but the effect spreads to other rats in the cage. If an antagonist is given which stops the oxytocin functioning, then this effect does not take place, so oxytocin is definitely implicated in the increase in prosocial behaviours (Ågren *et al.* 1997). In humans, too, we know that happiness is almost contagious. One study found that a person is 42 per cent more likely to be happy if a friend who lives less than half a mile away becomes happy, but that this is seen in only 22 per cent if the friend lives over two miles away (Fowler and Christakis 2008).

Carsten de Dreu (2011) found that oxytocin enhances group cooperative behaviour in humans, increasing 'tend and defend' altruistic and caring acts, at least for those in our 'in-group' but not necessarily for those deemed different to us. Paul Zak found that empathy is contagious and that when someone acts generously, other people coming into contact with such generosity often also act generously, and in turn release higher levels of oxytocin (Zak 2012). Maybe one of the questions for us as individuals, parents, but also for those organising neighbourhoods, work environments and political policy, is how to create more oxytocin-fuelled and -fuelling environments.

Other hormones: serotonin

While I have concentrated on oxytocin, other hormones play a central role in moral, altruistic and empathic behaviour, not least serotonin. Serotonin is of course the hormone that is targeted by anti-depressant drugs like Prozac, and is very linked to good feelings. We see low levels of serotonin in depression, alongside irritability and aggression (Carver *et al.* 2008). Bad experiences have a powerful effect on serotonin levels. For example, monkeys removed from their mothers at birth have chronically low levels, tend to become violent and are often ostracised from groups (Shannon *et al.* 2005). Childhood adversity such as maternal depression or trauma is linked to lower serotonin levels (Field 1995).

Such effects are partly mediated by genes. One can have one of two versions of the *5HT* gene, and those with the short version are more vulnerable to childhood trauma and neglect, releasing even less serotonin (Canli *et al.* 2008) and in the face of bad experiences being more prone to aggression, anxiety and depression. Adverse early experiences have an effect on how genes are expressed (Lesch 2011). It is clear that abusive early experience equates generally with lower serotonin levels, even more so if one has a short version of the *5HT* gene, and we know that many on the fringes of society, such as aggressive psychiatric patients, prisoners and others, have low levels of this hormone (Davidson *et al.* 2000). In humans, poor early emotional regulation by parents, and exposure to violence, neglect or abuse, can all have a devastating effect on these hormonal systems.

Serotonin levels also have an effect on how we approach moral issues. For example, in the Ultimatum Game, which I describe more in the next chapter, people with low serotonin levels are more likely to make less generous offers to others, and be more rejecting of ungenerous offers to them (Emanuele *et al.* 2008). When given drugs which increase serotonin levels, people become more likely to act in ways that avoid harm to individuals, and are more wary of unfair behaviours (Crockett *et al.* 2010). Basically, higher levels tend to make people more prosocial and altruistic. This links with a central theme of this book. Good experiences and feeling good lead people to be more prosocial, particularly as when experiencing emotional wellbeing our threat system is dampened down.

It seems that serotonin works on morality in a different way to oxytocin, in a more 'top-down' as opposed to 'bottom-up' way, activating higher-level brain functions, such as in the prefrontal cortex, which inhibit fear and threat responses in the emotionally important limbic areas. Interestingly, increases in prosocial behaviour are not present when adrenaline is artificially introduced, suggesting again the opposite pulls of stress and being prosocial (Tost and Meyer-Lindenberg 2010).

The main medical research about serotonin has been pharmacological, especially with regard to modern anti-depressants. However, what we know from the developmental literature is that if children feel safe, accepted and cared for and have sensitive attuned parenting, then they will more than likely have higher serotonin levels, be happier, be more worried about harm to other people, be less aggressive and reactive and more likely to fit into social groups, as well as having good peer relations and good relationships generally.

Testosterone

Our countervailing tendencies for selfishness and aggression also have a hormonal aspect, seen particularly in the hormone more associated with males, testosterone. For example, violent prisoners, both male and female, have higher testosterone levels (Dabbs and

Dabbs 2000). While oxytocin enhances cooperation and mutual kindness, testosterone has the opposite effect, making people more egocentric and less collaborative (Wright, Bahrami *et al.* 2012). Similarly, people, even infants, with higher levels of testosterone are less able to read the emotions of others and tend to have less empathy (Baron-Cohen 2011), while artificially giving people testosterone has a negative effect on empathy levels. High testosterone levels are also seen more in grandiose people (van der Meij *et al.* 2012).

However, testosterone also has positive effects, such as increasing confidence and resilience. Indeed it has anti-depressant qualities and low levels of it are linked with depression (Giltay *et al.* 2012). Maybe most importantly for thinking about morality, we know that with high levels, there is less caring of others, more risk taking and quicker arousal to aggression and conflict. In fact, in one study of over 1,000 people, the ratio between index and ring fingers, believed to be linked to exposure to prenatal testosterone, even predicted how altruistic people would be in trust games: longer ring fingers tend to equate with higher testosterone (Brañas-Garza *et al.* 2013).

Interestingly males, on becoming fathers, tend to experience a lowering of testosterone levels, at least if they are living with the mother; and presumably this is to enhance the nurturing and loving behaviours which testosterone can inhibit (Kuzawa *et al.* 2009). Thus biology, culture and life history interweave, and while people can be born with lower or higher levels of testosterone, life events and culture inscribe their influences on bodily processes.

Given that on average females release more oxytocin and males have higher levels of testosterone, the research seems to suggest at least some gender-based differences in levels of caring, openness, trust, altruism and empathy, unfortunately backing up a range of gender stereotypes. These, of course, are at most only *on-average* tendencies.

When faced with a decision about whether to kill a close relative in order to save the lives of ten unknown people, most people struggle terribly. As discussed already, a utilitarian decision would be based on rationality and not emotion, on what is best for the greatest number. High testosterone levels predict such utilitarian decision-making (Carney and Mason, 2010). It seems likely that testosterone quietens the ventromedial prefrontal cortex, which has a crucial role in empathy and caring for others (Mehta and Beer 2010). This might be a similar mechanism to that which leads to high-testosterone people being very successful in business and the financial world, as well as being involved in criminality. High testosterone generally goes with less sensitivity to the feelings of others.

It is important to reiterate that our levels of these and other hormones are not simply biological givens, and will always be mediated by cultural and socioeconomic factors and life experiences. For example testosterone levels are higher when sportsmen play in front of their home crowd (Neave and Wolfson 2003). Similar effects are seen in other cultures. For example, when forager-horticulturalist males of the Bolivian Amazon compete they too have higher testosterone (Trumble *et al.* 2012). In fact, on the night when Obama won the presidential election over McCain, Obama supporters had higher testosterone levels (Stanton *et al.* 2009). Hence culture and experiences hugely influence our hormonal responses.

In what are called 'honour' cultures, prevalent in southern rather than northern US states, males show higher aggressiveness, reactivity and retaliatory responses, with more rapid testosterone and cortisol responses (Nisbett and Cohen 1996). Pupils in schools in states where such honour cultures are common were twice as likely to be involved in shooting as those in non-honour states, even when all other demographic factors were screened out (Brown, Osterman *et al.* 2009).

Other research shows that adverse experiences such as poor parenting affect testosterone levels. Young people living in poor, violent neighbourhoods where there were more empty and boarded-up properties were more likely to show aggressive and externalising behaviours, and have higher levels of testosterone (Tarter *et al.* 2009). This links to the 'life history' evolutionary model which suggests that, when confronted with cues suggesting that life is dangerous, we develop a more stress-based and risk-taking 'fast' life-course, in which empathy and altruism play a smaller role. These high-octane young people also had a range of other psychological vulnerabilities, including increased use of drugs.

Summary

I have been looking at how hormones, and in particular oxytocin, are implicated in altruistic, prosocial and moral behaviours. Due to space I have been somewhat selective, and for example, have left out the central role of dopamine, which is profoundly implicated in the degree of attunement seen in new mothers to their offspring (Mileva-Seitz *et al.* 2012). Depressed mothers, for example, have lower dopamine levels, higher cortisol and are less responsive to their infants.

We have seen how oxytocin and testosterone can work against each other, although there is a danger of suggesting simplistic one-to-one relationships between hormones and emotional states; the issues are far more complex, given the multifaceted interactions between hormones and other biological systems (Glenn *et al.* 2011; Strathearn 2011). Part of my rationale for presenting research about hormones is to stress the profound interplay between parenting, culture, context and bodily states, all influencing the way we relate to others, all playing a role in tilting us towards either prosocial or antisocial behaviours.

Overall I have been suggesting that life experiences, social influences and genetic inheritance all get written into our bodily states, leading to different propensities for altruistic behaviour, and also different approaches to morality. With more oxytocin, and to a smaller extent and differently serotonin, we see more empathy, compassion and altruism. Both hormones are released more when living in safe, loving environments. On the other hand, more testosterone can lead to more aggression, self-centredness, and a utilitarian moral decision-making divorced from emotionality. Other hormones have different effects.

Thus, a complex array of factors influences the kind of social and moral beings that we become. Empathy, generosity and trust smooth the wheels of social and group existence, but for these to come to the fore, people need a calmed parasympathetic nervous system in which the 'smart vagus' is dominant. Such an apparently oxytocin-rich state of mind helps the forging of bonds, allowing humans to successfully undertake tasks that isolated individuals could never manage. Some argue that there is currently a risk of such prosocial cooperative traits taking a back-seat to more competitive, individualistic ones as aggressive market models become dominant in contemporary societies. Humans lived for at least 25,000 years in small hunter-gatherer communities where the emotional states for which oxytocin is central, like empathy, were needed and valued. The more close-knit and bonded the group, the more likely everyone would survive and thrive. This central aspect of our evolutionary inheritance, which possibly is now more at risk, is what I now go on to consider.

Chapter 10

Evolved both to cooperate and compete

Non-human origins

A striking and often-used metaphor that has grown out of brain research is that we are part reptile, part mammal, and part a uniquely sophisticated primate, and that we can be driven by motivations originating from any of these evolutionary inheritances (see Figure 10.1). In this chapter I introduce some evolutionary thinking, and in particular research about how humans lived in our hunter-gatherer past, a time when it seems likely that many of our more prosocial traits became more developed. I want to avoid the idea that a hunter-gathering or any other way of living is any more *natural* than any other. I introduce this research because I believe it helps in understanding the range of human possibilities, as well as the social conditions needed for potentials like altruism to become prominent.

In evolutionary development, nothing is built from scratch or designed from new, but rather older inherited tendencies can find new uses and co-exist with newly forming ones. The prominent neuroscientist Jaak Panksepp (Panksepp and Panksepp 2000) has suggested, using compelling evidence, that just about all the human biological systems involved in emotional and social lives, such as caring for others, rage, fear, playing, seeking, panic or sex, are rooted in ancient, subcortical areas of the brain. These are systems that we share not only with other primates, like chimpanzees, but indeed with all mammals. Unflatteringly many of our brain pathways remain remarkably similar to those of pre-mammalian reptile species.

Many moral dilemmas can be thought about using the metaphor of conflict between these different inherited systems. Take the

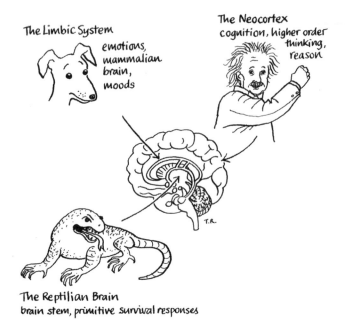

Figure 10.1 The triune brain

Source: MacLean, P.D., 1973. *A triune concept of the brain and behavior.* Toronto: University of Toronto Press.

Illustration © Teresa Robertson

example of Martin, aged six. He is at a party with his friend Stephen. They thought the food was finished but they find one delicious-looking chocolate left on a table. Martin, driven by naked desire, makes a grab for it, but is pulled back by another more prosocial internal pull, and looks at Stephen whose worried expression betrays his own desire for the goody. Martin is obviously in a quandary. He wants the chocolate but knows Stephen does too. He seems stuck, almost paralysed. Eventually, looking at Stephen again, he takes a bite and passes the rest to his friend. The tension abates and they start to play happily together, closely bonded, and this lasts for the rest of the party.

These are two reasonably well-adjusted children but even so, events could have panned out differently. In a different mood, Martin and Stephen might have got into a fight. A boy more troubled and angry than Martin, like some of the abused children

I work with, might have simply resorted to overt cold aggression, or even gobbled the chocolate and gloated in triumph. Such a child might not have had the more empathic and social parts of their brains turned on. Some more anxious children who need to please others might have taken none for themselves. Such a complex range of motivations is all too present in most of us.

That classic tension between selfishness and cooperation can be viewed, albeit in a simplified metaphorical way, in terms of the traits humans inherited through our shared ancestry with creatures such as chimpanzees and bonobos, alongside newer developments in the last 70,000 years or so. The later shifts include culture, language, symbolism and also more egalitarian, empathic and prosocial behaviours. Again many of these traits existed, in rudimentary forms, in other mammals that have lived in complex social groups.

Our evolutionary paths have diverged from other mammals, and indeed other apes, and so inevitably human nature is unique in certain ways. We split with our common ancestor, named Ancestral Pan by Christopher Boehm (2012), at least 6,000,000 years ago. As a species our very existence was under huge threat around 80,000 years ago, when as few as 10,000 of us seemingly survived. Archaeological and other evidence points to major changes from this time.

Comparisons with chimpanzees have been used to fuel the idea that we humans are innately as aggressive, uncaring and bellicose as our genetic cousins. Despite having some empathic traits, chimps can be violent, not care much for outsiders or offspring other than their own, and rarely cooperate. They have strict male-dominance hierarchies, engage in lethal warfare and theirs is a much more dog-eat-dog world.

Much of this is also true of course of humans. However, with the advent of culture and banding together in larger groups, the proto-empathic capacities that we share with many mammals were enhanced as we developed a new strain of personality characteristics alongside self-interested and aggressive ones. These promoted group cohesion and enhanced levels of altruism, empathy and mutual support. One might use the conceit of thinking of these as opposing tendencies within us, each of us having more or less altruistic traits. More importantly different families, organisations and societies will promote and enhance either more altruistic or selfish tendencies.

Some species like bees and ants are known as eusocial, and while human levels of sociality is not at ant levels, the degree of our sociality is unusual in primates and mammals. In humans there is a battle, as E.O. Wilson states (2012, p. 56), between 'honor, virtue and duty' as opposed to 'selfishness, cowardice and hypocrisy', which might be thought of as the conflict between good and evil. This issue is the heart of what this book is about.

Traits such as altruism did not just form from thin air and would have built on already existing capacities. Even chimps have some limited altruistic and empathic capacities (De Waal 2013), and indeed so do rats, who will forego food for themselves if eating it is accompanied by pain inflicted on a fellow rat (Decety *et al.* 2012). Humans share very close common ancestry and genetic profiles not only with chimps but also with another closely related ape, the bonobo. Bonobos are less well known, partly as they are confined to a shrinking stretch of Congolese forests and have been less studied. Bonobos and chimps have evolved into quite different creatures. In bonobo social groups, authority is shared between males and females, there is more likelihood of female dominance and males are less aggressive with outsiders and rivals. Bonobos are more capable of acting cooperatively and better at reconciliation after conflict. In fact their conflicts are commonly defused by having sex.

Bonobos are also better at forming strategic alliances, especially females who do not allow alpha males too much power. Sometimes would-be alpha males are viciously attacked and even killed. Such a predisposition to form alliances and gang up against dictatorial tendencies, seen so forcefully in bonobos, is possibly an evolutionary precursor of human tendencies to form coalitions and rebel against dictators and bullies.

Some think we are more like bonobos in other ways. We mate at any time of the year like them, whereas chimps only mate when females are in heat. In chimps homosexuality is almost unheard of, whereas in bonobos, like humans, it is quite common. Bonobos have been described as our 'make love not war' relative, the 'hippies' to chimpanzees' more patriarchal ways of being.

Many human prosocial traits resemble bonobo rather than chimp traits. Bonobos have a more upright gait, use tools in more sophisticated ways and are nearer language use than chimps. They have more capacity to understand other minds and certainly are more likely to cooperate than chimpanzees. They are one of the few creatures other than humans who pass the mirror self-recognition test described earlier. Other species that manage this are dolphins and elephants, highly social and cooperative large-brained species; chimps tend to fail it. In addition, bonobos are more altruistic and there are many apocryphal stories of bonobo good deeds, such as rescuing and setting free trapped birds.

DNA evidence suggests that early human societies, like bonobo ones, tended to be organised far more around the female line and with more female authority, something that only changed when, with more settled pastoral living, patrilineal societies become dominant (Knight 2008). In this respect we might say that we have moved, with more settled societies, from being more bonobo-like to chimp-like. The bonobo–human metaphor can only stretch so far; we are not by any means the same as bonobos, one of many major differences being that we humans pair bond, are not as promiscuous, and we are also cooperative breeders who tend to raise our young in groups. Humans diverged from bonobos millions of years ago and went our own way. Something distinctive is apparent in human social organisation compared to all other apes, and many of our most notable traits have been extremely evident in hunter-gatherer societies in which we lived for tens of thousands of years, and in which much of our distinctiveness evolved.

Hunter-gatherer pasts

Christopher Boehm (2012) has studied ethnographic reports of just about every hunter-gatherer group known about in any detail, in an attempt to make sense of how humans might have evolved our personality traits, and particularly our moral capacities. He above all focused on societies living in conditions nearest to the Pleistocene, the time before about 10 to 12,000 years ago when we saw the first-known settled communities. Indeed, he discounted any culture which had any contact with modern or settled societies. He found that whatever the climate or continent, from the Arctic to the Sahara, the same egalitarian pattern emerged. Altruism, generosity and group cooperation were highly valued and selfishness, laziness and free-riding were punished. All such hunter-gatherer groups exercised powerful social control via clear moral rules, to try to ensure a cooperative and egalitarian lifestyle. These are the societies in which human populations stabilised and began to expand across the planet, and the traits Boehm described, our groupness and cooperative and altruistic tendencies, were central to this.

Aggression, warfare and murderousness were also, of course, part of this heritage, seen most obviously in some bellicose cultures. Similarly selfishness and greed was endemic but in the hunter-gatherer societies that have been studied such tendencies became relatively suppressed and controlled, while altruistic and co-operative personality traits were more valued. Evolutionary anthropologists such as Boehm and Wilson agree that there is a clear rule: selfish individuals out-compete altruistic individuals, but altruistic groups out-compete groups made up of selfish individuals. We might think of the analogy of sports. For individual sports you need a different kind of competitor to team sports, and a band of superb individualists is unlikely to succeed in team competitions.

There is a conflict between the needs of individuals and of groups, and each exerts its own evolutionary selection pressures. The theory of multi-level selection (Nowak and Highfield 2011) suggests that there is competition between the tendencies that favour altruism, selflessness and even heroism as opposed to those that favour individualism, selfishness, alpha-maleness and competition. In multi-level selection, different to Dawkins' (2006) theory about the selfish gene, selfish tendencies can be powerfully suppressed by group pressures.

This tension is often played out in how we compete (for status, possessions, sexual favours, etc.) within a group, but we also favour group cohesion and cooperation, often in competition with other groups. The team huddle in sports is a typical sign of this, and interestingly also raises oxytocin levels. Due to pressures within groups to be generous and cooperative, people with altruistic traits gain higher status and become more successful at attracting mates and reproducing, while selfish people will reproduce less, or even be ostracised, and thus the gene pool altered. While such genetic change might take at least 1,000 generations, Boehm believes that the archaeological and anthropological evidence suggests that for a minimum of 25,000 years humans lived in hunter-gatherer groups, plenty of time for more prosocial traits to become more prominent in the human gene pool.

Like Boehm, E.O. Wilson argued that cooperation bestowed huge advantages on groups. A cooperative and mutually altruistic group will stand firmly together in the face of danger, out-compete rival groups and thus increase chances of survival and reproductive success. The advent of hunting large game, as well as cooking, required social cohesion, and cooperative groups, something that Boehm believes might have been central to the temporary quashing, but not demise, of alpha-male dominance.

Until recently most evolutionary thinkers believed altruism to be either reciprocal (Trivers 2002), the 'I'll scratch your back if you scratch mine' kind, or driven primarily by the push to reproduce one's own genes, and by extension kin who share one's genes. E.O. Wilson is among many who have argued strongly that the data suggesting kin selection as the main driver for altruism simply do not stack up (e.g. Nowak and Highfield 2011; Pagel 2012; Henrich, Boyd et al. 2001; Bowles and Gintis 2011). All hunter-gatherer bands have consisted not only of genetically related individuals, but rather a mixture of kin and non-kin. Each society studied has been found to strongly preach the virtue of generosity to others in the group, including non-kin.

Interestingly, all these writers have focused on slightly different explanations of the main drivers for group cooperation, all of which must have played a role. For Boehm, it was the collaboration needed for large-game hunting, while for E.O. Wilson the prime driver was having a territory. He shows that every eusocial species has a nest or territory, and similarly bands of humans lived in defendable sites. Grouping by family does not lead to eusociality, he found, but having a definable nest with access to food does. He argues that high levels of genetic relatedness to other group members is the consequence and not cause of eusocial behaviour.

There are other linked drivers of altruism and cooperation. Hrdy (2009) stresses the importance of being a cooperative breeding species which rears its young in groups. This is unlike other apes and nearly all primates. She argues that this led to the development of the extraordinary capacities for empathy and understanding other minds which I outlined earlier. It makes sense that even relatively young human infants become adept at signalling to other adults and children, and non-mothers become soft and gooey at the sight of other people's infants and children. To survive and thrive infants need to attract and communicate with alternative carers. In hunter-gatherer communities, being able to attract an adult, whether by smiling or crying, could be the difference between life and death. Cooperative breeding species, including wolves, meerkats and a variety of birds and a few primates, tend to be more prosocial. Cooperative breeding marmosets, for example, are much more sensitive to the needs of others and are more likely to help a stranger marmoset in trouble than, for example, one larger-brained chimpanzee would help another.

Another eminent evolutionary anthropologist, Mark Pagel (2012), has emphasised the development of culture and symbolisation which require the empathic and mind-understanding skills that Hrdy described. Culture of course has a particular role in distinguishing one group from another. Even babies prefer their own culture and people who look and sound 'like us'. A group in which members can read each other's intentions and cooperate would have huge advantages, especially in competing with rival groups. Humans have a unique capacity for symbolisation, complex language, sophisticated tool use, and both religious and cultural traditions.

An idea that works well with those of Boehm, Wilson and Hrdy is the Social Brain Hypothesis, put forward by Robin Dunbar (1998). Our brains, particularly our neocortices, are very large, and this is fundamentally linked to increasingly complex social skills needed for intimate group life. We developed complex social brains because we lived in larger groups requiring sophisticated skills in mind-reading, empathy and synchronisation. Primates in smaller groups tend to make do with grooming, and there is a correlation between group size and size of neocortex. Dunbar and others have argued that language might initially have developed as a more successful mechanism than grooming for ensuring group cohesion, cultural transmission and for maintaining social bonds, alliances and mutual cooperation.

Humans in traditional hunter-gatherer societies acted less as a group of disparate individuals in the way most primates do. Humans have lived in societies with clear and strict mechanisms to quell individualistic and selfish tendencies and ensure that no one takes more than their share, or shirks responsibility. Egalitarianism was almost definitely, for at least 25,000 years, the basis of human group life, with food sharing, cooperation and the lack of formal leadership central. It is possible that such curtailing of individualistic, selfish tendencies is being reversed in contemporary market economies.

It is likely that all the drivers mentioned contributed to the extraordinary human propensity for altruism and cooperation;

these include collaboration for large-game hunting, cooking, cooperative breeding, having a nest to defend, language and culture, the increase in brain size and the advantages of operating in larger cohesive groups. Our alpha-male tendencies never went away of course. However, almost definitely in our hunter-gatherer pasts, as in all the existing hunter-gatherer societies studied, selfish or alpha-male tendencies would have been actively challenged in a way we might not see so much in Western market societies. The mechanisms used to ensure cooperation included social distancing, ridicule, shaming, expulsion from the group, both physical and capital punishment and also supernatural sanctioning, such as witchcraft, all mechanisms which ensure social cohesion, as discussed in Chapter 13.

This is, of course, not to suggest that altruistic and egalitarian traits are any more or less natural than selfish, aggressive or competitive ones. To the extent that any trait has survived, it is 'natural'. There is often of course a battle to capture the word 'natural' for the cause we believe in. Some think homosexuality is not natural, for example. There still exists a discourse arguing strongly that selfishness and competitiveness are what are really natural. I believe that for those of us who have a predilection for fairness, compassion, cooperation and more egalitarian lifestyles, it is worth taking seriously what a central role such altruistic traits have played in human history, and examine the kind of social conditions in which they are likely to thrive.

Hunter-gatherer life was basically egalitarian and cooperative, with few possessions, no land ownership, and life centred on group activities such as hunting or cooking. It is harder to be very selfish when one's actions are likely to be noticed by everyone else. These societies lacked the impersonal forms of interaction of our modern age: there were no call centres, anonymous sales assistants, business via cyberspace or privately hatched marketing campaigns. The people one interacted with yesterday were mostly those one would interact with tomorrow. As noted, hunter-gatherer bands always consisted of both kin and non-kin, but were tightly bound hives of mutual solidarity and cooperation. People firmly took action against selfishness, bullying, greed or meanness. Despite social stratification and status hierarchies, no one person became too powerful or greedy. People were appreciated for prosocial behaviours and high status was conferred on those who were group players.

Strangers and warfare

Relationships with strangers and those in other groups were not as consistently altruistic. Altruism towards strangers was still common in many societies. Hrdy described the widely seen but complex gift-exchange systems, such as the 'kula ring' of Melanesia, where people travel hundreds of miles in canoes to circulate precious objects. There were also the elaborate 'giveaway' ceremonies seen in many Native American tribes. She points out that most groups could not survive on their own and describes a study in South America which showed that just about every family would probably, over time, starve if they just relied on themselves; here food sharing and mutual reciprocation with nearby groups ensured survival. It was expected amongst the Bushmen of the Kalahari, for example, that tools and other objects, however highly treasured, would soon be passed on as gifts, most possessions being held only transiently, and it would not have been acceptable to keep hold of anything for very long.

Thus, even where warfare and violence between groups was common, people still needed their extended networks. As Hrdy suggests, if my water runs out but I, or my family, helped you last year, you might help us next time. Over lifetimes such encounters develop into a rich system of mutual support and obligation, albeit of a more reciprocal altruistic form. Such systems of exchange live on in different forms today, such as how neighbours help out others who have helped them, and even 'special arrangements' between countries.

Small human hunter-gatherer societies were not necessarily all a peaceful idyll, and some anthropologists have suggested that certain groups had homicide levels close to those in modern urban societies (Pagel 2012). Writers such as Chagnon (2013) have for many decades been arguing that many pre-modern societies showed extreme levels of violence, murderousness and lethal rivalry. Pinker (2011) agrees, suggesting that, in contrast, murder and violent deaths have been decreasing over recent centuries.

The evidence Pinker used has, though, been hotly disputed by many recent in-depth accounts. Typical is R. Brian Ferguson's aptly named chapter 'Pinker's List', which shows that Pinker was in fact highly selective in the examples he used to back up his thesis (Ferguson 2013b). Hrdy too argues that such warfare was uncommon, especially due to the models of complex cooperation and far-reaching gift-exchange networks. Recent work, in fact, has demonstrated convincingly that in pre-history war was extremely rare (Fry 2013), and there is very little empirical evidence for it (Haas and Piscitelli 2013). Ferguson (2013a), for example, looking in depth at the archaeological record across Europe and the Near East for the Neolithic period, found that war was certainly at most a later development, little seen for at least half a millennium of peace.

Archaeologists have found evidence of complex gift-exchanges as far back as 40,000 years ago (Stringer 2011) but of course there is also some evidence of ancient weapons and death by violence, mostly from later Neolithic times onwards. The anthropological literature suggests that while both fairly peace-loving and war-mongering hunter-gatherer communities existed, war and inter-group fighting to the death were rare in hunter-gatherer societies and a later development. Intra-species violence is of course rare in mammals anyway and often not in a species' interests. Many writers examining the anthropological and archaeological record argue that humans do not have an evolved predisposition for war, in the sense that warring is not 'just natural' and that humans will become warlike only under certain social conditions.

These conditions include competition for resources, and new forms of social organisation, particularly more static and stratified societies. The anthropological literature contains many examples of extremely peaceful societies in which war and murder were almost unknown, such as the Batek of Malaysia (Endicott 2013), or the Hadza of Tanzania (Butovskaya 2013). What Hobbesian evolutionary theory defines as 'natural', such as warlike aggression and particular forms of individualism, in fact are relatively recent in human history and require particular social conditions. This implies that it is possible to create social formations which minimise the likelihood of intergroup and interpersonal violence, as many ancient forager groups did.

Fry (2013), Hrdy (2009) and several other researchers have shown that as hunter-gatherer life gave way first to more pastoral lifestyles, and then to large conurbations, new needs arose such as to protect cattle and property, and partly for these reasons in the last 10,000 years intergroup warfare has become a more central feature of human life. This was less possible in fluid, small anarchic forager groups but changed as settled chiefdoms came into being, and even more so when the first ancient civilisations appeared, a mere 5–6,000 years ago. Nation states of course have only existed for about 500 years. Increased warfare has coincided with more patrilocal, chimp-like as opposed to matrilocal bonobo-like forms of social organisation with increased inequality, male-dominance structures and warfare against other groups (Kelly 2013).

We know from historical and anthropological accounts that peoples from warlike, highly stratified societies have often expanded at the expense of those living in more cooperative, egalitarian and sociocentric lifestyles. We can we think of Columbus and the Native Americans or the decimation of Australian aborigines or swathes of African and Asian indigenous cultures. As Hrdy states, 'altruists eager to cooperate fare poorly in encounters with marauders' (2009, p. 28).

Ironically, warfare and aggression against other groups might have gone hand-in-hand with high levels of cooperation within such groups, much of which would have been highly ritualised. There is archaeological evidence of group rites from ancient burial sites. Rituals activate brain areas central to emotional modulation, self-regulation and morality (Wain and Spinella 2007). The evidence from many hunter-gatherer groups, whether the Ache and Hadza, or tribes in South America such as the Sironio of Eastern Bolivia, shows how ritual is central to enhancing a sense of group belonging, which also has repercussions for those who do not belong. Research on oxytocin similarly shows that it enhances both in-group loyalty and distrust of out-groups (De Dreu 2011).

A few contemporary residues from our evolutionary past

The urge for reciprocity runs deep in the human psyche and we see many of its effects in the contemporary world. An interesting experiment took place in the 1970s when a college professor sent out hundreds of Christmas cards to complete strangers, and what was surprising was just how many hundreds he received in return (Kunz and Woolcott 1976)! Other researchers left wallets around town with an address inside as well as money, and most were returned to the address with the money still inside (Hornstein *et al.* 1968). Such reciprocal altruism remains a central human predisposition, although one that varies by historical period and geographical location. For example, considerably fewer of the deliberately dropped letters are reposted in very deprived environments (Holland *et al.* 2012), although other forms of altruism, such as helping someone who drops something, do not seem to differ according to the relative affluence of an area (Nettle *et al.* 2011).

There are advantages to working out who we can trust and who it is safe to cooperate with. Julia Pradel of the University of Cologne demonstrated how humans are often altruistic and generous in one-off encounters with people they are never likely to see again, and most of the time recognise altruistic traits in others (Pradel and Fetchenhauer 2010). Interestingly, in her experiments altruists tended to band together which also meant that egotists had little choice but to join together as well. Groups of altruists generally stand by each other, out-compete groups made up of more selfish egotists, and thus, Pradel argues, altruistic traits have survived and thrived.

Some kinds of cooperation and altruism are more pragmatic and less empathically driven than others, such as the reciprocal altruism described by Trivers. Chimpanzees are more likely to share food with other chimps who have helped them in the past, and in humans, too, all manner of reciprocal acts help bind alliances, whether food sharing, grooming, looking after young or even sex, as the anthropological literature shows. For example, with the Ache of Paraguay, those who are most generous in good times are also the ones who reap the most rewards when times get tough (Gurven *et al.* 2000).

Typical of the kind of traits that facilitate socially cohesive living is embarrassment, interestingly unpacked by the Berkeley Professor, Dacher Keltner (2009). Most of us care what others think and try to abide by the dominant expectations of our group. When we step outside of such expectations then the group will often try to shame or embarrass us to fit in. Similar kinds of social signals are seen in placatory smiles when subordinates approach superiors, in both humans and other apes.

Keltner suggests that embarrassment is an evolved mechanism that helps ensure social order. In embarrassment we turn our heads away, rather than look someone in the eye, or in other words we take a 'one-down' position. The infancy researcher Vasu Reddy has even shown traits like coyness in four-month-old babies (Reddy 2008). Most of us look embarrassed if we make a social gaffe, transgress someone's boundaries or break a rule.

Some show less embarrassment than others including, as Keltner found, people who are antisocial, and children diagnosed with conduct disorders or ADHD, and boys who fight, bully or steal. Maltreatment, abuse and neglect can lead to this too, as we saw in Chapter 4. When Keltner gave a group of boys a test which they were bound to fail, it was the well-adjusted boys who showed embarrassment; they cared what others thought of them and wanted to do well. However, the acting-out, less emotionally regulated boys tended to show anger instead, for example threatening to stomp out. Embarrassment, says Keltner, is a sign of our commitment to the social and moral order. Those lacking commitment to group norms would have struggled more in our hunter-gatherer past, although possibly less so in our contemporary more individualistic world.

Keltner's research showed that cooperativeness, altruism and being prosocial remain highly valued traits. He found that, maybe surprisingly, kinder people tend to have happier and closer marriages, for example. Julia Pradel also found that when looking for a long-term partner altruism is a very sought-after character trait. Most of us prefer to have enduring relationships with people we can trust, who are cooperative, compassionate and trustworthy. Children with higher empathy have wider networks of friends (Goetz et al. 2010) as do adolescents with more agreeable traits. A development I often see with children who come from abusive backgrounds is that if they thrive in good adoptive families, or make hopeful progress in psychotherapy, they begin not only to feel better in themselves, but also to have better peer relationships. A classic anecdotal sign of such a child's progress is starting to be invited to birthday parties or play-dates.

Of course, there are forms of empathy, over-the-top altruism and self-sacrifice which seem less healthy, at least for the individual concerned, whether being stuck in what are called co-dependent relationships, or worse, more masochistic ones with abusive, violent partners. Interestingly, many acts which seem not to be in the best interests of the person doing them might well be good for the group. This includes dramatically self-sacrificing acts, as seen in heroic risks in war, or risking one's life to save an unknown drowning baby. Other traits which seem bad for the individual are also good for the group. For example, people high in survivor guilt and other psychological problems were found to be more cooperative than most and so helped group cohesion (O'Connor et al. 2012).

Even if some have termed such kinds of altruism *pathological* (Oakley *et al.* 2012), presumably such traits have survived and been passed down the generations for good evolutionary reasons. For example, women in abusive relationships are more likely to give birth to sons (Kanazawa 2008), which might well have been an advantage in our evolutionary past where inherited high-testosterone males would be an advantage. These, of course, can only ever be *post-hoc* explanations. Psychiatric diagnoses such as Dependent Personality Disorder describe traits such as excessive helpfulness which certainly do not seem to be to the advantage of the helper. The same might be said for forms of self-sacrifice such as suicide bombing or the Japanese *kamikaze* tradition. The way many patients with serious eating disorders feed everyone else but put their own lives at risk is another hard to explain behaviour. Thus altruism sometimes seems good for groups but not necessarily for the altruist. Evolutionary theorists suggest that at times we act in the interests of our genes rather than our own lives.

Summary

In this chapter I have outlined some key research about our evolutionary history which explains how more altruistic, prosocial and cooperative predispositions would have been enhanced through living in cohesive hunter-gatherer communities. Here, group-mindedness was greatly valued and group-minded people probably were advantaged for reproducing their genes, while cheats, free-riders and self-aggrandisers would not have fared so well.

Sometimes altruistic acts are not in the altruist's interest, but might be in the interests of their genes, or of the group. I have particularly stressed the importance of traits that enhance group cohesion, such as embarrassment as described by Keltner (2009). Even depression might serve the group, given that a brain area called the subgenual cingulate cortex is active in not only depression, but also in guilt and in charitable donations (Zahn *et al.* 2009).

While sometimes altruistic acts work against the altruist's personal interests, more often, of course, being empathic and altruistic in fact is to people's advantage, especially when the world seems safe and beneficent. Then we often act well, not because we calculate that it is to our advantage but rather because we want to, it feels good and we cannot help ourselves. In blood donations or other charitable acts the real reward is doing what we care about (Costa-Font *et al.* 2012). Mostly we want to help. Dan Ariely (2009) asked people to do a fairly boring task, such as dragging as many circles as they could from one side of a computer screen to the other. Some were given a reasonable sum of money for this ($5), others were offered only 50 cents, and still others were asked to do this 'as a favour'. Maybe surprisingly, the people who scored highest were those asked to do it as a favour.

The same is seen in children, as Michael Tomasello (2009) found in experiments where toddlers helped others because they found helping rewarding, but helped less if the reward was extrinsic, say sweets or another treat. Such willingness to act for what is seen as the greater good was probably a trait that was greatly enhanced through our evolutionary history of living in cooperative bonded groups.

This propensity for helping others might make sense of the finding by Lara Aknin and colleagues that money can indeed make one happy, but mainly if we spend it on other people! Looking at samples from 142 countries with very different levels of income, they found that, irrespective of other factors, spending money on others predicted happiness (Aknin *et al.* 2013). They go as far as to say that it is a psychological universal that human beings across diverse cultures derive emotional benefits from using their financial resources to help others. Similarly, Harvey James of the University of Missouri analysed data from the World Values Survey which showed that people who were less sympathetic to immoral or unscrupulous acts were happier, and interestingly also healthier, than those who seemed less moral (James 2011).

It is, I am sure, no coincidence that a range of brain areas central for empathy and understanding other minds light up when we co-operate, as do a range of reward circuits. When people in experiments play a financial-reward game, those who cooperate have more activity in brain areas central to empathy. We have evolved so that working together is its own reward (Elliott *et al.* 2006).

Such findings might make us wonder how standard economic theories about human nature could be so wrong, particularly the belief that innate self-interestedness is our *only* real driver. We are not prisoners of our evolutionary past, but we certainly are powerfully constrained by our biological, genetic, neuroscientific and hence also our psychological inheritances. We, of course, also have an evolutionary history dating back much further than even our hunter-gatherer past, and share aggressive, selfish and competitive traits with chimps and many other species. As E.O. Wilson suggested, our moral quandaries might partly be explained by the tension between these very different propensities.

Research by Henrich and colleagues (2001; 2010) showed that the likelihood of humans being generous varies hugely depending on the kind of society we live in and the values that are espoused. In monetary games, the Machiguenga, a people from Peru in whose culture there was rarely any cooperation, gave away less than half of that given away by the Lameala of Indonesia, a culture in which people depend on each other much more for survival. Societies where there is more equality and social cohesion are the ones where people tend to feel more trusting, believe that each has responsibility for others, and also experience greater emotional wellbeing (Uslaner and Brown 2005). Egalitarian cultures in which mutual dependence is valued seem to be healthier and happier.

We, of course, need to be cautious about stating that a particular way of living or bringing up children is 'natural', but we should also remember that for 99 per cent of our history, by many people's calculations (Narváez 2013), we lived in small hunter-gatherer communities. It was in these environments that many traits that we consider prototypically human become central. Here people lived in small tight-knit communities which were cooperative and prosocial and in which infants were always held, carried, responded to swiftly and had constant human companionship. Possibly much that we value in human nature, such as empathy, mutual care and interpersonal tenderness, will most fully come online in just such environments.

Constant responsive care is in fact seen in just about every hunter-gatherer community studied and is possibly what infants are born to 'expect' even if they can survive in less benign environments. Similarly we might survive in fast, stressful and competitive environments but we did not evolve to expect constant anxiety or fear. Such small hunter-gatherer communities, we now know, were not very aggressive or even overly stressful, and war, trauma and stress tended to be the exceptions and not the rule (Fry 2013). We might well have evolved to expect such low-stress environments for adults and constant attuned care for infants. The consequences of not receiving them are unknown but might include much of what we are seeing in contemporary societies: worse mental health, lower social cohesion and less empathic, altruistic and prosocial ways of relating.

It is possible that the advantages of being altruistic, generous or moral might be diminishing somewhat in a contemporary world in which being group-minded might not be as big an advantage as it once was. As I discuss later, success in modern market economies often favours more self-interested individualistic traits. While any of us can be self-serving, greedy and not pull our weight, some forms of social organisation make this more or less likely, possibly including our more monetised, competitive and impersonal contemporary societies. I now turn to an interesting body of research, the science of game theory, which has investigated in great detail our human propensities for fairness and cooperation, and for selfishness and greed.

Chapter 11

Moral games

Games and the good

We all have times when our loyalty is tested. One client, Michelle, was recently in this position. A few years back she began working for a small company in a field she really believed in, doing exciting research on environmentally sustainable food production. They were developing alternatives which had a fraction of the ecological cost of equivalent conventional methods. This was work with a team she felt at home in, with people she respected and admired. She had recently described herself as feeling fulfilled and inspired. Then an offer arrived from a rival company, needless to say for far more money, but a company whose ethical basis left a lot to be desired. She could nearly quadruple her salary; her family could at last buy the home they wanted, all their debts would soon be paid off. We spent many weeks pondering this terrible dilemma, as she teetered, nearly jumped, stepped back, and in the end stayed. She wanted to be true to her values and what 'felt right' but was also pulled towards the financial interests of her family. I would not want to judge her either way. However, I am fairly sure that earlier in her therapy Michelle would have been unlikely to resist the allure of status and money. Starting therapy and before the oxytocin rush of children she was maybe more ambitious, and maybe more importantly, did not yet really know which of the conflicting messages inside herself she could trust.

We are often faced with such dilemmas in small or big ways. Does the classmate snitch on the peer who wrote on the wall, for which the whole class has to stay behind? Do I give to that homeless person, or the charity that my friend is running a race to support, or help out in the local community event? Much light has been shed on how we act in such scenarios, particularly about how altruistic or self-interested we are likely to be, in a series of ingeniously devised experiments using what scientists call experimental game theory. These games confirm much of what I have been arguing so far, that humans have a propensity to cooperate and be generous to others, but also to be selfish, and we are hugely influenced not only by our personalities but also factors such as the context we are in, who will find out what we do, and whether the other players are known to us.

Typical of such clever formats is the Ultimatum Game, originally devised in the early 1980s in Germany (Güth *et al.* 1982). Here a sum of money such as £50 is given to one player, and they must offer a proportion of this to a co-player unknown to them. If the offer is accepted then they can both keep the agreed sums, but if the offer is rejected then neither player gets to keep any of the money. Interestingly, despite some cultural variations, just about everywhere that this has been tested, the first person feels that they need to make an offer which is good enough to be accepted and the second player will reject an offer which is deemed too low. Yet it does not make sense, from the standpoint of traditional economic theory, to reject even a fairly low offer. If I am offered £5 and I reject it I am then left with nothing, and so is the other player; so surely I am better off accepting the £5? This would be even more the case in a one-off unrepeated encounter as there is little incentive, logically, to either curry favour with, or punish, someone who we are unlikely to ever come across again. However, maybe surprisingly, even in such one-off encounters most people tend to be fair when making offers and also tough about what offers we think are unacceptable. If the other person is likely to be encountered again then there is even more incentive to either make good offers or reject bad ones.

It is interesting that in most cultures offers average somewhere between 40 per cent and 50 per cent of the total, and people nearly everywhere tend to reject offers of less than about 20 per cent (Oosterbeek *et al.* 2004). The fact that people reject low offers, and are prepared to go away with nothing, suggests that we are more likely to operate from a principle of fairness than solely from immediate self-interest. This is irrespective of the size of the sums played with. The game has been played with fairly insignificant amounts such as a mere $10 in affluent parts of

America to sums that equate to several weeks' wages in other countries, and most people make similarly high offers, and reject low ones. In a recent version, other rewards, not money, were used. Subjects were made very thirsty by drinking a salt solution, and knew they could expect nothing else to drink for quite some time. Despite their thirst, when their partner offered them a much smaller amount of water than they kept for themselves, the subjects tended to refuse it (Wright, Hodgson *et al.* 2012). People often make decisions which support their sense of justice, even if this has a personal cost.

Psychological and neurological research casts some light on these matters. If players making the offers are given oxytocin intranasally (Zak *et al.* 2007) then they tend to make higher offers, which makes sense given that we know that oxytocin increases generosity, trust and empathy. Also in response to low offers, brain areas such as the insula, involved in disgust, become especially active, and people show physiological signs of emotional arousal such as sweating (Van 't Wout *et al.* 2006). We reject low offers on emotional rather than logical grounds, irrespective of personal economic benefit.

However, rejections are, less virtuously, also motivated by a desire to punish. When I refuse your offer, I prefer to cut off my nose to spite my own face and get nothing rather than let you have much more than me. Even young children and adolescents reject unfair offers, and interestingly also often refuse offers that give *them* more than the other (Sutter 2007). What is maybe less savoury is how we take pleasure in punishment, which activates the brain's reward circuits, such as our nucleus accumbens (Strobel *et al.* 2011). While we may not be purely motivated by maximising personal gain, we are no angels either.

Another game devised by the Nobel prize-winning economist Daniel Kahneman, the Dictator Game, was invented partly to refute the idea that people will always put their interests first. Once again a sum of money is allocated to a player who unilaterally decides whether or not to give any to the other player, who in this case can do nothing about what they are offered. Over 130 scientific papers later, Kahneman's original hunch has been backed up (Engel 2011). About 70 per cent give some of their money away, even if it is a very small amount. This is even more likely if we think the other person deserves it or if we receive a social cue from them which taps our innate sociality. Indeed in some countries, particularly less industrialised ones, people tend to give more away anyway, another lesson in how a society's values and dominant discourses affect traits like generosity.

However, these experiments by no means demonstrate just fairness, let alone altruism. When the parameters of the game are shifted, and people are told that they can give any or none of their money away, and also told that they can take money *away from* the other person, a surprising number give nothing or even take money away (List 2007). We also give more away if our actions are apparent to other people, and this is because we care hugely about our reputation. We are less happy when we donate more and our motive is not to be viewed as mean, but we do act to enhance our reputations (Reyniers and Bhalla 2013).

Human societies have always depended on reputation. As an increasingly complex market economy has penetrated further, ever more ingenious ways have been found to try to ensure that we can trust the person we are dealing with, and for example, check out the credentials of sellers of goods or travel via their ratings on well-known websites. It is no coincidence that similar reward circuits fire up in our brains when trying to earn money as when trying to build a reputation (Saxe and Haushofer 2008), and of course money is often used to enhance reputations, hence designer labels. We seemingly want status symbols because we want to be thought well of, and the brain regions that light up when we gain financial rewards are very linked to those engaged when we receive praise for personal attributes such as generosity.

Prisoner's dilemma

In maybe the most famous game in 'game theory', the Prisoner's Dilemma, loyalty is pitched against personal gain. This has been tested literally thousands of times in many different ways, perhaps most famously by Robert Axelrod (2006), and also Martin Nowak of Harvard University (Nowak and Highfield 2011). The Prisoner's Dilemma also asks fundamental questions of human nature. An example of the scenario is that you and a partner in crime are in jail. You are both interrogated separately and the police are out to make a deal.

- If you betray your partner and your partner remains silent, you will get off very lightly, with a very short jail sentence, say a year, and your partner will go to prison for at least four years.

- If you both remain loyal and neither betrays or incriminates the other, then there will not be enough evidence to commit either of you and you will both get a short sentence, maybe of two years in jail, but not as short as if you betray your partner.
- If you both betray each other then you will both be convicted, but as you helped the police your sentence will be reduced to about three years.

This is quite a quandary. From a purely self-interested perspective the best thing to do is defect, as at most you get three years and maybe just one. It might appear to be logical to be loyal if your partner is also loyal and then you would both get two years. However, if your partner stays loyal and you defect you get just one year in jail, while if he defects you are definitely better off defecting too, and thus receiving three years rather than four. If we just act on logic and self-interest then defecting is the best option.

However, people will often not betray their partner. Loyalty is highly valued, as is trust and decency. As one might expect, the easiest way to encourage loyalty rather than defection is to be clear that one is going to play the game at a later time again with the same people. Defecting means risking losing a potential ally for the future and also one's reputation. Yet even if there will be no likelihood of a future rerun of the dilemma, loyalty very often still wins out.

As in the other games, whether one is loyal or betrays the other player is heavily influenced by reputation, and we cooperate more with people who have a good reputation (Nowak and Highfield 2011). In some trust games we can give away a sum of money, say $5, knowing that the amount our co-player receives will be tripled. They can then decide how much to give back to us, and we are much more likely to give more when the other player has a reputation for being generous and fair (Wedekind and Milinski 2000).

Another way of thinking about the power of reputation is that it facilitates a form of *indirect reciprocity*. If I do a good deed I might not get a reward from the person I help, but I will probably reap my reward further down the line due to my reputation as a helpful person. The basic rules for successful indirect reciprocity in stable groups seem to include being cooperative to those reputed to be good cooperators, while punishing those who do not cooperate (Ohtsuki and Iwasa 2006). Folk sayings such as 'what goes around comes around' seem to be emblematic of beliefs engrained deep within the human psyche.

Huge amounts of research using complex mathematical and computer models have tried to work out which strategy will be most successful if repeated over time on games like the Prisoner's Dilemma. Axelrod organised huge virtual tournaments in which scientists put forward many strategies, at one point examining 240,000 choices to see which worked best. The aim was to cast light on how and why humans get on and cooperate.

Axelrod himself put forward a strategy where one randomly cooperates and defects. This was not all successful. In another, a protagonist would never trust anyone again once they have cheated, which of course leaves no room for forgiveness; and this strategy, it turns out, is spectacularly unsuccessful. In fact, in Axelrod's research the easy overall winner was a very simple tactic called 'tit-for-tat'. This always starts with a cooperative move and then always repeats the other player's last move; for example, if the other player betrayed you last time then this time you betray him. It is worth noting that just being nice does not work.

Such strategic logic might explain the rationale behind our often petty reactions, and maybe also the nuclear arms race and the other ways in which good behaviour prevails partly out of fear of retribution. Axelrod found that crucial for success was not being the first to defect. Old Testament lack of forgiveness is also an ineffective strategy and bearing grudges ultimately backfires.

Martin Nowak, using powerful computer programs, let a range of strategies 'slug it out' over thousands of generations of games to see which would be the most successful. Rather like in evolution, the most successful were rewarded with offspring. Remember how 'always defect' was the self-interested choice, at least in one-off encounters, the cold-hearted tactic that logically should reap the most rewards. Well, indeed it did, after about 100 generations of the game. However, a few 'tit-for-tat' strategists hung on in there, surviving. Once the 'always defect' cold-eyed strategists had run out of anyone else to exploit, they in fact began to die out and 'tit-for-tat', a kinder and more reciprocal strategy, began to dominate. Slightly nicer strategies tend to win out in the longer term. In fact, Nowak found an even more successful strategy which he called 'win stay, lose shift'. In this I change strategy if my last move did not work but otherwise I stick to it. This was the best recipe for success after hundreds of generations of such games.

Of course, caution is needed about whether laboratory findings can really be translated into real-life behaviours. However, what we see overall is that strategies which contain a fair degree of cooperation are likely to outlast and triumph over those based entirely on self-interest, while pure altruists do not last long either. Neither being overly selfless, nor too selfish, is a good idea. These computer models of games did not even add empathy into their equation. When empathy for the partner was induced in a variant of the Prisoner's Dilemma, amazingly cooperation increased about five-fold, which might be more true to real life (Batson 2011). Indeed, such games stripped of usual cultural expectations or ordinary human contact can give a false picture. When the Ultimatum Game was played with Kalahari Bushmen, they were quite stingy, whereas in real life they were very generous with others as well as punitive of unfairness (Wiessner 2009). The anonymity of these games, as well as the lack of normal social expectations, can give a false and maybe more selfish picture.

On the other hand, as David DeSteno found (2012), people are very watchful for social cues which signal untrustworthiness. These cues are not the usual suspects of avoiding eye-contact or fidgeting. Rather the four typical gestures that induced distrust were leaning away from someone, crossing arms in a blocking fashion, touching, rubbing or grasping their hands together and touching themselves on their face, abdomen or elsewhere. Both when students played with other students, and surprisingly, when the other 'person' was a robot speaking with a female voice, these gestures led to a lack of trust.

Other contextual factors will also affect how people act in such games. Our moods affect behaviours, as will the way the questions are framed (Pastötter et al. 2013). David Rand, looking at over 2,000 subjects in different countries, found that when people were prompted to act spontaneously in such games they were far more generous than when given more time to think, or when they took on a more rational or calculating mind-set (Rand et al. 2012). We know that a whole range of seemingly random factors affect our decisions about morality or justice. Judges even tend to give harsher sentences before lunch, when they are hungry, compared to after eating (Danziger et al. 2011).

A hopeful note was sounded by the work of Les Ross and his colleagues who invented a new version of the Prisoner's Dilemma (Liberman et al. 2004). They told one group of players that the game was called the 'Wall Street Game', and another group that it was called 'The Community Game'. Amazingly, 70 per cent of those playing the 'Community Game' cooperated, as opposed to only 33 per cent of those playing the 'Wall Street Game', even though there was no difference in the games other than the name. There may be important lessons here about the potential for changing behaviour via challenging dominant discourses about people being primarily self-interested consumers as opposed to being public-minded. A discourse which values community and being prosocial can prod people to act more selflessly.

The public good

Many believe that the human race and the planet are facing threats of huge proportions, such as rising populations, the earth's resources depleting, man-made pollution having powerful effects and the planet heating up. Not surprisingly there are games which model this kind of dilemma, and cast light on human behaviour. These are called 'public goods' games and the most famous of these is the Tragedy of the Commons. This was devised by the ecologist Garrett Hardin who published the first paper on this in 1968 (Hardin 1968). In the Tragedy owners of livestock allow pasture which is common land to be over-grazed, even though everyone is aware that soon it will be so over-used that future grazing would become impossible. People have a choice about whether to let another of their animals graze on the common land or act in the interests of the general good. Mostly players think that they *would* stop but *only if* everyone else would. They worry that if they stop their animals grazing then others would just continue anyway, and so other people's animals would get fat and healthy and theirs would lose out.

This kind of scenario can be applied to a variety of situations, from diminishing fish-stocks to population explosion to the threat to any natural and limited resources. It does not arise when stocks seem infinitely bountiful, as was the case when Europeans first arrived in America. The Tragedy can also be used to think about what is put into the environment, such as pollutants and toxic waste. It is a classic example of the conflict between individual and communal interest. It benefits me (or my company) if I dump more waste, but it does not benefit the local community, wildlife or future generations, just as it will benefit me but not others if I send out one more fishing trawler or use large quantities of fossil fuels.

Hardin's work was a challenge to the idea that freedom should be given free rein, and he urged that we might be in danger of doing irreversible damage to the human race by acting in such short-sighted and selfish ways. To cast light on this he developed further versions of public goods games. A typical example is that four people are handed a sum of money, say €10 each. They are told that there is a communal pot into which they can invest as much or as little of their €10 as they choose and the total contributed is then added to by 50 per cent and then the new amount is divided between all the four players. Obviously we are all better off the more we all contribute. If we all invest our whole €10, and 50 per cent is added to this before it is redivided, then we would all get €15 back.

However, there is always the temptation of becoming a free-rider. If only three of the four invest their €10, and that total of €30 is topped up by 50 per cent, making €45, and that new total of €45 is divided, then we just about all come out on top, with just over €11 each. However, there is one free-rider amongst us who has the €11 plus their original €10. The other players know this and it generally irks them. In such games people tend to start with a lot of optimism and generosity but once they realise that someone has not contributed, they become tempted not to contribute themselves. This is maybe a kind of tit-for-tat mentality, so successful in the Prisoner's Dilemma, and presumably in life generally. Of course, if we all went down this route then in no time we would have no one contributing and everyone would lose out. It is not just self-interest that leads people to withdraw but also disgruntlement at unfairness. Society benefits if selfishness and cheating are not rewarded. On a larger planetary scale though, a scale humans have not evolved to think about, the situation presents a huge challenge.

This is seen even more clearly in a version of the game devised by Manfred Milinski from the Max Planck Institute with over 150 students, focusing on climate change and how people might pool resources for the common good (Milinski *et al.* 2006). The subjects were asked to contribute their own money to a pot, and whatever was collected was then doubled and used to pay for an advert about climate change in a widely circulated newspaper. What most pre-dicted success was excellent information and also that the donations were made publicly. When the students had been given reliable and helpful facts about climate change, then they were far more likely to help. They also behaved more altruistically when everyone knew what everyone else was contributing. As has been consistently shown, reputation hugely influences how altruistic people are, and we also feel less incentive to contribute if others do not. There are lessons here for how we organise public life, both in terms of transparency and also what information people have with which to make decisions.

What is heartening about these experiments is that if we get it right there is a good chance that we can pull together for the public good, as Milinski confirmed in later experiments. Again, climate change was the issue and the aim was to see if a group could work together to reach a collective target, and if they failed there was potential disaster. The disaster scenarios were based on projections by climate theorists such as James Lovelock, with a point of no return being reached for the planet due to global heating and ecological catastrophe (Lovelock 2006). The donations were linked to people foregoing things, such as taking planes or using heating, with each sacrifice represented in monetary form.

Players were given a sum of money and after ten rounds the game was won (and the world saved) if the team contributed €120. Players had three choices in each round: they could give nothing or €2 or €4, which translated into behaviour that was *selfish, fair* or *altruistic*. If all players played *fair* then the sum in the climate bank would reach the necessary €120, the planet would be saved and in addition everyone would still have another €20 to keep.

In all such public-goods games, researchers see a mix of altruistic and selfish behaviour. Some will invest nothing, and others the maximum, and the selfish ones will be hoping the altruists will donate enough to both save the planet and allow them to go home with more money than the rest. This probably is not so different from how many of us justify taking that one plane flight, or buying that beautiful item of clothing from an unethical manufacturer.

Milinksi added a twist which had important implications. He set up three separate versions of the game, in which losing led to a 10 or 50 or 90 per cent chance of climate disaster. Fascinatingly, where there was a 90 per cent chance of disaster, half the groups actually succeeded, which might seem either good or bad depending on one's expectations. The groups that failed only just did so, averaging €113 of the €120 needed. However, when the stakes were lower and disaster a bit less likely, the incentive to be altruistic diminished further. With a 50 per cent chance of disaster, only a single group stumped up the needed amount, while where there was only a 10 per cent chance of disaster, not a single group made the €120.

Milinski's results might have serious implications. We need to know just how dangerous the situation is if we are to feel sufficient urgency to make sacrifices for a cause. Humans have what we call an 'optimism bias' (Sharot 2012) anyway; we avoid believing the worst, a strategy that has often served us well over our evolutionary history, but maybe not now when our problems are global, and disasters threaten. We need the right information and to be able to take this in, which means providing honest, open, scientifically reliable information, whether about climate change, over-fishing or the economic situation. Vested interests and ideologically or financially motivated disinformation can confuse people of course, for example lobbies funded by energy companies arguing that climate change is a myth. Then people are likely to struggle to know what to believe and will resort to a mixture of selfishness and over-optimism as well as the fear of other people's selfishness.

The importance of fairness and transparency is seen as crucial time and again. The size of contributions is transformed when it is clear who is and is not contributing. Shaming has always been a central way in which humans have ensured fairness and decency, especially in small-scale communities. We see modern variants in which people publicly 'out' and demonstrate against big companies and senior figures who do not pay their fair amount of tax.

Summary

I have introduced the science of game theory which illustrates that the version of human nature that economists have depended on, *homo economicus*, is not the whole story. Game theory has shown the importance of traits such as being generous, helpful and forgiving, that fairness matters, as does being able to punish, and that fear for one's reputation is a powerful weapon. Irrespective of the genetic, psychological or social inheritance of those playing, for people to act in the public interest certain conditions must be in place. These include the ability to impose sanctions, that their acts should be made public, and that there should be reliable information about the consequences of not contributing to the common good.

What the research also shows is that one cannot simply appeal to human nature to solve such problems, or state that human nature is to blame and that selfishness is inevitable. Our natures, as this book has emphasised throughout, are complex and contradictory and influenced by dominant social discourses, immediate context, family history and power structures. While humans have both a propensity for selfishness and competitiveness, and also for fairness and generosity, it is a major challenge to create the social conditions that will enable more prosocial aspects of human nature to thrive. This is all the more the case because our altruistic and prosocial traits evolved to ensure fairness and cooperation within small local groups, not on a global scale. They also did not evolve in situations where the rules of the game can be changed without people really understanding what is happening, as seen in financial deregulation, the complex mechanisms devised in the financial sector and the power of lobbyists to change regulatory processes in favour of the groups they represent.

Developing a way of implementing fairness on a non-local and global scale would require something different, a new kind of extension of human prosociality. Rifkin (2010) and others have been trying to think about more global forms of empathy and interconnection. We are group creatures through and through, and can be very loyal and cooperative, but these traits have normally manifested themselves within parochial alliances, such as families, ethnic groups, hunter-gatherer bands, and in contemporary manifestations such as football teams, social class, even nation states. Such group formations have tended to define themselves in relation to those who are 'not like us', and so are not ideal for seeking more global solutions. I now turn to group life, which so often has extraordinary cooperativeness and prosociality at its heart, but which can also lead to terrible violence and damage perpetrated against those outside the group.

Chapter 12

Group-minded and narrow-minded

Be like me and like me

Paradoxically, our group nature is a force that drives the most moral and caring of our behaviours but also some of our most terrible acts. As a hypersocial and cooperative species, most humans want to be accepted and fit in. Standing out from the crowd can be an uncomfortable process, as any of us know in anxious moments such as worrying if our dining etiquette is wrong or clapping at a concert and suddenly fearing it is the wrong time!

Being excluded from one's group, whether being given the silent treatment by work colleagues, or cold-shouldered by neighbours or family, is literally painful. Kipling Williams of Purdue University investigated the effects of very brief episodes of ostracism in over 5,000 people (Williams and Nida 2011). These might include, for example, setting up a ball game and then ensuring that someone is left out. He found that when ostracised, the same brain areas are involved as in physical pain, particularly the dorsal anterior cingulate cortex. Unlike physical pain, with ostracism the pain can return each time the incident is thought about. Being excluded has a surprisingly powerful effect on most people, even when the person doing the shunning is unlikely ever to be encountered again.

As stated earlier, human adaptive capacities have depended on this ability to fit in, cooperate and learn from each other. We are neither particularly strong nor fast, but have enormous social brains. As perhaps the most adaptive species on earth we have passed down information about how to survive in a huge range of environments, from rain forests to arctic ice to Polynesian waters to the Sahara. Each culture has its own forms of knowledge, beliefs and expectations that are eagerly learnt, adapted to and transformed for new situations. This makes us very different from other primates.

In a classic experiment, children and chimpanzees were invited to copy the actions of an adult in order to retrieve a sweet from a box. This involved pushing a stick into various crevices and tapping on hidden parts of the interior. The children copied every gesture, as did chimpanzees when it was their turn. However, it was later revealed, by repeating the exercise but this time with a see-through Perspex box, that many of the actions were completely superfluous, and in fact one could skip stages one, two and three and thus get the sweet far more quickly. The chimpanzees cut to the chase and retrieved the sweet without the unnecessary steps but the human children diligently, perhaps stupidly, copied exactly what the adults did (McGuigan et al. 2007). Human adults also tend to imitate unnecessary aspects of tool use (McGuigan et al. 2011), and this might make us seem not very clever compared with chimps. In humans, only autistic children do not imitate superfluous actions (Marsh, Pearson et al. 2013), and they of course often struggle to fit in.

Imitating is in fact a huge advantage: it is how we learn. A more recent study by Lewis Dean and colleagues at St Andrews gave human children, young chimpanzees and capuchin monkeys tasks that became more complex, but also yielded increasing rewards. For example, they had to turn various switches and push buttons to get doors to open. The chimps took about 30 hours to get to level two, the capuchins much longer but human children made it in just three hours. This is because the human children learnt from each other, talked together and were keen to help and be helped. Chimps still did not manage even when there was also a chimp present who had been trained to do all the tasks (Dean et al. 2012). We might lose out to chimps on some tasks but overall the gains of communication, passing down knowledge and working as a group far outweigh the disadvantages. It is extremely rare to see any other ape co-operating, but in humans cooperation motivates us and fires reward circuits in our brains (Rekers et al. 2011).

This fits with so much else we know about humans. We have extraordinary capacities to imitate and synchronise body movements, and we like to be copied. We tend to unconsciously mimic those we like or feel rapport with (LaFrance 1979). In one study college students were found to unwittingly mimic the posture of their teacher. When the teacher placed his right hand under his chin, some students mirrored this by placing their left hand under their chin. It was those who reported having good rapport with their teacher who unconsciously mirrored his posture most of all. Feeling good is partly a function of being in synchronous harmony with those around us.

These are subtle processes that occur fast and out of consciousness. If we are exposed to pictures of faces expressing feelings such as anger or sadness then our own faces react in 300 to 400 milliseconds, and the moment we see a smiling face, our own face starts to form a smile, and at speeds too fast to have consciously registered the pictures (Dimberg and Thunberg 1998). Beatrix de Gelder from Tilburg University has shown how we respond extraordinarily swiftly to the meaning of body postures (Schindler *et al.* 2008). If someone makes a threatening gesture we instantaneously show fear, maybe with shallow breathing and tense bodies, irrespective of whether the person's verbal messages are friendly.

The very form of our embodied actions is profoundly affected by the cultures we happen to inhabit; language, postures and ways of moving are culturally distinctive. Most Italians when speaking use their hands much more animatedly than English speakers, while Native American Kutenai people move differently when speaking Kutenai or English (Birdwhistell 1970). Even infants quickly learn to act in culturally expected ways. Sometimes such imitation makes little obvious sense, such as smoking cigarettes to appear cool, or natives of the New Guinea highlands eating the brains of diseased relatives, and thus dying too. Mostly, though, imitation is a sensible strategy, enabling fitting in, cooperation, cultural transmission and successful group life.

Generally we like to be in tune with those around us and we like to feel understood. This explains why waitresses who repeat back what has been ordered ('two lightly poached eggs with tomatoes and no pepper') earn more tips than those who just say something positive (e.g. 'coming right up' or 'lovely day') (van Baaren *et al.* 2004). The same research found, not for the first time, that prosocial good feelings are contagious and their effect spreads. People who are imitated empathically are then much nicer to other people, being more likely to help someone who drops something, for example. In fact, after being imitated people are also likely to be more generous to third parties, and even 18-month-olds are more prosocial after being imitated (Carpenter *et al.* 2013). Walking, singing or other acts undertaken in synchrony all increase cooperativeness and helpfulness (Wiltermuth and Heath 2009). We are primed to join with others, and cooperate.

Them and us

Babies can imitate minutes after birth (Meltzoff 2007) and are like barometers of emotional atmospheres. A four-month-old is likely to smile when the ambience is jolly, and become fretful if things get tense. Researchers such as Ben Bradley, Jane Selby and Cathy Urwin (2012) even found that babies as young as eight months, when placed in groups of three or four, strive to be accepted and be 'in' rather than 'out'. Much research shows that babies have what are called *in-group* preferences. Three-month-olds prefer faces of those of their ethnic group over those of other races (Kelly *et al.* 2007). Eleven-month-olds prefer individuals who share their own taste in food and even expect them to be nicer than those with different tastes.

Indeed, a different part of our brains lights up when we look at a familiar kind of face as opposed to one with less-known features (Dawson *et al.* 2002). Sixteen-month-olds, when presented with food that they were uncertain about, chose the same food that kinder rather than antisocial strangers preferred (Hamlin and Wynn 2012). More worryingly, babies of only nine months old preferred those who treat people 'like them' well and treat people who are 'not like them' badly (Hamlin *et al.* 2013). Prejudice starts early.

It seems that, troublingly, it is harder to even sympathise with people we see as dissimilar. We even use different parts of our brains if we try to empathise with those who see the world differently. A left-leaning atheist academic asked to empathise with a creationist Christian fundamentalist will probably struggle. With people whose views or cultures are very different we rely more on abstract cognitive and deductive parts of our brains, whereas with people we feel are like-minded we use brain areas dominant for empathy and emotional understanding, in fact similar areas to those used when thinking about oneself (Mitchell *et al.* 2006). We are also more generous to members of our own group when they violate social rules than to those from out-groups, recruiting more mentalising and empathic brain circuitry (Baumgartner *et al.*

2012). This all poses real problems for international, cross-cultural and cross-group linking.

We have a natural tendency to divide the world into 'them and us', even when the belonging is based on the most spurious of grounds. Typical is a well-known experiment in which boys were shown pictures constructed using lots of dots. They were asked to estimate how many dots were in each picture. They were then told randomly, with no grounding in reality, that they had either over- or under-estimated the number of dots, and so were labelled either as 'over-estimators' or 'under-estimators'. Surprisingly, they later tended to favour and be more generous to others who were labelled in the same group as them (Tajfel and Turner 1979). In another experiment, a teacher divided her class into brown- and blue-eyed pupils and announced that the brown-eyed pupils were better in various ways (Peters 1987). The children with the low-status blue eyes showed a marked worsening in performance, while previously well-functioning friendships between blue- and brown-eyed children deteriorated.

The chances of reaching out to those in other cultures and groups are even more compromised by the fact that belonging and group loyalty increases self-esteem (Hewstone *et al.* 2002), so it is good for us to belong. Prejudice about ethnicity, class or nationality are extreme examples of this double-edged predisposition.

Indeed it seems that group bonding might be a common way of bolstering a fragile sense of self by feeling part of a particular in-group, hence gang membership and the increase in racism and xenophobia witnessed so often when times are difficult. Claire Ashton-James and Jessica Tracy of the University of British Columbia (2011) demonstrated how people showing a hubristic over-blown pride had higher levels of prejudice than those with ordinary self-confidence. The latter they call 'authentic pride', which might derive from hard work and a genuine sense of achievement, which is more likely to lead to a compassionate and empathic attitude to others. On the other hand, pride based on hubris, and presumably geared to bolstering fragile self-esteem, is a more arrogant and less genuinely self-confident kind, and suggests attempting to feel better by diminishing others. Such studies back up the psychoanalytic idea that we can cope with bad feelings about ourselves by projecting them onto others. Those with more authentic pride were not only more empathic but they harboured less prejudice.

Prejudice and dehumanising

The tendency to divide into groups can have dreadful implications, as seen in the famous if shocking Stanford Prison experiment in 1971. Here, adults were randomly assigned to play the role of either prisoners or guards. In a very short time the two groups, whose members were in fact similar in terms of social class, ethnicity and educational level, took on their respective roles. The prisoners became distrustful of and angry with the guards who in turn became surprisingly vindictive to the prisoners (Zimbardo *et al.* 2000). Their over-identification with these roles led to mutual hostility, a prisoners' revolt and guard violence.

Such experiments ask profound questions about this trait that we call cooperation. In probably the most famous of such experiments, Stanley Milgram (1974) asked subjects to participate in what they believed to be a method of helping students learn. The method included giving someone they thought was a student (in fact an actor) mild electric shocks when they got an answer wrong. Sometimes it was slipped into the conversation that the 'student' had a heart condition. Shockingly around 65 per cent of the subjects were prepared, under pressure from a white-coated male in authority, to administer what they believed were potentially fatal levels of electric shock. When a participant showed reluctance, the experimenter used verbal prods such as 'the experiment requires that you continue'. Subjects were allowed to stop if their reluctance remained after four such prods.

This experiment has been replicated on numerous occasions, with both men and women, and has consistently shown that over 60 per cent follow the instructions, irrespective of the harm that might ensue. This confounded all predictions. Of course if asked what we would do in such situations we probably all would say, and firmly believe, that we would do the ethical thing, but this sadly is probably self-deception. The parallels with Nazi Germany and collaboration are striking and despite what we like to believe about ourselves, it is the very few who resist such pressures. I still feel shame about not standing up to a bully who mercilessly teased my friend in primary school, and I am sure we all constantly have dilemmas about whether to put our head above the parapet for something we believe in.

Our group biases can be extremely unsettling. In a typical experiment in America, white subjects were shown both black and white faces for 30 milliseconds, too short a time for the conscious mind to register. When shown black faces, scans revealed heightened amygdala response, suggesting non-conscious fear. When the pictures were shown for long enough to register consciously, the scans showed activation in brain areas involved with conflict resolution, suggesting that the subjects now were grappling with their own racism (Cunningham *et al.* 2004). Interestingly when the face was well known, such as Nelson Mandela, then the same prejudices were less present in white participants. Such biases are non-conscious and implicit, often develop early in childhood, and can play a powerful role in how we define ourselves (Baron and Banaji 2006).

Such research chillingly shows how easy it is to diminish or even dehumanise people we do not know. Non-conscious prejudice is very common, whether to those of another ethnic group, social class, country, or the poor or drug-users. A mixed group were shown images of a range of people, such as a female college student, a male American fire-fighter, a business woman and rich man, a disabled woman, a female homeless person and male drug addict. They were asked to imagine a day in the life of each of these people, an exercise that generally induces empathy. Strikingly, while the empathy circuits in the volunteers' brains lit up for all the others, for both the homeless person and the drug addict areas dominant for disgust, such as the insula, were most active (Harris and Fiske 2011). Indeed very worryingly, given the current social trend towards inequality and social divisions, for many the areas linked with disgust lit up in response to poor people generally.

We similarly know that when shown pictures of people in pain, if the other person is of one's own ethnic or cultural group, such as African-American or Caucasian American, distinct parts of the brain, those involved in empathy, are active (Mathur *et al.* 2010). Such dehumanisation seems to be at the heart of many atrocities based on prejudice such as homophobia, Nazi anti-Semitic murder, race crimes against black people or genocides such as between Hutus and Tutsis.

Fellow feeling, good and bad

Thus, identifying with a group is an extremely mixed blessing. Belonging makes us feel better, is good for the group as a whole, and is one of the roots of genuine mutual care and cooperation. However, it can also lead to dehumanisation of others and will inhibit cooperating with those we deem different. Surprisingly, oxytocin, which mainly has such prosocial effects, can be implicated. In close-knit and bonded groups, such as the huddles of sportsmen before games, oxytocin levels rise. Yet when given oxytocin intranasally, people become more likely to help those in their own ethnic group, and less likely to aid those from other groups (de Dreu *et al.* 2011). Even infants have been shown to prefer those who harm people who are different over those who harm people like them (Hamlin and Wynn 2012).

In a trust game in Belgium, a country with high levels of ethnic tension between Flemish and Walloon citizens, members of both groups made lower offers to those from the other ethnic group and similar results were seen in Israel between Hasidic orthodox and non-religious Jews (Fershtman and Gneezy 2011).We tend to be even tougher on people who violate norms if they come from another social group, as research with two cultural groups in New Guinea recently found (Bernhard *et al.* 2006). Bernhard, one of the researchers, termed such survival strategies 'parochial altruism', or in other words, we are nicest to people in our group, but can be nice to people in other groups as well as being competitive with them. If one is too nice to everyone, one might not survive, but selfishness within groups has a diminishing return.

Thus our loyalty can be blind and not the least bit ethical, something that, maybe not surprisingly, can be seen in business. Elizabeth Umphress (2010) from Texas found that if people identify with the organisation they work for, then they are very likely to undertake unethical acts seen as 'for the good of the organisation'. We can justify bad acts if undertaken for an 'us' we identify with.

Empathy-induced altruism can be similarly unfair. One of Batson's experiments concerned Sheri, a 10-year-old with a terminal illness. Empathy for Sheri was manipulated by asking some subjects to listen to her talking about her illness from an objective position while others were to really try understanding her feelings. The subjects were later given a chance to help Sheri by moving her up a hospital waiting-list ahead of children who might have worse illnesses or have been waiting longer. Perhaps not surprisingly those in the high-empathy condition were more likely to move her up the list.

While some of us have more of a predisposition for altruism than others, due to factors such as how we were parented and also our genes, our altruism is also hugely influenced by current contexts and environments, as well as by the social systems we live in. Israeli soldiers showed more in-group cohesion during the Israeli–Hezbollah conflict in 2006 than either before and after the conflict, for example making lower offers to outsiders in ultimatum games during the conflict and displaying more in-group generosity in trust games (Gneezy and Fessler 2011). Similarly in Burundi, those who were themselves victims of recent genocides or whose family were, acted more altruistically to close neighbours (people like them) than to those less affected by the conflict (Voors *et al.* 2011). During wars, punishment of group members who violate norms and rules tends to increase (Sääksvuori, Mappes and Puurtinen 2011). A classic example is the severe punishments, often including death, meted out to soldiers who desert.

How much this human tendency towards powerful group solidarity was the result of inter-group conflict in our evolutionary history remains controversial. Samuel Bowles and his colleague Herbert Gintis (2011) examined archaeological evidence for lethal fighting between groups in pre-history, finding evidence of frequent death by violent means. Many others such as Fry (2013) and Hrdy (1999), on the other hand, found little evidence of warfare in the time of our hunter-gatherer past, and much more since settled societies took root. It is likely that both are right, that even irregular warfare would enhance the pressure for cohesive groups and parochial altruism, as would group competition, but violence also probably increased with the advent of fixed property and the move into static communities, initially pastoral ones and later larger conurbations and states.

Martin Nowak argues convincingly that such loyalty to our in-groups and those we identify with makes evolutionary sense, given that strong, tight-knit and cooperative groups were so important to survival (Nowak and Highfield 2011). Altruism and cooperation might not immediately benefit the individual cooperator, but groups of cooperators do well and maybe paradoxically inter-group conflict breeds altruism. Computer models devised by Samuel Bowles are typical of research suggesting that when there is competition between groups the strongly bonded ones, containing people prepared to make sacrifices for others, are more likely to survive than bands of individualists. Mathematical models suggest that a self-sacrificing gene is likely to disappear after about 150 generations unless group conflict is brought into the equation, and then even with fairly infrequent group conflict, seemingly costly altruistic traits spread rapidly and survive.

Summary and the question of hope

Much of this book has emphasised the positive value of being in a group, giving rise, for example, to loyalty, kindness and generous behaviour. However, in this chapter I have emphasised how group life most definitely has a dark side, something that group psychoanalysts have known clinically for a long time (Bion 1961; Foulkes 1984). The kind of research reviewed in this chapter poses a fundamental challenge to hopes for a better world. We have not evolved to empathise with people on the other side of the planet, or even those from other cultural groups. The parochial nature of our altruism poses serious issues.

Maybe there is hope in how we can have shifting and multiple identifications. In a study in Liverpool (Levine *et al.* 2005) an actor wore either a Manchester United or Liverpool football shirt whilst lying on the ground feigning illness. He was far more likely to be helped if wearing the native Liverpool shirt! Yet when students were asked to write an essay on the joys of being a football fan generally, they were much more likely to stop and help anyone in any team's kit. Similarly, a doctor can have one set of values in one context, such as when working as a clinician, and yet if also working as a manager they might find themselves acting from quite other belief systems (Leavitt *et al.* 2012). This at least shows the possibility of broadening the range of our identifications towards less parochial allegiances.

There is a range of projects and initiatives that have attempted to break down such parochial barriers. Examples include the long history of conflict resolution and peace studies. Much work is in small-scale local projects aiming to enhance empathy between rival groups. These include brave attempts to diminish hatred and distrust between Protestants and Catholics in Northern Ireland, or Israelis and Palestinians. Such work has been pioneering, sometimes successfully helping one side to see the other's viewpoint, activating empathy towards members of an out-group who might otherwise be dehumanised.

In one ingenious experiment, which might have wider applications, a radio soap opera was used in Rwanda to promote reconciliation between Hutus and Tutsis. In the widely listened-to programme, characters grappled with issues such as inter-racial marriage in a way that aimed to diminish prejudice. Listeners became more tolerant of their out-group and more accepting than non-listeners (Paluck 2009). Of course such prejudices are not just in people's minds, but are often fuelled by conflicts between huge vested interests, such as the historic economic ascendancy of Protestants over Catholics in Northern Ireland. Without challenging these, little change will take place. Nevertheless such studies do suggest that there is hope for shifting attitudes.

There have been many initiatives, from smaller-scale ones such as the Jigsaw project (Aronson and Patnoe 1996) to international ones, which suggest the possibility of challenging the inevitability of our parochial and often prejudiced group nature and enhancing empathy between people who otherwise might not care much about each other. Jeremy Rifkin (2010) similarly argued that the cross-national and cultural worlds of the internet and of global manufacturing can challenge parochial altruism. For example, he argues that global media allows communication that can confront and break down racial and national boundaries.

Rifkin might be being overly optimistic, and his argument is by no means universally agreed with, but it is a brave attempt to try to theorise something that few have taken seriously. A parochial altruism based on group loyalty might well be the evolutionary root of genuine care of others. It was probably also hugely instrumental in enabling humans to expand across the globe and exploit the earth's resources with such great success. That same parochial altruism and inability to care much for either distant people or future generations has also been the source of much cruelty and conflict and might now be contributing to a threat to our very futures.

Chapter 13

Reputations, shaming, gossip and punishment

Reputations and gossip

Whatever our levels of empathy or our altruistic predispositions we can all be tempted to stray from the straight and narrow, to be less than honest, kind or generous. In all societies something more than spontaneous altruism and empathy have been necessary to oil the wheels of cooperative group life and minimise self-interest. Group rules, moral precepts, gossip and the use of both shame and punishment have nearly always been present. In other words, social rules and structures are needed to ensure a moral way of life.

Shame and the fear of being judged have a powerful effect on curbing individualistic and antisocial actions. Melissa Bateson and Daniel Nettle from the University of Newcastle looked at what led students to contribute to an honesty box for tea or coffee. Just above the box they experimented with hanging two kinds of pictures; the first was simply of a pair of eyes and the second was of a flower. Astonishingly, when the picture of eyes was above the honesty box the students contributed three times as much! The eyes seemed to non-consciously nudge people to follow their consciences. Similarly café users were found to be far more likely to put litter away when posters of eyes were on the wall rather than of flowers (Ernest-Jones *et al.* 2010). This is a potent effect and illustrates something about how much humans generally care about how we are perceived.

Most research suggests that shame, the fear of a bad reputation and of being punished are massive drivers of better behaviour. Shame is different to guilt, and is evoked in response to how we expect to be perceived, whereas guilt is more a matter of individual conscience. We watch out for unfairness and misdemeanours in others and most of us want to be thought well of. By about six years old, children actively dissemble so as to be thought fairer than they are (Shaw *et al.* 2012) and for example they give more stickers away when they can be seen than when they think they are invisible (Leimgruber *et al.* 2012).

Tilting away from morality

Dan Ariely, Professor of Psychology and Behavioural Economics at Duke University, experimented by giving people a test, and letting them know that they would earn more money the better they performed, but also making sure that there was plenty of room to cheat! Half of those taking the test were asked beforehand to recall ten books they had read in high school, while the other half were asked to recall as many of the Ten Commandments as they could. Fascinatingly those who had been asked to recall the Ten Commandments, irrespective of how many they in fact remembered, were far less likely to cheat (Ariely 2009). Just being in touch with a moral prompt makes a difference to how ethically we behave.

Triggers which remind us of moral expectations definitely help to keep us on the straight and narrow. The psychoanalyst Glen Gabbard, who works a lot with therapists and medics who have contravened sexual boundaries, found that about 50 per cent of medical students would cheat, given the chance (Gabbard and Hobday 2012). Similarly John List discovered high levels of academic misconduct, from falsifying data to the exchange of grades for gifts, money or sex (List *et al.* 2001), while Ferric C. Fang reported a 10-fold increase in known fraudulent publications in 20 years (Fang *et al.* 2012).

It is possible that this increase in fraud reflects a central theme of this book, that anxiety and pressure increase the likelihood of dishonesty. Typical of the high levels of fraud by prominent academics from a number of countries was how anaesthesiologist Yoshitaka Fujii was dismissed from Tokyo University for fabricating data in 183 articles (Hunsucker 2013). Most academics are under huge pressure to publish by their institutions and for career advancement. A report on nearly 150 cases of misconduct suggested that the fear of a stalling career was a huge motivator in a system where high-quality publication equates with increased income (Kornfeld 2012).

Cheating or acting immorally is of course far easier when one is unseen, and may have increased in our large-scale anonymous cultures compared to the smaller-scale close-knit communities in which humans lived for tens of thousands of years. Possibly the complex financial instruments that led to a financial crisis, and that so few understood, might be examples of what can happen when a social system allows people to act hidden from public gaze, with few moral prompts, and with individual gain rather than the common good being valued.

Moral prompts will have a greater effect on some of us than others, depending on how much being moral is central to our self-identity. Dr Karl Aquino (2009) and his colleagues at their research centre, appropriately called the 'The Immorality Lab', found that people with a stronger moral identity were more generous and prosocial than those for whom it is less important. Interestingly, for the people who were more moral anyway a prime of reading the Ten Commandments had less effect on whether they cheated than on those with a weaker moral identity. For those who waver, moral prompts are far more influential.

We are very influenced by subtle contextual influences. Simply wearing sunglasses that we are told are counterfeit, as opposed to identical ones we believe are an authentic brand, predisposes us to be more dishonest (Gino *et al.* 2010). If people read stories containing moral statements then they are more likely to do a good deed than if they read a story about very selfish people being rewarded, or if they are exposed to a cunning selling technique. However, once again the people most easily influenced are those who have a weaker moral self-identity anyway.

Such subtle experimental moral nudges have real effects, although the most powerful nudges in contemporary society are probably from advertising and the mass media, and we are more likely to buy a product that might make us look better, than to be implored to do a good or kindly deed. There are obviously political questions about whether these kinds of influences, and the social forces from which they arise, are best for people and society.

Shame

Ensuring social conformity via shaming would have been much easier in the small hunter-gatherer groups that humans once lived in than in contemporary large-scale industrial societies. There were no police or courts of law in such societies so people took justice into their own hands. Furthermore, as we have seen, the fear of ostracism and being an outcast runs deep. Yet public shaming does not sit well with most of us any more; we do not like to put people in stocks, or to tattoo criminals or make people who are 'different' wear yellow stars. Few of us would have approved of French women consorting with Nazis but how do we feel about their heads being shaved after the war as they were jeered at by furious crowds? Yet in many earlier human societies shaming was a central mechanism for maintaining social cohesion and ensuring norms.

Jennifer Jacquet has examined the moral questions in environmental issues such as the likely extinction of many fish species due to over-fishing and the perhaps surprising lack of collaborative international action to prevent environmental disasters. As in the famous Tragedy of the Commons or other public-goods games, if everyone felt that everyone else was being fair, there would be more likelihood of individuals or countries not self-interestedly exploiting resources.

As already discussed, in public-goods games people are given a sum which they can contribute to the public pot and what they do not contribute they can keep. The public pot is then multiplied before redistribution so in fact everyone does better the more is contributed to the pot. What consistently happens is that people start by contributing generously but if they get a whiff of others acting selfishly then they too become withholding and put less into the pot. In two recent versions of this game Jacquet (Jacquet *et al.* 2011) let players know either that all the players would get to know who the most generous donors were, or alternatively all the players would find out who the least generous were. The likelihood of being seen as the least generous, or of being known as the most generous, led to doubling the overall contributions, compared to a control group. Shaming ungenerous behaviour and rewarding big-heartedness are powerful motivators, often more so than individual gain.

Thus, shaming can work, but otherwise people tend to follow the public-goods scenario whereby if everyone is not doing their bit, then people think, 'why should I?' Spanish fishermen will not stop over-fishing if British fishermen continue at the same level, and vice versa. In the financial realm, bankers gaining massive bonuses are far less visible and harder to shame than a hunter-gatherer who takes most of the spoils of a hunt. Unlike in hunter-gatherer societies, people cannot take the law into their own hands to protest and dispense justice when acts that are deemed wrong are in fact legal, whether tax evasion, the exploitation of fish stocks, industrial emissions, environmental pollution or indeed the increasing inequality in Western societies. Indeed, the law often protects those who gain from such acts.

The increased likelihood of meeting someone regularly is also usually a deterrent against taking advantage of them. People value their reputation and it does not pay to be seen as untrustworthy or a cheat. Indeed in most hunter-gatherer communities a reputation for generosity can be traded on when times are hard. A study of the Ache showed that in times of need the previously most philanthropic were helped the most while those considered mean fared the worst (Boehm 2012, p. 296). In hunter-gatherer communities, and maybe still today, being generous is a kind of insurance policy; paying in now can provide cover when bad times come. It also has been advantageous in terms of popularity and seeking mates in both hunter-gatherer (Boehm 2012) and also contemporary societies (Keltner 2009).

Shame has historically been one of the most effective ways of ensuring human cooperation. Remember that in the Ultimatum Game, those who received very low offers that they were determined to reject had heightened activation in areas of the brain associated with disgust, particularly the insula. Contempt, anger and disgust are emotions that trigger the shaming of others, and are potent socialising forces. In groups where shaming is more common, there will be stronger conformity and in-group allegiance and a more sociocentric attitude.

Our anonymous monetary-exchange system and impersonal city lives can give rise to opportunities for dishonesty and antisocial acts which are less likely to be discovered, let alone punished, than in days of yore. Contemporary Western societies rely less nowadays on public shaming and more on the law, police and regulations as well as on individual conscience. Shame, though, remains powerful, especially at local levels. No teacher in a school wants to be seen as a bad teacher, no bank clerk as dishonest or employee as unreliable. Occasionally public shaming is effective, especially when a media frenzy is whipped up, such as British MPs' expenses scandals or major media corporations being vilified for infringements of privacy such as phone-tapping. However, such shaming is rarer in large-scale societies with more one-off exchanges. The anonymity of contemporary life allows sub-sets of people to get away with acts which otherwise would attract public opprobrium, whether in the financial sector or practices such as pornography or internet fraud.

Gossip

Many of us know only too well how either office or community gossip can make or destroy reputations. Fear of gossip and worry about reputation are staples of all known human societies. As Wiessner (2009) found in her in-depth study of the !Kung, and as Boehm's accounts also attest, the main topic of gossip in hunter-gatherer societies was 'big-shot' non-cooperative, non-egalitarian behaviour, as well as laziness, stinginess, and generally being antisocial.

Gossip has remained a really vital form of ensuring social conformity, and maybe surprisingly it has beneficial side-effects, as Dr Robb Willer and his colleagues of the University of Berkeley found (Feinberg, Willer, Stellar et al. 2012). They got participants to play a trust game, in which money or points were to be shared. In one game it became obvious that a particular participant was hoarding more than their fair share, and observers often gossiped about this player to newcomers to the game. Interestingly, on observing the cheat in action, the observers' heart rates rose but when they gossiped their heart rates came down. It seems that such prosocial gossiping is good not only for the group but also for the gossiper's health.

In such trust games, the higher someone scored on scales of altruism the more they were upset by cheating, and the more likely they were to engage in gossip about the cheat. Thus gossiping is not undertaken only from malicious intent but is often motivated by strong feelings about fairness and a desire to stop cheating. Participants even sacrificed some of their own pay from being in the study in order to pass gossip onto others. This was more remarkable as they knew that this would not even affect the selfish player's score.

This need to gossip, fear of being gossiped about and commitment to fairness seem to be wired into us. Even young children do it. In an experiment at the famous Max Planck Institute (Vaish et al. 2011) three-year-olds watched a puppet draw a picture.

When this puppet left the room another character destroyed the absent puppet's creations. Three-year-olds protested when the damage was being done, but also 'tattled' on the actor/puppet when the harmed puppet returned. Indeed, equally young children have been found in experiments to actively use moralistic and normative language to prod peers not conforming to group norms (Schmidt and Tomasello 2012).

Gossip gets a bad press, and can of course be both self-righteous and vindictive, but it can also be a force for social good. Willer and colleagues (Feinberg, Willer, Stellar,*et al.* 2012) found that when people knew that they might be the subject of gossip they played considerably more fairly, and the biggest change was seen in those with the lowest levels of altruism. These are powerful results. Most people feel upset at unfairness, feel better when they can do something about it, and are even prepared to make personal sacrifices to ensure fairness. It is unclear whether a materialistic and individualistic culture, in which the market remains the ultimate arbiter of value, militates against such tendencies to enforce fairness.

Some people are less likely than others to act prosocially without the threat of gossip and punishment, apparently males more so than females. When people had the opportunity to donate money, they were observed by attractive people either of the same sex or of the opposite sex. While the level of donations given by the women did not change according to who was watching them, the peacockish men were far more generous when they were being observed by an attractive woman (Van Vugt and Iredale 2012). Possibly such seemingly superficially motivated acts might have useful social benefits, as seen in Native American 'giveaway' *potlatch* rituals in which giving away what one owns is central and takes place in a culture that values not conspicuous consumption but conspicuous generosity.

We are more likely to be dishonest and duplicitous if circumstances allow this, when there is less transparency and more secrecy, obfuscation and anonymity. There is even more cheating in dimly lit rooms than brightly lit ones, as researchers Zhong, Bohns and Gino found in their aptly entitled paper 'Good lamps are the best police' (Zhong, Bohns *et al.* 2010). They also found that just wearing sunglasses could make people more prone to cheat. In both the dim lighting and the sunglasses experiments the apparent anonymity inhibited moral behaviour, presumably because such anonymity increases the likelihood of trying to get away with something.

Punishment

If shaming does not work then we often resort to stronger methods like overt punishment. In public-goods games when the possibility of punishing non-contributors is introduced then contributions increase by up to 90 per cent (Fehr and Gachter 2002). In games where there is a chance of real and effective punishment a brain region called the dorsal striatum, also central to processing rewards, is very active. Those with the most activation (and rewards) were the most disapproving of the antisocial actions (de Quervain *et al.* 2004). As already stated, we even punish when we cannot change the outcome, such as in the last round of a public-goods game when it is too late to change anyone's behaviour. This again suggests that punishment has its own rewards.

Boehm's and other anthropological studies showed that when shaming and gossip do not work, in hunter-gatherer societies powerful mechanisms were in place whereby alpha-male tendencies were policed, sometimes violently, and groups of males generally stood up to bullies, dictators and inveterate cheats. This is almost unique to humans, but Boehm suggests it was the norm in such communities. He reports that over half the executions on the ethnographic records were about issues of sharing and egalitarian values (p. 156). While those thieves and cheats seen as capable of reforming suffered lesser punishments, serious self-aggrandising cheats, who presumably were seen as less likely to change, were most likely to be executed. It is possible that nowadays bullies, free-riders and self-aggrandising people, or indeed psychopaths, can more easily become extremely powerful without punishment.

Punishment though has drawbacks if over-used. Martin Nowak found consistently that people who punished the most in such games became embroiled in an endless cycle of mutual retribution (Nowak and Highfield 2011). He found that rewarding good behaviour was far more effective than punishing bad behaviour, something that those teaching parenting programmes have long known. None the less we need both reward and punishment to most effectively ensure prosocial communal activity.

One large cross-cultural 16-nation study (Herrmann *et al.* 2008) using the public-goods game found big cultural differences in altruistic contributions to the public pot. When punishment was allowed into the equation, and participants could use their own resources to punish, in some countries, in fact including the USA, Switzerland and the UK, the punished free-riders seemed to hold their hands up, accept the chastisement and then become fairer. However, in other countries the game deteriorated into one of mutual revenge and punishments as retribution. The authors hypothesise that there is a link between low levels of revenge and countries where the law is more respected and police more trusted. Where there was less trust of public authority, people vengefully took events into their own hands. Culture has a big influence on our attitudes to fairness and punishment.

Summary

I have described the typical ways in which societies and smaller social groups ensure conformity to group expectations, including shaming, gossip and the importance of reputation as well as more overt forms of punishment. This has meant taking seriously the prosocial impact of character traits we might not feel that good about, such as gossip or the pleasures of punishment, vengefulness, and other unsavoury but equally 'natural' ones like envy and what the Germans call *Schadenfreude*, that pleasure in someone else's downfall. The brain regions activated in envy (the anterior cingulate cortex) are very linked to those involved in *Schadenfreude*. After witnessing someone's fall from grace, the stronger the anterior cingulate cortex activation (associated with envy) then the stronger the ventral striatum activation, associated with *Schadenfreude* (Takahashi *et al.* 2009). Just as our brain's reward and pleasure circuits light up in response to punishment, we can get other rewards from the failure of those we envy (Strobel *et al.* 2011). Presumably such responses are motivated by an archaic human wish for fairness.

Anger, disgust, envy and *Schadenfreude* might be feelings we wish to disown but they are part of the human repertoire that ensures fairness and social norms. Even very young children have been shown to feel *Schadenfreude* (Schulz *et al.* 2013). There has been much revealing recent research about the role of the brain area called the insula in recent years, which is active in disgust, and relatedly, in ostracism. For many of us it fires away when seeing vomit, rats, or flea-ridden decomposing bodies. It is also involved when we actively disapprove of others, particularly if we hear about sexual misconduct such as abuse or incest. Being made a low offer in the Ultimatum Game also gives rise to heightened insula activity. Such moral disgust and disapproval is another central mechanism whereby social rules and morals are enforced, even if at times it can also unleash a braying mob mentality.

Once again there tend to be gender differences. In one set of experiments, subjects were paired up with others who either played fairly or unfairly. Then people's brains were scanned as they watched their play partner receive a reasonably mild electric shock. Both men and women showed empathy in fairly equal measures when seeing a fair co-player receiving shocks, and their pain-related brain regions lit up. With the players who cheated, women not surprisingly tended to show a reduction in empathy, but men not only showed less empathy, but also an activated reward circuitry when watching the shocks, which correlated with how much they desired revenge (Singer *et al.* 2006)!

We have finely tuned antennae to pick up how prosocial others are. People make reasonably good estimates of how kind, considerate and prosocial others are just by watching 20 seconds of them listening to their romantic partner and observing their gestures and body language (Kogan *et al.* 2011). We are built to watch out for bad behaviour and to know that we are likely to be watched. Possibly the relative anonymity of contemporary life mitigates against such sensitivity to being seen and judged.

The urge to shame and protect moral, environmental or prosocial values can often run counter to other consumerist and self-interested tendencies. Jennifer Jacquet described how a morally minded minority go to great lengths to avoid eating endangered fish, taking tape measures to supermarkets to avoid buying baby fish, while overall consumption of such fish increased. In supermarkets, of course, there is no shaming, nor subliminal priming messages, let alone punishment for buying threatened species or polluting products. Each society will have its own predominant messages, whether more materialistic and consumerist, environmentally aware, or more egalitarian and generous. Some cultures even have ritualised ways of ensuring public generosity, such as the *potlatch* or 'giveaway' ceremony of some Native American peoples. Here high status was bestowed on the most generous, rather than on those who have the most.

I have outlined how human innate prosocial tendencies can dovetail with the use of punishment, shame, gossip and other mechanisms to ensure a more egalitarian, altruistic way of being, and greater compliance with social norms and rules. We have seen how the influence of one's context and environment can activate different behaviours, such as the dime in the phone booth that triggered altruistic helpfulness. This might give hope that, as well as focusing on parenting and children's development, we can also work towards social systems and lifestyles that promote more prosocial actions. Clever psychological primes will not achieve this but they can indicate our potential for change. However, organising institutions, communities and social and economic forces according to more prosocial values could have a huge impact. I now turn to look at the impact of some societal shifts on altruistic and prosocial actions, in particular the rise of consumerist culture, and the effect this seems to be having on our very brains.

Chapter 14

Consumerism, society and our divided brain

Materialism

The values of the society we live in, and the kind of social messages we receive, have a profound impact on how self-reliant and selfish, or kind and altruistic, we are. In one fascinating experiment subjects were given words to rearrange into sentences. Some had in front of them a random selection of words whereas others had similar ones but also some words linked with finance such as 'profit' or 'high salary'. After this task they had a more complex puzzle to do, and they could both ask for help, and also offer help. Those who compiled sentences using the financial words took about five minutes longer to ask for help and were also less likely to offer help (Vohs *et al.* 2006). Being primed with financial words prods people to act more selfishly and self-reliantly. Presumably more consumerist and money-oriented cultures and influences would have a different effect on moral behaviours to more altruistic or spiritual societies.

Tim Kasser (2003), Professor of Psychology in Illinois, has spent his professional life analysing the impact of materialistic values on individuals and society. He has carefully defined the concept of materialistic values as a cluster of traits that tend to arise together. These include aspiring to expensive consumer goods, wanting to be viewed as attractive or to be famous. He calls these *extrinsic* values, denoting being motivated particularly by how one is perceived by others. The opposite of extrinsic values he and others call *intrinsic*, meaning valuing a cluster of attributes like being community- and family-minded, being kind to others and living by deeply held beliefs.

He found a very clear relationship between materialistic values and behaviours. People with more extrinsic values tended to have higher levels of prejudice, less concern for human rights and overall were less caring. They also were more negligent about environmental issues, which makes sense given that there is a close link in young people between being kind to others and caring about the world and future generations (Lawford *et al.* 2012). All too frequently such materialistic values come with emotional insecurity and unhappiness. More materialistic desires are often an attempt to compensate for not feeling very good inside, acting as 'defences' or ways of coping with inner distress.

Many of the young people I work with, including a large number who have been in public care, hugely value material things, whether new trainers or a gadget they aspire to. Dee was typical, complaining vociferously about her foster carer who did not buy her what she wanted, and whom she accused of 'only looking after her for the money'. Typically of many maltreated young people, Dee moved quickly between anger at others, self-hatred, suspicion and cruelty. I have though found that, movingly, young people like Dee, as they begin to feel some trust that they have a place in the hearts and minds of those who look after them, become more motivated by relationships, and also more caring of others around them. As this happens, their extrinsic desires recede more into the background. Unfortunately I only have anecdotal clinical rather than research evidence of this, albeit seen many times in cases I have worked with or supervised (Music 2011; 2012). Such changes fit with research showing that a sense of wellbeing and feeling cared for makes us more prosocial, while emotional insecurity, perfectionism and a preoccupation with how one is viewed by others come with insecure attachment and social isolation (Chen *et al.* 2012).

We are all capable of moving into either more competitive or caring states of mind. As we have seen, the extent to which we do either is influenced by early experiences and family life, and also the kinds of work environments, communities and societies we inhabit. In competitive environments we are more likely to see others as rivals, compare ourselves with them and make judgements. When people feel compared to others, irrespective of whether these comparisons are positive or negative, then several days later they are less empathic and prosocial than control groups (Yip and Kelly 2013). The huge amount of data on the devastating effects of inequality on levels of trust underscores this (Wilkinson 2005; Wilkinson and Pickett 2009).

In one simple study (Bauer *et al.* 2012) people were asked to imagine there was a water shortage, and the available water should be shared with several other people. The water users were either described as *consumers* or as *individuals*. Those described as *consumers* were less trusting of the others, less helpful and less likely to work in partnership than those designated as *individuals*. The only difference between the groups was the label, and personality differences between the participants did not affect the result. This is very similar to the previously mentioned study (Liberman *et al.* 2004) in which two groups played exactly the same game. For one group it was called the 'Wall Street Game', and the other the 'Community Game', and 70 per cent of those playing the 'Community Game' did indeed cooperate, as opposed to only 33 per cent of those playing the 'Wall Street Game'. There are lessons here about how subtle messages can enhance or diminish cooperative and helpful behaviour.

Kasser and colleagues have undertaken much research into the effects of advertising. Its messages, whether on billboards, TV screens or the web, are of course designed to induce people to spend money and buy into lifestyle choices, perhaps that a new car will make us more powerful, or that a skin cream will make us look younger and more glamorous. What the evidence is not clear about is whether advertising for a specific product, like a new kind of computer, will necessarily increase sales of that particular computer. However, exposure to such advertising does prime people for more extrinsic values, and we are more likely to aspire to be consumers and to become more materialistic as a result of it.

One simple natural experiment (Greenberg and Brand 1993) compared children in several American schools with other children of similar age, race and socioeconomic background. In some schools a TV news station called Channel One was introduced, aimed at school children. Channel One showed ten minutes of news followed by two minutes of adverts. The teenagers in the schools which showed Channel One had higher levels of materialistic extrinsic values, more desire for advertised goods and generally more consumerist attitudes. Many findings point in this direction. Advertising need not even influence people's conscious attitudes, but simply seeing excited faces using an item, or hearing a celebrity endorsement of a product, can change implicit attitudes, albeit outside of consciousness (Nairn and Fine 2008).

Materialistic values are in opposition to intrinsic motivations such as 'social justice', 'equality' or making the world 'a better place'. For example, people and businesses that place a high value on money and possessions also tend to 'objectify' others, perceiving them less as fellow humans to be related to, but more as a means to an end, perhaps as a potential source of sales (Kasser, Vansteenkiste et al. 2006). Those with more extrinsic values tend to be less community- and other-minded and more selfish. When playing games such as the Tragedy of the Commons they tend to take more for themselves (Sheldon and McGregor 2000). People with higher levels of extrinsic values are also more likely to be suspicious of out-groups and to perceive threat (Duriez et al. 2012).

Maybe not surprisingly, while most people are highly rewarded by positive social cues, individuals with high levels of antisocial personality traits are much more motivated by monetary rewards (Pfabigan et al. 2011). As Kasser and others have shown, the more people value material things, the less they care for more prosocial and intrinsic values such as 'helpfulness', 'loyalty', 'friendship' or 'committed relationships' (Richins and Dawson 1992). Research shows that there is a kind of see-saw effect. As materialistic values go up then prosocial values go down. The more we care about money, image and status, then the less we are likely to care much about the future of the planet or the poor or even a neighbour who might be in trouble. Those with more materialistic values consistently have worse relationships, with more conflict. This is significant if the perceived shift towards more materialistic values in the West is accurate.

Less wellbeing, more extrinsically motivated

The less people feel good about themselves, the more they tend to try to bolster a fragile sense of self-worth with status-enhancing symbols. It even happens on a very small scale. Researchers found that people who felt unconfident in the activity that they were involved in, whether tennis, business or law for example, tended to compensate by buying the latest equipment and accessories, seemingly in an attempt to bolster their self-esteem (Braun and Wicklund 1989). When people feel bad, fear social exclusion or are nursing emotional wounds they are more likely to compensate by purchasing high-status consumer goods (Sivanathan and Pettit

2010). This is a very simple example of ordinary human defences against vulnerability. After all, how many of us need the protection of buying a new outfit for an important event, for example? Yet it also suggests that poor emotional health might be in the interests of those selling such goods.

In the USA, individual per capita spending has risen by nearly 100 per cent in recent decades, partly fuelled by easy credit and advertising, yet study after study shows that overall levels of personal happiness and satisfaction have not risen, while mental health problems have. There is a vital lesson here, one drawn out in James Roberts' book, *Shiny Objects* (2011). Urges and desires for material things become addictive in their own right, indeed in a similar way to that which occurs in some forms of addiction. In fact, achieving an aim or desire generally increases the sense of wellbeing of those pursuing intrinsic motivations but not those motivated by extrinsic motivations (Sheldon *et al.* 2010). Extrinsically motivated people can become increasingly driven to seek the reward that ironically will not really make them feel better.

Not surprisingly, adolescents whose parents have a less nurturing or sensitive parenting style tend to be more insecure about their intrinsic worth. These same adolescents tend to place a higher value on consumerism, high status and ambitions, as opposed to the teenagers of more nurturing parents who on average place greater value on relationships, community life and self-acceptance (Kasser *et al.* 1995). Similarly, in families with a lack of emotional resources, of love, caring support and stability, we see more individualistic beliefs and also more of what researchers called 'compulsive consumption' (Rindfleisch *et al.* 1997).

Those with more extrinsic values also tend to experience less psychological wellbeing, are more prone to depression, anxiety and even substance abuse, and are more likely to report ailments from stomach problems to headaches. Patricia and Jacob Cohen (1996) looked at 700 young people in New York and clustered them according to their values. Those clustered as materialistic were more admiring of 'having valuable possessions', 'being seen as attractive' or 'wearing expensive clothes'. Another group of young people valued characteristics such as 'being a good person' or 'getting on with others'. Both groups were assessed for their risk of psychiatric diagnoses such as ADHD, depression or anxiety. Those with more materialistic beliefs had far higher levels of mental health problems across over 20 diagnostic categories.

Young adults who pursue intrinsic rather than extrinsic motivations have better psychological health, and this seems to be mediated by possessing more autonomy and better relatedness (Niemiec *et al.* 2009). Such research has been replicated in countries such as Singapore, Turkey, Germany, Romania, India, China and Korea. Extrinsic and materialistic values come with increased psychological problems and less contentment, and the less content people are the more they seem driven to consume.

Contented people, then, win each way, as do those around them, as they are more likely to have good health, good friends and be more prosocial. Much of the most pertinent research goes back to the 1970s, such as how people who found a dime in a phone booth became more helpful (Isen and Levin 1972). Around that time in another experiment (Aderman 1972) people were induced into either good or bad moods by having statements read to them. Those induced into a good mood also became more helpful, which chimes with other research that shows that when we feel better we tend to also volunteer and help more (Harris and Huang 1973). Even young children in good moods are more generous (Isen *et al.* 1973).

Those with higher levels of 'psychological well-being' (Konow and Earley 2008) are more likely to be outward looking and generous and to give to charity. As we saw in earlier chapters, doing good also makes us feel good and that 'warm glow' has a corollary in our brains. Volunteering leads to people feeling better and happier (Meier and Stutzer 2008); engaging in random acts of kindness can leave a warm afterglow of positive feelings for days (Lyubomirsky *et al.* 2005), and indeed is also good for one's health, for example reducing levels of cholesterol and inflammation (Schreier *et al.* 2013). Volunteering also leads to better relationships. Nine- to eleven-year-olds who in experiments undertook a mere three acts of kindness a week were, compared to control groups, much more accepted by peers than those who did not, and on top of this their sense of emotional wellbeing improved (Layous *et al.* 2012). Once again we see that Aristotle's views on the Good Life seem right, that being good and feeling good are fundamentally linked.

Increased wealth and higher class not only do not make us happy, they also seem to make us less generous and prosocial. Dacher Keltner and colleagues at Berkeley reviewed a range of literature, and also used their own experimental designs, and found that the higher up the social-class ranking people are, the less prosocial, charitable and empathically they behaved (Piff *et al.* 2010). For example, they were less likely to feel compassion for a family in which a child had cancer, or for colleagues who were stressed. Consistently those who were less rich showed more empathy and more of a wish to help others, and when watching people in distress had lower heart rates, a known signature for compassionate feelings.

In Keltner's studies it was the richer subjects who were liable to be distracted, doodle and avoid eye-contact whereas the less well-off made better eye-contact and nodded their heads frequently to show they were listening. Placing electrodes on their chests demonstrated that the less affluent had stronger emotional responses to images of starving children than rich people.

Rather than money, it is the pursuit of other activities that increases wellbeing, whether committing to a cause one believes in, a career one is dedicated to, being surrounded by loving friends and family or having wide cultural interests. A study of over 50,000 adults in Norway (Cuypers *et al.* 2011) found that those who engaged in more cultural activities, such as going to the theatre or art galleries, had better health, more life-satisfaction and lower levels of depression and anxiety. Being interested in things broader than oneself, and not just material rewards, seems to be good for us (Wallman 2013).

People who spend their money on experiences, like holidays or cultural activities, are generally more optimistic, outgoing and happy than those who spend their money on consumer goods (Howell *et al.* 2012). When people start to think of their time as money, then their ability to be in the moment and be satisfied with what they are doing diminishes. People also volunteer less when their time begins to be billed by the hour (DeVoe and House 2011).

Some caution is needed in thinking about what we mean by happiness and wellbeing. More recent positive psychology research has been differentiating between two very different kinds of happiness (Diener and Chan 2011), and interestingly each seemingly has different effects on our health and wellbeing. Some researchers (Fredrickson *et al.* 2013) recently divided a considerable sample in terms of whether their happiness was of a more *hedonic* kind, such as from buying consumer goods or having an exciting time, or of a more *eudaemonic* kind, that is, happiness derived from engaging in meaningful activity based on personal values such as a passionate interest or a cause. The two kinds of happiness had surprisingly very different effects, right down to a genetic and cellular level.

Those whose sense of happiness and wellbeing derived from being motivated by a strong sense of meaning and purpose had lower levels of inflammation and higher levels of immune response and antibodies than those whose version of happiness was more hedonic. In other words, the Good Life, as the Greeks might have defined it, gives rise to emotional and physical health, a win-win situation. On the other hand if we are motivated by a more hedonic buzz of immediate desire or a wish to achieve or consume, then physiologically this is not so good for us. It leads to more inflammation of our cells, and worse health. This is presumably the kind of happiness that is promoted in contemporary consumerist societies, the buzz of acquiring something new, the thrill of success.

Such research can be linked to the effects of creeping monetisation and marketisation which have been widely documented. Michael Sandel has, for example, described how it is now possible to buy and sell what used to have no price, whether a traffic-free lane in a motorway, priority-access to flights or tourist sites, access to politicians, medical care and much more (Sandel 2012). Market values are different from moral ones, and encourage a more extrinsic and less relationship-oriented approach to many areas of life. Indeed, one recent study showed that, while people mostly don't approve of practices such as child labour, land grabs or cruelty to animals, when induced into a market mentality they are far more likely to override their principles (Falk and Szech 2013). Values shift depending on context. In this study, people induced into a non-market state of mind would not accept money if doing so led to harm to an animal, whereas in a market-based mindset they went along with less moral behaviour if it enhanced their success.

There has been a move towards lifestyles increasingly influenced by market values, such as health or local government organisations describing people as customers or consumers. Most strikingly recent decades have witnessed a huge commercialisation of children's lives as documented by many such as Juliet Schor in her book *Born to Buy: The Commercialized Child and the New Consumer Culture* (Schor 2006). American children apparently spend about

40 billion dollars themselves each year and influence parental spending of about 700 billion dollars. They are spending increasing amounts of time shopping rather than playing. Nearly half of American youngsters dream 'a lot' about becoming rich, and more and more define themselves in terms of what they wear and look like, and think that money will make them happy. Extrinsic values seem to be on the increase and with them come, we know, less prosocial and altruistic values and behaviours.

Our different hemispheres

These like any social changes are almost definitely having a profound effect on how our very brains function. We have recently begun to see how regular internet users who were over 55, for example, had far more activity in left prefrontal brain areas than less internet-savvy people (Small *et al.* 2009), and that just a few weeks of intensive internet usage changed these brain patterns in novices as well. Just as taxi-drivers' brains change as they learn, and meditators' brains change as they practise, so will our brains change in response to social environments and value systems.

Psychiatrist Iain McGilchrist develops this thesis in a synthesis of research that has challenged our understanding of the relationship between our brain's left and right hemispheres. Debunking old pop psychology notions of left and right brains, he has none the less found that each hemisphere tends to view the world in different ways. The left in most species is used for a very focused kind of attention, looking at detail, analysing, taking things apart and observing components. Medicine and much science works like this. We use our right hemispheres when we are scanning in a more open and uncertain state of being, and it is the right hemisphere that is most involved in empathy and in caring for others. Some people have better links between these two brain areas than others, and people can also be dominant in one or other hemisphere.

While there is a danger of using a homunculus metaphor, as if each hemisphere is an autonomous being, there is surprisingly some truth in this. McGilchrist has found that more of the nerve endings in the corpus callosum, which links the hemispheres, are involved in stopping communication between the left and right sides than facilitating it. People whose corpus callosum was severed in an attempt to treat serious epilepsy have been shown to often literally have battles between their left and right hemispheres. Their left hand might be doing a button up while the right tries to get it undone, for example (Sperry 1961).

When patients have strokes or other damage to their right hemisphere, they lose their ability to empathise and are less attuned to the feelings, hopes and concerns of others, giving rise to more calculating, utilitarian and instrumental ways of relating, typical of left-hemisphere activity (Koenigs *et al.* 2007). When cooperating with others, being empathic or altruistic, we use more right-hemispheric brain areas, whereas competition activates more left-sided ones. More utilitarian, non-emotional decisions are seen in people with damage to emotional areas of their brains, especially if the damage is to right prefrontal areas (Martins *et al.* 2012). As McGilchrist notes, the right hemisphere is not dominant for all emotions. The left is dominant for anger, and researchers are finding that the one emotion that often is very present in people who tend to make utilitarian moral judgements is anger (Choe and Min 2011).

Not only people but societies can have different hemispheric balances, and cross-cultural research describes a clear bias in Western market-based cultures towards more individualist, atomised ways of experiencing the world, which suits left-hemisphere dominance. Anthropologists have long thought about this in terms of a distinction between cultures that are more egocentric, mostly seen in the West in modern times, as opposed to sociocentric cultures seen in many pre-industrial and also Eastern cultures (Geertz 2000). More interdependent cultures are geared to ensuring that people grow up more aware of being embedded in a community.

As Richard Sennett (2012) has described, this is enshrined in the Chinese idea of *guanxi*, a complex and highly developed system of mutual obligation central even to modern capitalist relationships in China. The Japanese have a concept of *amae*, not fully translatable into English but describing an expectation that one will be cared for by others (Doi 1973). In Japanese preschool, empathy is highly prized and *amae* and *omoiyari* (responding with empathy to expressions of *amae*) are the most highly valued form of learning, enabling emotional awareness of the importance of social connection (Hayashi *et al.* 2009).

On the other hand, more egocentric cultures value autonomy and individuality more, as seen in Western market societies, where the development of the person as a separate individual is more highly prized. Shand writes:

> In Japan the infant is seen more as a separate biological organism who, from the beginning, in order to develop, needs to be drawn into increasingly interdependent relations with others. In America, the infant is seen more as a dependent biological organism who in order to develop, needs to be made increasingly independent of others.
>
> (Shand 1985, pp. 52–67)

Close bodily contact, such as between mothers and infants, is generally taken for granted in more interdependent cultures, whereas there is more distal, face-to-face communication between Western mothers and babies which encourages separation and increased reliance on verbalising and left-hemispheric abstraction. The language we use is telling. Western parents often talk of the need to train infants to be 'self-reliant', 'independent', and worry about 'dependency', while mothers in more sociocentric cultures emphasise qualities of 'interdependence'.

As the cross-cultural researcher Heidi Keller found, in sociocentric cultures immediate bodily comfort of infants, as in breast-feeding, is believed to be 'obviously' what is needed. Such attuned contact sustains right-hemisphere bodily sensibilities, emotional awareness and secure attachment. Rural Cameroonian Nso mothers watching videos of German mothers trying to comfort their children without picking them up or breast-feeding could barely believe what they saw, and several wondered if German mothers were forbidden to hold their babies, even questioning whether they were really watching the actual mothers! In Heidi Keller's studies (2007), three-month-old German babies spent 40 per cent of their time out of physical reach of their mothers, whereas infants in interdependent farming communities were never alone. Early attuned mother–infant interactions are marked, as neuroscience researcher Alan Schore (2009) has helped us see, by more right-brain to right-brain communication. Indeed the patterns of our emotional life and internal models of relationships are laid down in the first few years of life, primarily via our right hemispheres. Indeed, the left hemisphere is much less online in those early months and years.

Sociocentric practices emphasise the importance of tradition and respect for cultural values, ritual, social cohesion, interdependence and community expectations, all needing high levels of right-hemisphere activation. As the influence of the market, Western education, industrial development and urban life increases across the world, parenting has tended to move to a more independent 'egocentric' model. Research (Hofstede 2001) examining cultural attributes in 50 countries showed that the USA, Australia, Britain and Canada ranked highest in individualism.

Keller looked at free-play scenarios between German mothers and children in the 1970s and again in 2000 (Keller and Lamm 2005). Twenty-first-century German mothers gave less bodily contact, responded more to positive signals rather than signs of distress, typical of left-hemisphere dominance, and encouraged more face-to-face, distal contact, more use of object manipulation and toys and more use of language that supports autonomy and separateness. This suggests a clear move towards left-hemisphere ways of interacting within a single culture in only a few decades. Contemporary market-dominated societies seem to be moving more in such individualistic and egocentric directions. Interestingly, research (Cameron *et al.* 2013) is suggesting that the one-child policy in China, alongside huge economic change, might be having a very specific effect on personality traits, giving rise to less-trusting and other-centred people.

McGilchrist states that we are in danger of living in an increasingly mechanistic, fragmented decontextualised world which he links to growing left-hemisphere dominance. The world of scientific advance, business attitudes and mechanistic, technological and goal-oriented aspirations, all are signs of this. Other people and their feelings are of little consequence when left-hemisphere traits are dominant. The left hemisphere is used to control and manipulate, to organise, be logical and analyse with a calculating mind-set. This is a great advantage for financial planning, for technological advance, for bureaucratic control, but not for achieving what the Greeks called *eudaemonia*, sometimes translated as a 'Good Life' or as human 'flourishing' (Seligman 2012).

Empathy and caring for others depend on right-hemisphere areas such as the right ventromedial and orbitofrontal cortex central to moral behaviour. Strokes in these areas lead to people acting in a colder, even psychopathic manner. People with secure attachments are generally in touch with the emotional aliveness of what has happened to them and can create a coherent auto-biographical narrative about their lives. Such narratives are based on a good working relationship between the right and left hemispheres. Those who are more avoidant and live in a more emotionally cut-off left-hemisphere-dominated world tend to be more optimistic but often in an overly positive way. They are less interested in people, in feelings, in relationships, in closeness. Indeed many mental health problems are marked by left-hemisphere dominance, such as schizophrenia, autism and eating disorders, all of which are becoming far more common in urban centres and in the industrialised world.

Historical shifts

McGilchrist shows how there have been historical changes in hemispherical dominance, although maybe not as big a shift as we have been witnessing in recent decades. For example, the development of pictograms about 3,300 BC represented a move towards abstraction, which increased with the advent of the more formal written word in the Greek alphabet. Language use is processed in different areas of the brain in different cultures; readers of Arabic and Chinese use both hemispheres more fully than English, which is much more left-hemisphere led. McGilchrist suggests that there is plenty of evidence that in Eastern cultures the hemispheres are working much more in tandem than in the West where there is increasing left-hemisphere dominance.

Other inventions have profoundly influenced hemispheric balance. Cartography had a huge effect on voyaging. When maps appeared, travel and navigation were transformed, leading to much more abstract thinking and less reliance on sensory information, such as sight, smell and intuition. Reading, of course, has a huge effect on our brain structure, and literate people show very different brain activation to non-literate people (Ostrosky-Solís *et al.* 2004). Probably the technology that most affected hemispheric balance was the clock. With its appearance time was suddenly broken up into small pieces, allowing days to be divided into regimental units, very different from more circular rhythms of time in hunter-gatherer and agrarian societies. This facilitated more abstract thinking, relying less on other ways of being, which again would have changed the very way our brains were wiring.

McGilchrist argues that the increase of exchange by money has perhaps been one of the biggest drivers of the move towards abstraction and away from more direct and concrete valuing of things in their context. Money allows an exact science. If I give a gift to a neighbour, they will hopefully reciprocate some time, but this might be in a variety of ways. Financial transactions on the other hand encourage left-hemisphere exactitude. I owe you £10 and that is what I expect to return to you, no more, no less and no room for manoeuvre.

Richard Sennett (2012) has painstakingly described the shift away from lives lived with a profound sense of community, stability, continuity of belonging, with clear rituals, where work was stable if hard, whether down a coal mine or as a craftsman or in a school. Previously cooperation and mutual obligations were a given. Life was marked by rituals and civilised ways of associating with each other which allowed differences but ensured respect. Bauman's analysis of contemporary society as 'Liquid Life' (Bauman 2005) suggests a similar loss of intrinsic values in the face of materialism and a speeded-up, less secure world. For Sennett, as for Bauman and McGilchrist, contemporary life is marked by transient roles, little security, increased competition, where people are treated less as real, alive emotional beings, and more as consumers, or units of labour. Here technocratic efficiency, devoid of right-hemisphere emotion and ritual, alongside the quest for profit and success, are increasingly important motivators.

The left hemisphere is central to verbal discourse and has on its side language, logic and linearity. Patients whose connections between the left and right hemisphere are severed can read a word presented to their right side (which is linked to the left hemisphere) but will not be able to read the same word when presented to the left side (right hemisphere). We could barely function without the left hemisphere, but when not moderated by right-hemisphere functioning, it can go on its own merry way. According to McGilchrist, the left hemisphere is the 'Berlusconi of the brain, a political heavyweight who has control of the media' and whose propaganda is very convincing. Michael Gazzaniga, who has done a lot of research with split-brained patients, has called it the 'left hemisphere interpreter' or storyteller (Gazzaniga 2013). Its focus is on what it knows, and it can be an inveterate denier of any reality it does not want to acknowledge. Gazzaniga reported how one patient after a right-hemisphere stroke believed that the hospital she was in was her home. When asked about the elevators she replied convincingly, 'Doctor, do you know how much it cost me to have those put in?' (Gazzaniga 2006). Gazzaniga and others argue that the right hemisphere acts as a kind of 'bull-shit detector' via its use of what Damasio calls 'somatic markers' (Damasio 1999), such as bodily sense, intuition and emotions.

McGilchrist and others such as Daniel Siegel (2012) have been arguing that for emotional health we need both hemispheres, and we need them in balance with each other. This idea relies on a version of the brain that Gazzaniga describes as 'not an all-purpose, centralized computing device but rather is organized in a modular fashion, consisting of distributed, specialized circuits that ... perform specific subfunctions while preserving substantial plasticity' (Gazzaniga 2013). Given that, and assuming that particular areas of specialism become more dominant in particular historical eras, it seems fair to speculate with McGilchrist that we have moved into a more left-hemisphere-dominant world.

This shift, many argue, has come with a concomitant devaluing of human relationships, community, altruism, cooperation, and with utilitarian mechanisms increasingly predominating. Costs include a breakdown of community life and the social capital that comes with that (Putnam 2000; Bauman 2005), more uncertainty and less continuity and less reliance on tradition and rituals (Sennett 2012). It has also come with treating people, the natural world and our planet more instrumentally, as a means to an end. This is very different to living from the intrinsic values researched by Tim Kasser and others, values more concerned with real relationships, empathy, caring for others and living with less materialistic and instrumental goals, but rather with more prosocial ones.

Chapter 15

Conclusions

In this book I have asked questions about our tendencies for being either prosocial or antisocial, selfish or altruistic, individualistic or other-oriented. It is not that we humans are 'really' selfish and competitive or 'really' kind and generous. Both are central aspects of our inherited repertoire and we can be tilted more in one direction or another by an array of factors. A propensity to be kind, empathic and generous is present from infancy onwards. Prosocial, altruistic and cooperative behaviours are as much a part of human genetic inheritance as more selfish, competitive and aggressive ones.

We have seen how the kind of experiences we have, especially our early ones but also our immediate social contexts and the kind of society we live in, all influence the extent to which we become empathic, altruistic and moral, and how much we are able to participate in social groups and interpersonal relationships. The parenting we receive and our attachment styles are very influential, and the development of empathy and understanding other minds is a crucial achievement, without which altruism and good-hearted generosity do not occur.

I have also highlighted how issues of morality and altruism cannot be understood properly without taking seriously the pivotal role of emotion and emotional development. I have described how trauma, abuse and stress can lead to the atrophy of many of these traits, affecting how our nervous systems and brain pathways form, and influencing whether or not we can engage in reciprocal interpersonal exchanges or good relationships. Indeed, having bad experiences predicts the likelihood of ending up on the fringes of society and not abiding by its expectations, something we see in many abused children who become the prison inmates or psychiatric patients of tomorrow.

When we feel good about ourselves, we are less stressed and tense, and more likely to be generous and less selfish. Paradoxically doing good need not be 'do-goody', and huge benefits are gained from being kind, charitable and generous, including the triggering of reward circuits in our brains and hormonal systems. Thus in fact sacrificing some of our more selfish desires in order to fit in comes with benefits.

It is true that, as recent experiments showed (Berman and Small 2012), there is pleasure in being completely selfish when we feel absolutely entitled to be so. When people are given a windfall, they feel happier if they are told that they *have to* spend it all on themselves. On the other hand, if people are given a choice about spending it on, say, a charity, or on themselves, they tend to feel worse if they spend it on themselves. Our consciences and sense of responsibility generally override more selfish drives, the more so when our social context supports this rather than self-interested behaviours.

We feel better when we give to charity, help people in trouble or volunteer (Weinstein and Ryan 2010). Spending money on others rather than ourselves makes us happier (Dunn *et al.* 2008), and the same is true for children (Aknin *et al.* 2012). In fact, helping others not only makes us feel good, it makes us healthier. One study showed that the more hours of community volunteer work undertaken, the higher the psychological and physical health benefits (Thoits and Hewitt 2001). Being helpful, like volunteering, even reduces mortality rates, a finding that is not explained by demographic factors such as socioeconomic status or prior health (Oman *et al.* 1999). In other words, being good is not necessarily against our best interests at all.

This also works the other way around. Not only do we feel good when we are more selfless, but we also are more generous and helpful when we feel good. We saw this in the famous dime-in-a-phone-booth experiment. Remember how those who found a mere dime were much more helpful to an actress outside who pretended to drop a sheaf of paper (Isen and Levin 1972). I have quoted other research showing that when we feel good we are more likely to be kind and trusting.

We have also seen how particular contexts, such as individualistic and competitive ones, or frightening and stressful ones, lead to less altruistic or moral ways of being. On the other hand contexts where others are generous, or where we are expected to behave morally, precipitate moral and prosocial behaviour. Indeed, just hearing a story of another's virtue, compassion or goodness, leads us to want to act virtuously ourselves (Immordino-Yang *et al.* 2009). An interesting question is whether there is a lack of moral role models in a society that increasingly values extrinsic values such as money, wealth and status. This might link with the huge increase in narcissism in contemporary Western market societies (Twenge and Campbell 2009), a valuing of individual entitlement, leading to a lessening of social and other responsibility.

While I have relied hugely on academic and scientific research to think about morality, altruism and cooperation, the subject is far from an academic one. There are currently risks to humanity, such as deforestation, pollution, population growth, warfare, water shortages, dwindling fish supplies, species loss, depletion of natural resources, new diseases and other environmental issues that might require joining with peoples and groups who otherwise are defined as rivals. Much research suggests that inequality has powerful negative effects on health, trust and generosity (Wilkinson and Pickett 2009). The more unequal the society, or even region of society, the lower the levels of trust within it. There is evidence of deleterious health effects from austerity regimes and poverty, including large rises in suicide rates and other forms of early death (Stuckler and Basu 2013). This all raises serious moral issues linked to the conflicts between our inherited selfish traits and our potential for a more humane, altruistic and cooperative way of being.

As E.O. Wilson (2012) has stated, our genetic inheritance, with its in-group parochial altruism and its ability to adapt and conquer new terrains, has transformed the earth. However, the intelligence that evolved in our evolutionary past is not primed to think of the distant future, nor to care much about other human groups. Natural selection has privileged traits which favour immediate survival and reproduction of our genes. This is maybe the truth in the myth of original sin. Selfishness, greed, cunning and aggressiveness are part of us, as is the wish for immediate gratification. Many argue though that such traits are given an increasingly free rein in a contemporary market-led world (Olson 2013).

Our prosocial propensities, built on a range of mammalian traits, necessarily became more central to human life through the advantages of living in closely bonded groups in our hunter-gatherer evolutionary past. These characteristics include co-operativeness, altruism, empathy, loyalty, mutual support and personal sacrifice. A major contemporary challenge is whether these can be harnessed for the wider good of the species or the planet, especially as such traits appear to have evolved to support our in-group at the expense of outsiders who are deemed 'other'. These are the very traits that have allowed us to thrive, flourish and expand, via culture and technology, to form extraordinary civilisations and tame nature, but all this has also had serious downsides.

Humans tend to have an optimism bias (Sharot 2012) whereby we underestimate dangers and assume things will work out for the best, at least for ourselves. We are much more realistic about other people than ourselves. We also tend to discount the future, and value future generations less than the present one (Kahneman 1994). Christian de Duve (2011) argues that natural selection has no foresight, and indeed that maybe for the first time in human history the unbridled pursuit of expansion and immediate reward is risking the same fate that befell every other hominid species: extinction.

Hope?

There many things to be optimistic about and I have tried to highlight some of these. De Duve (2011), for example, argued that humans have the power to act against our genetic inheritance due to our superior brains. We have seen that love, touch and attuned, sensitive and reflective parenting can go a long way to raising children who can care about others, show empathy, be altruistic, fit into social groups and embrace moral codes. We have learnt a lot about the hormonal and neurobiological effects of different kinds of experiences, such as the role of stress hormones or the 'cuddle hormone' oxytocin, and the pernicious effect of trauma and neglect on such systems. We know nowadays that our brains are plastic to a greater extent than we used to believe, and that change is possible throughout the lifespan. We also know from epigenetic research that we are not ruled by our genes, and that our experiences have a great impact on which genetic potentials get turned on or off.

Projects such as the Roots of Empathy (Gordon 2009) have shown that we can facilitate children's empathic and nurturing potential to come online, against the odds, whilst research on the extraordinary effects of mindfulness on the brain backs up the idea that fundamental changes can take place throughout the lifespan (Davis and Hayes 2011). We psychotherapists know this very well from our practice.

As society and the global economy have become so huge and interlinked, we can no longer rely just on the forms of immediate social sanctions which were dominant in our hunter-gatherer pasts. These still work at a local level, such as in the workplace, communities and families, as people fear for their reputation and do not want to be ostracised or thought badly of. Action on an international level is necessary to tackle issues ranging from corporate abuse to climate change, human rights and a raft of other matters. As Rifkin (2010) has pointed out, our parochial altruism has already been extended in some quarters to wider circles than we might have anticipated, for example towards ethnic minorities, the disabled, those of various sexual orientations, religions and beliefs, and he argues that it is possible for this to extend further. History shows that he is right, and there are many examples of parochial warring groups being brought into relationships which become consistently cooperative (Fry 2013).

The work of Joseph Henrich has helped us to realise that cooperation is not disappearing and that certain forms of it increase as market forces penetrate (Henrich et al. 2010). As seen in moral games, researchers consistently reveal fair and caring behaviours in brief, one-off encounters, and we hopefully all know this from personal experience of kindness to or from strangers. These ideas link with Rifkin's suggestions, that there is now, with the internet and other technologies, genuine potential for people divided by continents and cultures to reach out to each other in new ways. As Fry (2013) and others have pointed out, there have been many examples in the historical past of feuding, warring, uncooperative groups being drawn into new social structures which have ensured peaceful co-existence and more cooperative ways of managing conflict. These might include the Iroquois Confederacy and even the European Union.

Others fear though that there are many trends working in the opposite direction. These include the increasing dominance of market-led forms of social organisation, more competition, less job security, rising inequality (Wilkinson and Pickett 2009), less sense of community (Putnam 2000), a dog-eat-dog competitive and individualistic world in which there is less trust, one in which increasing materialistic values have a detrimental effect on health and wellbeing (Kasser 2003). Alongside all this, corporate power has been growing out of the reach of national governments, and large corporations are primarily motivated by profits and serving shareholders, rather than the general good.

There has been an increase in all manner of mental health issues in the Western and particularly the Anglo-Saxon world and a huge growth of psychological disorders in children. McGilchrist has suggested that we are organising society increasingly via the left hemisphere's highly controlled and ordered way of functioning which is crowding out the right hemisphere's more empathic, intuitive and emotional way of being (McGilchrist 2010). In addition we have seen how we are living in an era where there is an increase in impulsivity and less ability to defer gratification, which might in part be both caused by, and cause, the increased reliance on screens and games. In effect, we have seen something of an epidemic of behaviours characterised by less capacity to self-regulate, less ability to be still and concentrate, and deficits in the kind of frontal-lobe capacities needed for sophisticated executive functioning skills. These are the very skills that are so important for prosocial reciprocal, empathy-induced interchanges (Barkley 2012).

I have raised the thorny question of whether we are well adapted as a species to aspects of modern life, and in particular modern childcare methods. As Narváez suggests (Narváez and Gleason 2012), a whole tranche of developmental outcomes that we equate with psychological health are also associated with forms of childrearing consistently seen in our Environment of Evolutionary Adaptedness but less so in contemporary societies. These include being held or very near others constantly, prompt attuned responses to signs of distress or upset, breast-feeding more or less on demand for the first years, co-sleeping, having several known alternative caregivers in addition to parents, high levels of social embeddedness and a lot of free-play with children of a range of ages. Such an approach to childrearing is strongly correlated with outcomes such as higher levels of empathy and emotional recognition, better emotional regulation and less impulsiveness, for example.

Narváez's research strongly suggests that such childcare practices have neurobiological results which profoundly affect moral development as children get older and these findings fit well with much of the research I have quoted in this book. On the other hand, many contemporary childcare practices are a far cry from such ancestral practices and indeed can induce higher levels of stress, less empathy and less ability to manage impulsivity. It is possible that the higher levels of mental health issues seen in children are linked to such developments. We have to be careful about calling one way of living more *natural* than another, but we can say, with Marshall Sahlins (2008), that the Western view of human nature, and the correlative childcare and other social practices, are certainly *abnormal* when considered in the light of human evolutionary history.

Sarah Blaffer Hrdy (2009) has perhaps sounded one of the most worrying warning shots. She has shown very clearly how in the hunter-gatherer environments in which humans evolved, children would only have survived if they were constantly held, cared for and looked after by their primary attachment figures or one of a range of trusted alternative carers. Without high levels of physical and psychological care survival was simply unlikely. Narváez (2013) suggests that compared to lives in our forager pasts where infants received almost constant holding and attention, much contemporary childcare is marked by 'undercare', with profound consequences for empathy and prosociality. Child mortality has plummeted and babies do not any longer need sensitive, loving, consistent caregiving to survive, maybe for the first time in human history. They can survive even in abusive and neglectful environments. This, Hrdy also argues, poses a danger. It increases the likelihood of abused, traumatised and neglected children reaching adulthood and passing on these experiences to the next generation. It also increases the likelihood that people with less caring, altruistic and prosocial sensibilities will thrive in our society, something that we saw Bob Hare believed was the case with psychopaths. who often make it to the top of our corporate and political world (Hare and Babiak 2007).

Some of these theorists suggest that the balance of the population might be shifting towards less sensitive, altruistic or empathic people being more dominant than in any society that our ancestors would have belonged to. We know that securely attached children develop caring, collaborative attitudes. These are the children capable of empathy, of generosity, and of altruism. Hrdy (2009) raises the worrying possibility that over time the traits for altruism, fairness and decency might become a less central part of the human gene pool, as temperamentally more ruthless and aggressive traits thrive and reproduce. She fears that as our prosocial and empathic tendencies become less necessary for survival, they might just wither and die. This worrying idea might give people ammunition to campaign for the kind of parenting and social systems in which empathy, altruism, cooperation and fairness can flourish.

It might be that society, or even humanity, is at some kind of cross-roads. I hope that this book can be useful to those who can make an impact on how some of these issues play out, whether those working with children or parents, academics, policymakers and younger people whose life trajectories are in the balance. It might with luck address an ache that many of us feel, a sense that we could be living better lives, lives we are proud of, in which we could be truer to who we want to be, whatever that might be, making a contribution to shaping the communities and society that might offer what the Greeks called *eudaemonia*, or in other words the Good Life.

References

Abraham, A., Pocheptsova, A., and Ferraro, R., 2012. The Effect of Mobile Phone Use on Prosocial Behavior. Manuscript in preparation.

Abu-Lughod, L., 1999. *Veiled Sentiments: Honor and Poetry in a Bedouin Society*. Berkeley, California: University of California Press.

Aderman, D., 1972. Elation, depression, and helping behavior. *Journal of Personality and Social Psychology*, 24 (1), 91.

Affonso, N., Guthrie, I.K., Murphy, B.C., Shepard, S.A., Cumberland, A., and Carlo, G., 1999. Consistency and Development of Prosocial Dispositions: A Longitudinal Study. *Child Development*, 70 (6), 1360–1372.

Ågren, G., Uvnäs-Moberg, K., and Lundeberg, T., 1997. Olfactory cues from an oxytocin-injected male rat can induce anti-nociception in its cagemates. *Neuroreport*, 8 (14), 3073–3076.

Aharoni, E., Vincent, G.M., Harenski, C.L., Calhoun, V.D., Sinnott-Armstrong, W., Gazzaniga, M.S., and Kiehl, K.A., 2013. Neuroprediction of future rearrest. *Proceedings of the National Academy of Sciences*, 110 (15), 6223–6228.

Ainsworth, M.D.S., 1978. *Patterns of Attachment: A Psychological Study of the Strange Situation*. Mahwah, New Jersey: Lawrence Erlbaum Associates.

Aknin, L.B., Barrington-Leigh, C.P., Dunn, E.W., Helliwell, J.F., Biswas-Diener, R., Kemeza, I., Nyende, P., Ashton-James, C.E., and Norton, M.I., 2013. Prosocial spending and well-being: Cross-cultural evidence for a psychological universal. *Journal of Personality and Social Psychology*, 104 (4), 635–652.

Aknin, L.B., Hamlin, J.K., and Dunn, E.W., 2012. Giving leads to happiness in young children. *PLOS ONE*, 7 (6), e39211.

Anderson, P., 2008. Is altruism possible? Royal Anthropological Institute Hocart Prize Essay. Available from: www.san.ed.ac.uk/__data/assets/pdf_file/0005/15269/080519-altruism_article.pdf.

Anderson, S.W., Damasio, H., Tranel, D., and Damasio, A.R., 2000. Long-term sequelae of prefrontal cortex damage acquired in early childhood. *Developmental Neuropsychology*, 18 (3), 281–296.

Anik, L., Aknin, L.B., Norton, M., and Dunn, E., 2009. Feeling good about giving: The benefits (and costs) of self-interested charitable behavior. *Harvard Business School Marketing Unit Working Paper* (10-012).

Aquino, K., Freeman, D., Reed, A., Lim, V.K., and Felps, W., 2009. Testing a social-cognitive model of moral behavior: The interactive influence of situations and moral identity centrality. *Journal of Personality and Social Psychology*, 97 (1), 123.

Ariely, D., 2009. *Predictably Irrational: The Hidden Forces that Shape Our Decisions.* New York: HarperCollins.

Aronson, E. and Patnoe, S., 1996. *The Jigsaw Classroom: Building Cooperation in the Classroom.* New York: Longman.

Arsenio, W.F., Adams, E., and Gold, J., 2009. Social information processing, moral reasoning, and emotion attributions: Relations with adolescents' reactive and proactive aggression. *Child Development*, 80 (6), 1739–1755.

Arsenio, W.F. and Gold, J., 2006. The effects of social injustice and inequality on children's moral judgments and behavior: Towards a theoretical model. *Cognitive Development*, 21 (4), 388–400.

Arsenio, W.F. and Lemerise, E.A., eds, 2010. *Emotions, Aggression, and Morality in Children: Bridging Development and Psychopathology.* 1st ed. Washington, DC: American Psychological Association.

Ashton-James, C.E. and Tracy, J.L., 2011. Pride and prejudice: How feelings about the self influence judgments of others. *Personality and Social Psychology Bulletin.* Available from: psp.sagepub.com/content/38/4/466.

Austin, M.A., Riniolo, T.C., and Porges, S.W., 2007. Borderline personality disorder and emotion regulation: Insights from the Polyvagal Theory. *Brain and Cognition*, 65 (1), 69–76.

Avinun, R., Israel, S., Shalev, I., Gritsenko, I., Bornstein, G., Ebstein, R.P., and Knafo, A., 2011. AVPR1A variant associated with preschoolers' lower altruistic behavior. *PLOS ONE*, 6 (9), e25274.

Axelrod, R., 2006. *The Evolution of Cooperation.* New York: Basic Books.

Baker, E., Shelton, K.H., Baibazarova, E., Hay, D.F., and van Goozen, S.H., 2013. Low skin conductance activity in infancy predicts aggression in toddlers 2 years later. *Psychological Science*, 24 (6), 1051–1056.

Bakermans-Kranenburg, M.J. and van IJzendoorn, M.H., 2011. Differential susceptibility to rearing environment depending on dopamine-related genes: New evidence and a meta-analysis. *Development and Psychopathology*, 23 (01), 39–52.

Bakermans-Kranenburg, M.J., van IJzendoorn, M.H., Caspers, K., and Philibert, R., 2011. DRD4 genotype moderates the impact of parental problems on unresolved loss or trauma. *Attachment & Human Development*, 13 (3), 253–269.

Barkley, R.A., 2012. *Executive Functions: What They Are, How They Work, and Why They Evolved.* New York: Guilford Press.

Baron, A.S. and Banaji, M.R., 2006. Evidence of race evaluations from ages 6 and 10 and adulthood. *Psychological Science*, 17 (1), 53–58.

Baron-Cohen, S., 2011. *Zero Degrees of Empathy: A New Theory of Human Cruelty*. London: Allen Lane.

Bartz, J., Simeon, D., Hamilton, H., Kim, S., Crystal, S., Braun, A., Vicens, V., and Hollander, E., 2011. Oxytocin can hinder trust and cooperation in borderline personality disorder. *Social Cognitive and Affective Neuroscience*, 6 (5), 556–563.

Bartz, J.A., Zaki, J., Ochsner, K.N., Bolger, N., Kolevzon, A., Ludwig, N., and Lydon, J.E., 2010. Effects of oxytocin on recollections of maternal care and closeness. *Proceedings of the National Academy of Sciences*, 107 (50), 21371–21375.

Batson, C.D., 2011. *Altruism in Humans*. Oxford: Oxford University Press.

Bauer, M.A., Wilkie, J.E.B., Kim, J.K., and Bodenhausen, G.V., 2012. Cuing consumerism: Situational materialism undermines personal and social well-being. *Psychological Science*, 23 (5), 517–523.

Bauman, Z., 2005. *Liquid Life*. Cambridge: Polity Press.

Bauman, Z. and Donskis, L., 2013. *Moral Blindness: The Loss of Sensitivity in Liquid Modernity*. Cambridge: Polity Press.

Baumgartner, T., Götte, L., Gügler, R., and Fehr, E., 2012. The mentalizing network orchestrates the impact of parochial altruism on social norm enforcement. *Human Brain Mapping*, 33 (6), 1452–1469.

Bechara, A., Damasio, H., Tranel, D., and Damasio, A.R., 2005. The Iowa Gambling Task and the somatic marker hypothesis: Some questions and answers. *Trends in Cognitive Sciences*, 9 (4), 159–162.

Beebe, B. and Lachmann, F.M., 2013. *The Origins of Attachment: A Microanalysis of Four-Month Mother/Infant Interaction*. London: Routledge.

Beijersbergen, M.D., Juffer, F., Bakermans-Kranenburg, M.J., and van IJzendoorn, M.H., 2012. Remaining or becoming secure: Parental sensitive support predicts attachment continuity from infancy to adolescence in a longitudinal adoption study. *Developmental Psychology*, 48 (5), 1277–1282.

Belsky, J., Houts, R.M., and Fearon, R.M.P., 2010. Infant attachment security and the timing of puberty: Testing an evolutionary hypothesis. *Psychological Science*, 21 (9), 1195–1201.

Belsky, J., Schlomer, G.L., and Ellis, B.J., 2012. Beyond cumulative risk: Distinguishing harshness and unpredictability as determinants of parenting and early life history strategy. *Developmental Psychology*, 48 (3), 662–673.

Belsky, J., Vandell, D.L., Burchinal, M., Clarke-Stewart, K.A., McCartney, K., and Owen, M.T., 2007. Are there long-term effects of early child care? *Child Development*, 78 (2), 681–701.

Berman, J.Z. and Small, D.A., 2012. Self-interest without selfishness: The hedonic benefit of imposed self-interest. *Psychological Science*, 23 (10), 1193–1199.

Bernhard, H., Fischbacher, U., and Fehr, E., 2006. Parochial altruism in humans. *Nature*, 442 (7105), 912–915.

Bezdjian, S., Tuvblad, C., Raine, A., and Baker, L.A., 2011. The genetic and environmental covariation among psychopathic personality traits, and reactive and proactive aggression in childhood. *Child Development*, 82 (4), 1267–1281.

Bion, W.R., 1961. *Experiences in Groups*. New York: Basic Books.

Birdwhistell, R.L., 1970. *Kinesics and Context*. Philadelphia, Pennsylvania: University of Pennsylvania Press.

Bischof-Köhler, D., 1994. Self object and interpersonal emotions. Identification of own mirror image, empathy and prosocial behavior in the 2nd year of life. *Zeitschrift für Psychologie mit Zeitschrift für Angewandte Psychologie*, 202 (4), 349.

——2012. Empathy and self-recognition in phylogenetic and ontogenetic perspective. *Emotion Review*, 4 (1), 40–48.

Blair, R.J.R., 2004. The roles of orbital frontal cortex in the modulation of antisocial behavior. *Brain and Cognition*, 55 (1), 198–208.

Bloom, P., 2010. The moral life of babies. *The New York Times*, 9 May.

Boehm, C., 2012. *Moral Origins: The Evolution of Virtue, Altruism, and Shame*. New York: Basic Books.

Bowlby, J., 1969. *Attachment and Loss. Vol. 1, Attachment*. London: Hogarth.

Bowles, S. and Gintis, H., 2011. *A Cooperative Species: Human Reciprocity and its Evolution*. Princeton, New Jersey: Princeton University Press.

Bradley, B.S., Selby, J., and Urwin, C., 2012. Group life in babies: Opening up perceptions and possibilities. In: C. Urwin and J. Sternberg, eds, *Infant Observation and Research: Emotional Processes in Everyday Lives*. London: Routledge, 137–148.

Brafman, O. and Brafman, R., 2008. *Sway: The Irresistible Pull of Irrational Behavior*. New York: Doubleday.

Brañas-Garza, P., Kováŕík, J., and Neyse, L., 2013. Second-to-Fourth Digit Ratio Has a Non-Monotonic Impact on Altruism. *PLOS ONE*, 8 (4), e60419.

Brandt, J.R., Kennedy, W.A., Patrick, C.J., and Curtin, J.J., 1997. Assessment of psychopathy in a population of incarcerated adolescent offenders. *Psychological Assessment*, 9 (4), 429.

Braun, O.L. and Wicklund, R.A., 1989. Psychological antecedents of conspicuous consumption. *Journal of Economic Psychology*, 10 (2), 161–187.

Brosi, M.W., Foubert, J.D., Bannon, R.S., and Yandell, G., 2011. Effects of women's pornography use on bystander intervention in a sexual assault situation and rape myth acceptance. *Oracle: The Research Journal of the Association of Fraternity/Sorority Advisors*, 6 (2), 26–35.

Brown, R.P., Osterman, L.L., and Barnes, C.D., 2009. School violence and the culture of honor. *Psychological Science*, 20 (11), 1400–1405.

Brown, S.L., Smith, D.M., Schulz, R., Kabeto, M.U., Ubel, P.A., Poulin, M., Yi, J., Kim, C., and Langa, K.M., 2009. Caregiving behavior is associated with decreased mortality risk. *Psychological Science*, 20 (4), 488.

Buber, M., 2002. *Between Man and Man*. London: Routledge.

Butovskaya, M.L., 2013. Aggression and conflict resolution among the nomadic Hadza of Tanzania as compared with their pastoralist neighbors. In: D.P. Fry, ed., *War, Peace and Human Nature*. New York: Oxford University Press.

Button, K.S., Ioannidis, J.P.A., Mokrysz, C., Nosek, B.A., Flint, J., Robinson, E.S.J., and Munafò, M.R., 2013. Power failure: Why small sample size undermines the reliability of neuroscience. *Nature Reviews Neuroscience*, 14 (5), 365–376.

Cameron, C.D. and Payne, B.K., 2012. The cost of callousness: Regulating compassion influences the moral self-concept. *Psychological Science*, 23 (3), 225–229.

Cameron, L., Erkal, N., Gangadharan, L., and Meng, X., 2013. Little emperors: Behavioral impacts of China's one-child policy. *Science*, 339 (6122), 953–957.

Canli, T., Congdon, E., Todd Constable, R., and Lesch, K.P., 2008. Additive effects of serotonin transporter and tryptophan hydroxylase-2 gene variation on neural correlates of affective processing. *Biological Psychology*, 79 (1), 118–125.

Carlo, G., Crockett, L.J., Wolff, J.M., and Beal, S.J., 2012. The role of emotional reactivity, self-regulation, and puberty in adolescents' prosocial behaviors. *Social Development*, 21 (4), 667–685.

Carlo, G., Mestre, M.V., McGinley, M.M., Samper, P., Tur, A., and Sandman, D., 2012. The interplay of emotional instability, empathy, and coping on prosocial and aggressive behaviors. *Personality and Individual Differences*, 53 (5), 675–680.

Carney, D.R. and Mason, M.F., 2010. Decision making and testosterone: When the end justifies the means. *Journal of Experimental Social Psychology*, 46, 668–671.

Carpenter, M., Uebel, J., and Tomasello, M., 2013. Being mimicked increases prosocial behavior in 18-month-old infants. *Child Development*, 84 (5), 1511–1518.

Carr, N., 2011. *The Shallows: What the Internet is Doing to Our Brains*. New York: Norton.

Carver, C.S., Johnson, S.L., and Joormann, J., 2008. Serotonergic function, two-mode models of self-regulation, and vulnerability to depression: what depression has in common with impulsive aggression. *Psychological Bulletin*, 134 (6), 912.

Casey, B.J., Somerville, L.H., Gotlib, I.H., Ayduk, O., Franklin, N.T., Askren, M.K., Jonides, J., Berman, M.G., Wilson, N.L., Teslovich, T., Glover, G., Zayas, V., Mischel, W., and Shoda, Y., 2011. Behavioral and neural correlates of delay of gratification 40 years later. *Proceedings of the National Academy of Sciences*, 108 (36), 14998–15003.

Chagnon, N.A., 2013. *Noble Savages: My Life Among Two Dangerous Tribes– The Yanomamo and the Anthropologists*. New York: Simon & Schuster.

Chen, C., Hewitt, P.L., Flett, G.L., Cassels, T.G., Birch, S., and Blasberg, J.S., 2012. Insecure attachment, perfectionistic self-presentation, and social disconnection in adolescents. *Personality and Individual Differences*, 52 (8), 936–941.

Choe, S.Y. and Min, K.H., 2011. Who makes utilitarian judgments? The influences of emotions on utilitarian judgments. *Judgment and Decision Making*, 6 (7), 580–592.

Christakis, D.A., 2009. The effects of infant media usage: what do we know and what should we learn? *Acta Paediatrica*, 98 (1), 8–16.

Cillessen, A.H.N. and Rose, A.J., 2005. Understanding popularity in the peer system. *Current Directions in Psychological Science*, 14 (2), 102–105.

Clearfield, M.W. and Jedd, K.E., 2013. The effects of socio-economic status on infant attention. *Infant and Child Development*, 22 (1), 53–67.

Coan, J.A., Schaefer, H.S., and Davidson, R.J., 2006. Lending a hand: Social regulation of the neural response to threat. *Psychological Science*, 17 (12), 1032–1039.

Coates, J., 2012. *The Hour Between Dog and Wolf: Risk-taking, Gut Feelings and the Biology of Boom and Bust*. London: Fourth Estate.

Cohen, P. and Cohen, J., 1996. *Life Values and Adolescent Mental Health*. Mahwah, New Jersey: Lawrence Erlbaum Associates.

Comte, A., 1966. *Catéchisme positiviste*. Paris, France: Flammarion.

Condon, P., Desbordes, G., Miller, W., and DeSteno, D., 2013. Meditation increases compassionate responses to suffering. *Psychological Science*, 24 (10), 2125–2127.

Costa-Font, J., Jofre-Bonet, M., and Yen, S.T., 2012. *Not All Incentives Wash Out the Warm Glow: The Case of Blood Donation Revisited*. CEP discussion papers, no. CEPDP1157. London: Centre for Economic Performance.

Cox, R., Skouteris, H., Dell'Aquila, D., Hardy, L.L., and Rutherford, L., 2013. Television viewing behaviour among pre-schoolers: Implications for public health recommendations. *Journal of Paediatrics and Child Health*, 49 (2), E108–E111.

Coyne, S.M., Nelson, D.A., Graham-Kevan, N., Tew, E., Meng, K.N., and Olsen, J.A., 2011. Media depictions of physical and relational aggression: Connections with aggression in young adults' romantic relationships. *Aggressive Behavior*, 37 (1), 56–62.

Crockett, M.J., Clark, L., Hauser, M., and Robbins, T.W., 2010. Serotonin selectively influences moral judgment and behavior through effects on harm aversion. *Proceedings of the National Academy of Sciences*, 107 (40), 17433–17438.

Crockford, C., Wittig, R.M., Langergraber, K., Ziegler, T.E., Zuberbühler, K., and Deschner, T., 2013. Urinary oxytocin and social bonding in related and unrelated wild chimpanzees. *Proceedings of the Royal Society B: Biological Sciences*, 280 (1755).

Cunningham, W.A., Johnson, M.K., Raye, C.L., Gatenby, J.C., Gore, J.C., and Banaji, M.R., 2004. Separable neural components in the processing of black and white faces. *Psychological Science*, 15 (12), 806–13.

Cuypers, K., Krokstad, S., Lingaas Holmen, T., Skjei Knudtsen, M., Olov Bygren, L., and Holmen, J., 2012. Patterns of receptive and creative cultural activities and their association with perceived health, anxiety, depression and satisfaction with life among adults: the HUNT study, Norway. *Journal of Epidemiology and Community Health*, 66 (8), 698–703.

Dabbs, J.M.B. and Dabbs, M.G., 2000. *Heroes, Rogues, and Lovers: Testosterone and Behavior*. New York: McGraw-Hill.

Dadds, M.R., Perry, Y., Hawes, D.J., Merz, S., Riddell, A.C., Haines, D.J., Solak, E., and Abeygunawardane, A.I., 2006. Attention to the eyes and fear-recognition deficits in child psychopathy. *The British Journal of Psychiatry*, 189 (3), 280–281.

Damasio, A.R., 1994. *Descartes' Error*. New York: Putnam.

——1999. *The Feeling of What Happens: Body, Emotion and the Making of Consciousness*. London: Heinemann.

Danziger, S., Levav, J., and Avnaim-Pesso, L., 2011. Extraneous factors in judicial decisions. *Proceedings of the National Academy of Sciences*, 108 (17), 6889–6892.

Darley, J.M. and Batson, C.D., 1973. 'From Jerusalem to Jericho': A study of situational and dispositional variables in helping behavior. *Journal of Personality and Social Psychology*, 27 (1), 100–108.

Darwin, C., 1860. *The Origin of Species by Means of Natural Selection: Or, the Preservation of Favoured Races in the Struggle for Life*. London: John Murray.

Davidson, R.J., Putnam, K.M., and Larson, C.L., 2000. Dysfunction in the neural circuitry of emotion regulation – a possible prelude to violence. *Science*, 289 (5479), 591–594.

Davis, D.M. and Hayes, J.A., 2011. What are the benefits of mindfulness? A practice review of psychotherapy-related research. *Psychotherapy*, 48 (2), 198–208.

Dawkins, R., 2006. *The Selfish Gene*. New York: Oxford University Press.

Dawson, G., Carver, L., Meltzoff, A.N., Panagiotides, H., McPartland, J., and Webb, S.J., 2002. Neural correlates of face and object recognition in young children with autism spectrum disorder, developmental delay, and typical development. *Child Development*, 73 (3), 700–717.

Dean, L., Kendal, R., Schapiro, S., Thierry, B., and Laland, K., 2012. Identification of the social and cognitive processes underlying human cumulative culture. *Science*, 335 (6072), 1114–1118.

Decety, J. and Cacioppo, S., 2012. The speed of morality: A high-density electrical neuroimaging study. *Journal of Neurophysiology*, 108 (11), 3068–3072.

Decety, J., Norman, G.J., Berntson, G.G., and Cacioppo, J.T., 2012. A neurobehavioral evolutionary perspective on the mechanisms underlying empathy. *Progress in Neurobiology*, 98 (1), 38–48.

Decety, J., Skelly, L.R., and Kiehl, K.A., 2013. Brain response to empathy-eliciting scenarios involving pain in incarcerated individuals with psychopathy. *JAMA Psychiatry*, 1–8.

De Dreu, C.K.W., 2011. Oxytocin modulates cooperation within and competition between groups: An integrative review and research agenda. *Hormones and Behavior*, 61 (3), 419–428.

De Dreu, C.K.W., Greer, L.L., Van Kleef, G.A., Shalvi, S., and Handgraaf, M.J.J., 2011. Oxytocin promotes human ethnocentrism. *Proceedings of the National Academy of Sciences*, 108 (4), 1262–1266.

Del Canale, S., Louis, D.Z., Maio, V., Wang, X., Rossi, G., Hojat, M., and Gonnella, J.S., 2012. The relationship between physician empathy and disease complications: An empirical study of primary care physicians and their diabetic patients in Parma, Italy. *Academic Medicine*, 87 (9), 1243–1249.

DeJong, M., 2010. Some reflections on the use of psychiatric diagnosis in the looked after or 'in care' child population. *Clinical Child Psychology and Psychiatry*, 15 (4), 589–599.

Delton, A.W., Krasnow, M.M., Cosmides, L., and Tooby, J., 2011. Evolution of direct reciprocity under uncertainty can explain human generosity in one-shot encounters. *Proceedings of the National Academy of Sciences*, 108 (32), 13335–13340.

Denson, T.F., Capper, M.M., Oaten, M., Friese, M., and Schofield, T.P., 2011. Self-control training decreases aggression in response to provocation in aggressive individuals. *Journal of Research in Personality*, 45 (2), 252–256.

Denson, T.F., DeWall, C.N., and Finkel, E.J., 2012. Self-control and aggression. *Current Directions in Psychological Science*, 21 (1), 20–25.

De Quervain, D.J.-F., Fischbacher, U., Treyer, V., Schellhammer, M., Schnyder, U., Buck, A., and Fehr, E., 2004. The neural basis of altruistic punishment. *Science*, 305 (5688), 1254–1258.

Derrida, J., 1992. *Given Time: I. Counterfeit Money*. Chicago, Illinois: University of Chicago Press.

DeSteno, D., Breazeal, C., Frank, R.H., Pizarro, D., Baumann, J., Dickens, L., and Lee, J., 2012. Detecting the trustworthiness of novel partners in economic exchange. *Psychological Science*, 23 (12), 1549–1556.

DeVoe, S.E. and House, J., 2011. Time, money, and happiness: How does putting a price on time affect our ability to smell the roses? *Journal of Experimental Social Psychology*, 48 (2), 466–474.

De Waal, F.B.M., 2008. Putting the altruism back into altruism: The evolution of empathy. *Annual Review of Psychology*, 59 (1), 279–300.

——2012. *The Age of Empathy: Nature's Lessons for a Kinder Society*. London: Souvenir Press Ltd.

——2013. *The Bonobo and the Atheist: In Search of Humanism among the Primates*. New York: W.W. Norton.

Diamond, L.M., Fagundes, C.P., and Butterworth, M.R., 2012. Attachment Style, Vagal Tone, and Empathy During Mother–Adolescent Interactions. *Journal of Research on Adolescence*, 22 (1), 165–184.

Diamond, M., 2009. Pornography, public acceptance and sex related crime: A review. *International Journal of Law and Psychiatry*, 32 (5), 304–314.

Dick, D.M., Latendresse, S., Lansford, J.E., Budde, J.P., Goate, A., Dodge, K.A., Pettit, G.S., and Bates, J.E., 2009. Role of GABRA2 in trajectories of externalizing behavior across development and evidence of moderation by parental monitoring. *Archives of General Psychiatry*, 66 (6), 649–657.

Diener, E. and Chan, M.Y., 2011. Happy people live longer: Subjective well-being contributes to health and longevity. *Applied Psychology: Health and Well-Being*, 3 (1), 1–43.

Dimberg, U. and Thunberg, M., 1998. Rapid facial reactions to emotional facial expressions. *Scandinavian Journal of Psychology*, 39 (1), 39–45.

Dodd, M.D., Balzer, A., Jacobs, C.M., Gruszczynski, M.W., Smith, K.B., and Hibbing, J.R., 2012. The political left rolls with the good and the political right confronts the bad: Connecting physiology and cognition to preferences. *Philosophical Transactions of the Royal Society B: Biological Sciences*, 367 (1589), 640–649.

Dodge, K., 2009. Mechanisms of gene–environment interaction effects in the development of conduct disorder. *Perspectives on Psychological Science*, 4 (4), 408–414.

Dodge, K., Lochman, J., Harnish, J.D., Bates, J.E., and Pettit, G.S., 1997. Reactive and proactive aggression in school children and psychiatrically impaired chronically assaultive youth. *Journal of Abnormal Psychology*, 106 (1), 37–51.

Doi, L.T., 1973. The Japanese patterns of communication and the concept of amae. *Quarterly Journal of Speech*, 59 (2), 180–185.

Dolan, M. and Fulham, R., 2007. Empathy, antisocial behaviour and personality pathology. In: T.F.D. Farrow and P.W.R. Woodruff, eds, *Empathy in Mental Illness*. New York: Cambridge University Press, 33–48.

Domes, G., Heinrichs, M., Michel, A., Berger, C., and Herpertz, S.C., 2007. Oxytocin improves 'mind-reading' in humans. *Biological Psychiatry*, 61 (6), 731–733.

Duckworth, A.L., Quinn, P.D., and Tsukayama, E., 2011. What no child left behind leaves behind: The roles of IQ and self-control in predicting standardized achievement test scores and report card grades. *Journal of Educational Psychology*, 104 (2), 439–451.

Dunbar, R., 1998. *Grooming, Gossip, and the Evolution of Language*. Cambridge, Massachusetts: Harvard University Press.

Dunfield, K.A. and Kuhlmeier, V.A., 2010. Intention-mediated selective helping in infancy. *Psychological Science*, 21 (4), 523–527.

Dunn, E.W., Aknin, L.B., and Norton, M.I., 2008. Spending money on others promotes happiness. *Science*, 319 (5870), 1687–1688.

Dunn, J. and Brophy, M., 2005. Communication, relationships, and individual differences in children's understanding of mind. In: J.W. Astington, ed., *Why Language Matters for Theory of Mind.* Oxford: Oxford University Press, 50–69.

Duriez, B., Meeus, J., and Vansteenkiste, M., 2012. Why are some people more susceptible to ingroup threat than others? The importance of a relative extrinsic to intrinsic value orientation. *Journal of Research in Personality*, 46 (2), 164–172.

Dutton, K., 2012. *The Wisdom of Psychopaths.* London: Heinemann.

Duve, C.D., 2011. *Genetics of Original Sin: The Impact of Natural Selection on the Future of Humanity.* Yale, Connecticut: Yale University Press.

Eagleman, D., 2011. *Incognito: The Secret Lives of The Brain.* New York: Pantheon.

Eisenberg, N., Eggum, N., and Di Giunta, L., 2010. Empathy-related responding: Associations with prosocial behavior, aggression, and intergroup relations. *Social Issues and Policy Review*, 4 (1), 143–180.

Eisenberg, N., Fabes, R.A., Murphy, B., Karbon, M., Smith, M., and Maszk, P., 1996. The relations of children's dispositional empathy-related responding to their emotionality, regulation, and social functioning. *Developmental Psychology*, 32 (2), 195–209.

Elbert, T., Sterr, A., Candia, C., Rockstroh, B., and Taub, E., 1996. Representational cortical plasticity as revealed by magnetic source imaging: how the brain learns to play the violin. In: *First Berlin Workshop On Cortical Plasticity.* Berlin, November 1996.

Elliott, R., Völlm, B., Drury, A., McKie, S., Richardson, P., and William Deakin, J.F., 2006. Cooperation with another player in a financially rewarded guessing game activates regions implicated in theory of mind. *Social Neuroscience*, 1, 385–395.

Ellis, B.J. and Essex, M.J., 2007. Family environments, adrenarche, and sexual maturation: A longitudinal test of a life history model. *Child Development*, 78 (6), 1799–1817.

El-Sheikh, M., Kouros, C.D., Erath, S., Cummings, E.M., Keller, P., and Staton, L., 2009. Marital conflict and children's externalizing behavior: Pathways involving interactions between parasympathetic and sympathetic nervous system activity. *Monographs of the Society for Research in Child Development*, 74 (1), vii–79.

Emanuele, E., Brondino, N., Bertona, M., Re, S., and Geroldi, D., 2008. Relationship between platelet serotonin content and rejections of unfair offers in the ultimatum game. *Neuroscience Letters*, 437 (2), 158–161.

Emde, R.N., 2009. From ego to 'we-go': Neurobiology and questions for psychoanalysis: Commentary on papers by Trevarthen, Gallese, and Ammaniti & Trentini. *Psychoanalytic Dialogues*, 19 (5), 556–564.

Endicott, K., 2013. Peaceful foragers. In: D.P. Fry, ed., *War, Peace, and Human Nature: The Convergence of Evolutionary and Cultural Views*. New York: Oxford University Press.

Engel, C., 2011. Dictator games: A meta study. *Experimental Economics*, 14 (4), 1–28.

Erez, A., Mikulincer, M., van IJzendoorn, M.H., and Kroonenberg, P.M., 2008. Attachment, personality, and volunteering: Placing volunteerism in an attachment-theoretical framework. *Personality and Individual Differences*, 44 (1), 64–74.

Ernest-Jones, M., Nettle, D., and Bateson, M., 2010. Effects of eye images on everyday cooperative behavior: a field experiment. *Evolution and Human Behavior*, 32 (3), 172–178.

Ersche, K.D., Turton, A.J., Chamberlain, S.R., Müller, U., Bullmore, E.T., and Robbins, T.W., 2012. Cognitive dysfunction and anxious-impulsive personality traits are endophenotypes for drug dependence. *American Journal of Psychiatry*, 169 (9), 926–936.

Eskine, K.J., Kacinik, N.A., and Prinz, J.J., 2011. A bad taste in the mouth: Gustatory disgust influences moral judgment. *Psychological Science*, 22 (3), 295–299.

Evans, G.W. and Schamberg, M.A., 2009. Childhood poverty, chronic stress, and adult working memory. *Proceedings of the National Academy of Sciences*, 106 (16), 6545–6549.

Ewoldsen, D.R., Eno, C.A., Okdie, B.M., Velez, J.A., Guadagno, R.E., and DeCoster, J., 2012. Effect of playing violent video games cooperatively or competitively on subsequent cooperative behavior. *Cyberpsychology, Behavior, and Social Networking*, 15 (5), 277–280.

Falk, A. and Szech, N., 2013. Morals and Markets. *Science*, 340 (6133), 707–711.

Fang, F.C., Steen, R.G., and Casadevall, A., 2012. Misconduct accounts for the majority of retracted scientific publications. *Proceedings of the National Academy of Sciences*, 109 (42), 17028–17033.

Fearon, P., 2013. Genetic and environmental influences on attachment. In: *Implications of Research on the Neuroscience of Affect, Attachment, and Social Cognition Forum*. London: University College London.

Fehr, E. and Gachter, S., 2002. Altruistic punishment in humans. *Nature*, 415 (6868), 137–140.

Feinberg, M., Willer, R., Antonenko, O., and John, O.P., 2012. Liberating reason from the passions overriding intuitionist moral judgments through emotion reappraisal. *Psychological Science*, 23 (7), 788–795.

Feinberg, M., Willer, R., Stellar, J., and Keltner, D., 2012. The virtues of gossip: Reputational information sharing as prosocial behavior. *Journal of Personality and Social Psychology*, 102 (5), 1015–1030.

Feldman, R., Gordon, I., and Zagoory-Sharon, O., 2011. Maternal and paternal plasma, salivary, and urinary oxytocin and parent–infant synchrony: considering stress and affiliation components of human bonding. *Developmental Science*, 14 (4), 752–761.

Felitti, V.J. and Anda, R.F., 2010. The relationship of adverse childhood experiences to adult medical disease, psychiatric disorders and sexual behavior: Implications for healthcare. In: R.A. Lanius, E. Vermetten, and C. Pain, eds, *The Hidden Epidemic: The Impact of Early Life Trauma on Health and Disease*. New York: Cambridge University Press, 77–87.

Felitti, V.J., Anda, R.F., Nordenberg, D., Williamson, D.F., Spitz, A.M., Edwards, V., Koss, M.P., and Marks, J.S., 1998. Relationship of childhood abuse and household dysfunction to many of the leading causes of death in adults: The Adverse Childhood Experiences (ACE) Study. *American Journal of Preventive Medicine*, 14 (4), 245–258.

Ferguson, R.B., 2013a. The prehistory of war and peace in Europe and the Near East. In: D.P. Fry, ed., *War, Peace, and Human Nature: The Convergence of Evolutionary and Cultural Views*. New York: Oxford University Press, 191–240.

Ferguson, R.B., 2013b. Pinker's List: Exaggerating prehistoric war mortality. In: D.P. Fry, ed., *War, Peace, and Human Nature: The Convergence of Evolutionary and Cultural Views*. New York: Oxford University Press, 112–131.

Fershtman, C. and Gneezy, U., 2011. Discrimination in a segmented society: An experimental approach. *Quarterly Journal of Economics*, 116 (1), 351–377.

Feshbach, N.D., 1989. Empathy and physical abuse. In: D. Cicchetti and V. Carlson, eds, *Child Mal-treatment: Theory and Research on the Causes and Consequences of Child Abuse and Neglect*. Cambridge: Cambridge University Press, 349–376.

Field, T., 1995. Infants of depressed mothers. *Infant Behavior and Development*, 18 (1), 1–13.

Foubert, J.D., Brosi, M.W., and Bannon, R.S., 2011. Pornography viewing among fraternity men: Effects on bystander intervention, rape myth acceptance and behavioral intent to commit sexual assault. *Sexual Addiction & Compulsivity*, 18 (4), 212–231.

Foucault, M., 2002. *Power: The Essential Works of Michel Foucault 1954–1984*, 3rd ed. London: Penguin.

Foulkes, S.H., 1984. *Therapeutic Group Analysis*. London: Karnac.

Fowler, J.H. and Christakis, N.A., 2008. The dynamic spread of happiness in a large social network. *British Medical Journal*, 337, a2338.

Francis, D.D., Champagne, F.C., and Meaney, M.J., 2000. Variations in maternal behaviour are associated with differences in oxytocin receptor levels in the rat. *Journal of Neuroendocrinology*, 12 (12), 1145–1148.

Fredrickson, B.L., Grewen, K.M., Coffey, K.A., Algoe, S.B., Firestine, A.M., Arevalo, J.M.G., Ma, J., and Cole, S.W., 2013. A functional genomic perspective on human well-being. *Proceedings of the National Academy of Sciences*, 110 (33), 13684–13689.

Freud, S., 1998. *The Essentials of Psycho-Analysis: The Definitive Collection of Sigmund Freud's Writing*. London: Penguin.

Frick, P.J. and White, S.F., 2008. Research review: The importance of callous-unemotional traits for developmental models of aggressive and antisocial behavior. *Journal of Child Psychology and Psychiatry*, 49 (4), 359–375.

Fries, A.B.W., Ziegler, T.E., Kurian, J.R., Jacoris, S., and Pollak, S.D., 2005. Early experience in humans is associated with changes in neuropeptides critical for regulating social behavior. *Proceedings of the National Academy of Sciences*, 102 (47), 17237–17240.

Frodi, A.M. and Lamb, M.E., 1980. Child abusers' responses to infant smiles and cries. *Child Development*, 51 (1), 238–241.

Fry, D.P., 2013. *War, Peace, and Human Nature: The Convergence of Evolutionary and Cultural Views*. New York: Oxford University Press.

Gabbard, G.O. and Hobday, G.S., 2012. A psychoanalytic perspective on ethics, self-deception and the corrupt physician. *British Journal of Psychotherapy*, 28 (2), 235–248.

Gallese, V., 2009. Motor abstraction: A neuroscientific account of how action goals and intentions are mapped and understood. *Psychological Research PRPF*, 73 (4), 486–498.

Gao, Y. and Raine, A., 2010. Successful and unsuccessful psychopaths: A neurobiological model. *Behavioral Sciences & the Law*, 28 (2), 194–210.

Gazzaniga, M.S., 2006. *The Ethical Brain: The Science of Our Moral Dilemmas*. New York: HarperCollins.

——2013. Shifting gears: Seeking new approaches for mind/brain mechanisms. *Annual Review of Psychology*, 64 (1), 1–20.

Geertz, C., 2000. *The Interpretation of Cultures*. New York: Basic Books.

Gentile, D.A., Anderson, C.A., Yukawa, S., Ihori, N., Saleem, M., Ming, L.K., Shibuya, A., Liau, A.K., Khoo, A., Bushman, B.J., and others, 2009. The effects of prosocial video games on prosocial behaviors: International evidence from correlational, longitudinal, and experimental studies. *Personality and Social Psychology Bulletin*, 35 (6), 752–763.

Gentile, D.A., Coyne, S., and Walsh, D.A., 2011. Media violence, physical aggression, and relational aggression in school age children: A short-term longitudinal study. *Aggressive Behavior*, 37 (2), 193–206.

Gentile, D.A., Swing, E.L., Lim, C.G., and Khoo, A., 2012. Video game playing, attention problems, and impulsiveness: Evidence of bidirectional causality. *Psychology of Popular Media Culture*, 1 (1), 62–70.

Gerhardt, S., 2010. *The Selfish Society: How We All Forgot to Love One Another and Made Money Instead*. London: Simon & Schuster.

Germer, C.K., 2009. *The Mindful Path to Self-Compassion: Freeing Yourself from Destructive Thoughts and Emotions*. New York: Guilford Press.

Germer, C.K. and Siegel, R.D., 2012. *Wisdom and Compassion in Psychotherapy: Deepening Mindfulness in Clinical Practice*. New York: Guilford Press.

Gershon, M.D., 1999. The enteric nervous system: A second brain. *Hospital Practice (1995)*, 34 (7), 31.

Ghiselin, M.T., 1974. *The Economy of Nature and the Evolution of Sex.* Berkeley, California: University of California Press.

Gilligan, C., 1977. In a different voice: Women's conceptions of self and of morality. *Harvard Educational Review*, 47 (4), 481–517.

——1982. *In a Different Voice: Psychological Theory and Women's Development.* Cambridge, Massachusetts: Harvard University Press.

——1988. *Mapping the Moral Domain: A Contribution of Women's Thinking to Psychological Theory and Education.* Cambridge, Massachusetts: Harvard University Press.

Gilligan, J., 1997. *Violence: Reflections on a National Epidemic.* New York: Vintage Books.

Giltay, E.J., Enter, D., Zitman, F.G., Penninx, B.W.J.H., van Pelt, J., Spinhoven, P., and Roelofs, K., 2012. Salivary testosterone: Associations with depression, anxiety disorders, and antidepressant use in a large cohort study. *Journal of Psychosomatic Research*, 72 (3), 205–213.

Gino, F., Norton, M.I., and Ariely, D., 2010. The counterfeit self. *Psychological Science*, 21 (5), 712–720.

Gleichgerrcht, E. and Young, L., 2013. Low levels of empathic concern predict utilitarian moral judgment. *PLOS ONE*, 8 (4), e60418.

Glenn, A., Raine, A., Schug, R.A., Gao, Y., and Granger, D.A., 2011. Increased testosterone-to-cortisol ratio in psychopathy. *Journal of Abnormal Psychology*, 120 (2), 389–399.

Glenn, A.L., 2011. The other allele: Exploring the long allele of the serotonin transporter gene as a potential risk factor for psychopathy: A review of the parallels in findings. *Neuroscience & Biobehavioral Reviews*, 35 (3), 612–620.

Gneezy, A. and Fessler, D.M., 2011. Conflict, sticks and carrots: War increases prosocial punishments and rewards. *Proceedings of the Royal Society B: Biological Sciences*, 279 (1727), 219–233.

Goetz, J.L., Keltner, D., and Simon-Thomas, E., 2010. Compassion: An evolutionary analysis and empirical review. *Psychological Bulletin*, 136 (3), 351–374.

Goldacre, B., 2012. *Bad Pharma.* London: Fourth Estate.

Gordon, I., Zagoory-Sharon, O., Leckman, J.F., and Feldman, R., 2010a. Oxytocin and the development of parenting in humans. *Biological Psychiatry*, 68 (4), 377–382.

——2010b. Oxytocin, cortisol, and triadic family interactions. *Physiology & Behavior*, 101 (5), 679–684.

Gordon, M., 2009. *Roots of Empathy: Changing the World Child by Child.* New York: The Experiment.

Gordon, P., 1999. *Face to Face: Therapy as Ethics.* London: Constable.

Graf, D.L., Pratt, L.V., Hester, C.N., and Short, K.R., 2009. Playing active video games increases energy expenditure in children. *Pediatrics*, 124 (2), 534–540.

Graham, A.M., Fisher, P.A., and Pfeifer, J.H., 2013. What sleeping babies hear: A functional MRI study of interparental conflict and infants' emotion processing. *Psychological Science*, 24 (5), 782–789.

Gramsci, A., 1995. *Further Selections from the Prison Notebooks*. Minneapolis, Minnesota: University of Minnesota Press.

Graziano, P.A., Keane, S.P., and Calkins, S.D., 2007. Cardiac vagal regulation and early peer status. *Child Development*, 78 (1), 264–278.

Greenberg, B.S. and Brand, J.E., 1993. Television news and advertising in schools: The 'Channel One' controversy. *Journal of Communication*, 43 (1), 143–151.

Greene, J.D., 2014. *Moral Tribes: Emotion, Reason and the Gap between Us and Them*. London: Atlantic.

Greene, J.D. and Haidt, J., 2002. How (and where) does moral judgment work? *Trends in Cognitive Sciences*, 6 (12), 517–523.

Greitemeyer, T., 2011. Effects of prosocial media on social behavior: When and why does media exposure affect helping and aggression? *Current Directions in Psychological Science*, 20 (4), 251–255.

Griskevicius, V., Tybur, J.M., Delton, A.W., and Robertson, T.E., 2011. The influence of mortality and socioeconomic status on risk and delayed rewards: A life history theory approach. *Journal of Personality and Social Psychology*, 100 (6), 1015–1026.

Guastella, A.J., Einfeld, S.L., Gray, K.M., Rinehart, N.J., Tonge, B.J., Lambert, T.J., and Hickie, I.B., 2010. Intranasal oxytocin improves emotion recognition for youth with autism spectrum disorders. *Biological Psychiatry*, 67 (7), 692–694.

Guastella, A.J., Mitchell, P.B., and Dadds, M.R., 2008. Oxytocin increases gaze to the eye region of human faces. *Biological Psychiatry*, 63 (1), 3–5.

Guéguen, N. and Jacob, C., 2005. The effect of touch on tipping: An evaluation in a French bar. *International Journal of Hospitality Management*, 24 (2), 295–299.

Gullhaugen, A.S., 2012. Redefining psychopathy? Is there a need for a reformulation of the concept, assessment and treatment of psychopathic traits? Norwegian University of Science and Technology. Doctoral thesis. Available from: urn.kb.se/resolve?urn=urn:nbn:no:ntnu:diva-16287.

Gullhaugen, A.S. and Nøttestad, J.A., 2011. Looking for the Hannibal behind the cannibal: Current status of case research. *International Journal of Offender Therapy and Comparative Criminology*, 55 (3), 350–369.

——2012. Under the surface: The dynamic interpersonal and affective world of psychopathic high-security and detention prisoners. *International Journal of Offender Therapy and Comparative Criminology*, 56 (6), 917–936.

Gunderson, E.A., Gripshover, S.J., Romero, C., Dweck, C.S., Goldin-Meadow, S., Levine, S.C., Croft, A.D., Duboc, K., Graham, L., and Griffin, J., 2013. Parent praise to 1–3 year-olds predicts children's motivational frameworks 5 years later. *Child Development*, 84 (5), 1526–1541.

Gurven, M., Allen-Arave, W., Hill, K., and Hurtado, M., 2000. 'It's a Wonderful Life': Signaling generosity among the Ache of Paraguay. *Evolution and Human Behavior*, 21 (4), 263–282.

Güth, W., Schmittberger, R., and Schwarze, B., 1982. An experimental analysis of ultimatum bargaining. *Journal of Economic Behavior & Organization*, 3 (4), 367–388.

Haas, J. and Piscitelli, M., 2013. The prehistory of warfare: Misled by ethnography. In: D.P. Fry, ed., *War, Peace, and Human Nature: The Convergence of Evolutionary and Cultural Views*. New York: Oxford University Press, 168–190.

Haidt, J., 2012. *The Righteous Mind: Why Good People are Divided by Politics and Religion*. London: Allen Lane.

Hamlin, J.K., Mahajan, N., Liberman, Z., and Wynn, K., 2013. Not like me = bad infants prefer those who harm dissimilar others. *Psychological Science, 24 (4), 589–594.*

Hamlin, J.K. and Wynn, K., 2012. Who knows what's good to eat? Infants fail to match the food preferences of antisocial others. *Cognitive Development*, 27 (3), 227–239.

Hamlin, J.K., Wynn, K., and Bloom, P., 2010. Three-month-olds show a negativity bias in their social evaluations. *Developmental Science*, 13 (6), 923–929.

Harbaugh, W.T., Mayr, U., and Burghart, D.R., 2007. Neural responses to taxation and voluntary giving reveal motives for charitable donations. *Science*, 316 (5831), 1622.

Hardin, G., 1968. The tragedy of the commons. *Science*, (162), 1243–48.

Hare, R.D., 1999a. *Without Conscience: The Disturbing World of the Psychopaths Among Us*. New York: Guilford Press.

——1999b. *The Hare Psychopathy Checklist-Revised: PLC-R*. New York: Multi-Health Systems.

Hare, R.D. and Babiak, P., 2007. *Snakes in Suits: When Psychopaths Go to Work*. New York: HarperCollins.

Harris, L.T. and Fiske, S.T., 2011. Dehumanized perception: A psychological means to facilitate atrocities, torture, and genocide? *Zeitschrift für Psychologie/Journal of Psychology*, 219 (3), 175–181.

Harris, M.B. and Huang, L.C., 1973. Helping and the attribution process. *The Journal of Social Psychology*, 90 (2), 291–297.

Hassan, Y., Bègue, L., Scharkow, M., and Bushman, B.J., 2013. The more you play, the more aggressive you become: A long-term experimental study of cumulative violent video game effects on hostile expectations and aggressive behavior. *Journal of Experimental Social Psychology*, 49, 224–227.

Hayashi, A., Karasawa, M., and Tobin, J., 2009. The Japanese preschool's pedagogy of feeling: Cultural strategies for supporting young children's emotional development. *Ethos*, 37 (1), 32–49.

Heim, C., Young, L.J., Newport, D.J., Mletzko, T., Miller, A.H., and Nemeroff, C.B., 2008. Lower CSF oxytocin concentrations in women with a history of childhood abuse. *Molecular Psychiatry*, 14 (10), 954–958.

Hembrooke, H. and Gay, G., 2003. The laptop and the lecture: The effects of multitasking in learning environments. *Journal of Computing in Higher Education*, 15 (1), 46–64.

Henrich, J., Boyd, R., Bowles, S., Camerer, C., Fehr, E., Gintis, H., and McElreath, R., 2001. In search of homo economicus: Behavioral experiments in 15 small-scale societies. *The American Economic Review*, 91 (2), 73–78.

Henrich, J., Ensminger, J., McElreath, R., Barr, A., Barrett, C., Bolyanatz, A., Cardenas, J.C., Gurven, M., Gwako, E., and Henrich, N., 2010. Markets, religion, community size, and the evolution of fairness and punishment. *Science*, 327 (5972), 1480–1484.

Hepach, R., Vaish, A., and Tomasello, M., 2012a. Young children are intrinsically motivated to see others helped. *Psychological Science*, 23 (9), 967–972.

——2012b. Young children sympathize less in response to unjustified emotional distress. *Developmental Psychology*, 49 (6), 1132–1138.

Herrmann, B., Thöni, C., and Gächter, S., 2008. Antisocial punishment across societies. *Science*, 319 (5868), 1362–1367.

Hewstone, M., Rubin, M., and Willis, H., 2002. Intergroup bias. *Annual Review of Psychology*, 53 (1), 575–604.

Hickok, G., 2009. Eight problems for the mirror neuron theory of action: Understanding in monkeys and humans. *Journal of Cognitive Neuroscience*, 21 (7), 1229–1243.

Hobbes, T., 1651. *Leviathan*. London: Andrew Cooke at the Green Dragon in St Paul's Churchyard.

Hobson, P., 2002. *The Cradle of Thought*. London: Macmillan.

Hobson, P., Patrick, M., Crandell, L., Garcia-Perez, R., and Lee, A., 2005. Personal relatedness and attachment in infants of mothers with borderline personality disorder. *Development and Psychopathology*, 17 (02), 329–347.

Hofstede, G., 2001. *Culture's Consequences: Comparing Values, Behaviors, Institutions, and Organizations across Nations*. Thousand Oaks, California: Sage Publications.

Holland, J., Silva, A.S., and Mace, R., 2012. Lost letter measure of variation in altruistic behaviour in 20 neighbourhoods. *PLOS ONE*, 7 (8), e43294.

Holmes, J., 1993. *John Bowlby and Attachment Theory.* New York: Psychology Press.

——2009. *Exploring in Security: Towards an Attachment-Informed Psychoanalytic Psychotherapy.* London: Routledge.

——2013. An attachment model of depression: Integrating findings from the mood disorder laboratory. *Psychiatry: Interpersonal and Biological Processes,* 76 (1), 68–86.

Holt-Lunstad, J., Birmingham, W.A., and Light, K.C., 2008. Influence of a 'warm touch' support enhancement intervention among married couples on ambulatory blood pressure, oxytocin, alpha amylase, and cortisol. *Psychosomatic Medicine,* 70 (9), 976–985.

Hölzel, B.K., Carmody, J., Vangel, M., Congleton, C., Yerramsetti, S.M., Gard, T., and Lazar, S.W., 2011. Mindfulness practice leads to increases in regional brain gray matter density. *Psychiatry Research: Neuroimaging,* 191 (1), 36–43.

Hornstein, H.A., Fisch, E., and Holmes, M., 1968. Influence of a model's feeling about his behavior and his relevance as a comparison other on observers' helping behavior. *Journal of Personality and Social Psychology,* 10 (3), 222–226.

Howell, R.T., Pchelin, P., and Iyer, R., 2012. The preference for experiences over possessions: Measurement and construct validation of the Experiential Buying Tendency Scale. *The Journal of Positive Psychology,* 7 (1), 57–71.

Hrdy, S.B., 1999. *Mother Nature: Natural Selection and the Female of the Species.* London: Chatto & Windus.

——2009. *Mothers and Others: The Evolutionary Origins of Mutual Understanding: The Origins of Understanding.* Camridge, Massachusetts: Harvard University Press.

Hubbard, J.A., McAuliffe, M.D., Morrow, M.T., and Romano, L.J., 2010. Reactive and proactive aggression in childhood and adolescence: Precursors, outcomes, processes, experiences, and measurement. *Journal of Personality,* 78 (1), 95–118.

Hunsucker, R.L., 2013. Bogus evidence. *Evidence Based Library and Information Practice,* 8 (1), 118–125.

Huxley, T.H., 1984. *Evolution and Ethics and Other Essays.* Eastbourne: Hodeslea.

Immordino-Yang, M.H., McColl, A., Damasio, H., and Damasio, A.R., 2009. Neural correlates of admiration and compassion. *Proceedings of the National Academy of Sciences,* 106 (19), 8021–8026.

Isen, A.M., Horn, N., and Rosenhan, D.L., 1973. Effects of success and failure on children's generosity. *Journal of Personality and Social Psychology,* 27 (2), 239.

Isen, A.M. and Levin, P.F., 1972. Effect of feeling good on helping: Cookies and kindness. *Journal of Personality and Social Psychology,* 21 (3), 384–388.

Israel, S., Weisel, O., Ebstein, R.P., and Bornstein, G., 2012. Oxytocin, but not vasopressin, increases both parochial and universal altruism. *Psychoneuroendocrinology*, 37 (8), 1341–1344.

Jackson, P.L., Brunet, E., Meltzoff, A.N., and Decety, J., 2006. Empathy examined through the neural mechanisms involved in imagining how I feel versus how you feel pain. *Neuropsychologia*, 44 (5), 752–761.

Jacquet, J., Hauert, C., Traulsen, A., and Milinski, M., 2011. Shame and honour drive cooperation. *Biology Letters*, 7 (6), 899–901.

James, J., 2011. Is the just man a happy man? An empirical study of the relationship between ethics and subjective well-being. *Kyklos*, 64 (2), 193–212.

Jazaieri, H., Jinpa, G.T., McGonigal, K., Rosenberg, E., Finkelstein, J., Simon-Thomas, E., Cullen, M., Doty, J., Gross, J., and Goldin, P., 2012. Enhancing compassion: A randomized controlled trial of a compassion cultivation training program. *Journal of Happiness Studies*, 1–14.

Johnson, S.C., Dweck, C.S., and Chen, F.S., 2007. Evidence for infants' internal working models of attachment. *Psychological Science*, 18 (6), 501–502.

Jones, A., Laurens, K., Herba, C., Barker, G., and Viding, E., 2009. Amygdala hypoactivity to fearful faces in boys with conduct problems and callous-unemotional traits. *American Journal of Psychiatry*, 166 (1), 95–102.

Joseph, J., 2004. *The Gene Illusion: Genetic Research in Psychiatry and Psychology under the Microscope*. Ross-on-Wye: PCCS Books.

Kahneman, D., 1994. New challenges to the rationality assumption. *Journal of Institutional and Theoretical Economics (JITE)/Zeitschrift für die Gesamte Staatswissenschaft*, 150 (1), 18–36.

Kanai, R., 2012. Brain structure and individual differences in social behaviors. In: *2012 AAAI Spring Symposium Series*.

Kanakogi, Y., Okumura, Y., Inoue, Y., Kitazaki, M., and Itakura, S., 2013. Rudimentary sympathy in preverbal infants: Preference for others in distress. *PLOS ONE*, 8 (6), e65292.

Kanazawa, S., 2008. Battered women have more sons: A possible evolutionary reason why some battered women stay. *Journal of Evolutionary Psychology*, 6 (2), 129–139.

Kanngiesser, P. and Warneken, F., 2012. Young children consider merit when sharing resources with others. *PLOS ONE*, 7 (8), e43979.

Kasser, T., 2003. *The High Price of Materialism*. Cambridge, Massachusetts: MIT Press.

Kasser, T., Ryan, R.M., Zax, M., and Sameroff, A.J., 1995. The relations of maternal and social environments to late adolescents' materialistic and prosocial values. *Developmental Psychology*, 31 (6), 907–914.

Kasser, T., Vansteenkiste, M., and Deckop, J.R., 2006. The ethical problems of a materialistic value orientation for businesses. In: J.R. Deckop, ed.,

Human Resource Management Ethics. Charlotte, North Carolina: Information Age Publishing, 283–306.

Keller, H., 2007. *Cultures of Infancy.* Mahwah, New Jersey: Lawrence Erlbaum Associates.

Keller, H. and Lamm, B., 2005. Parenting as the expression of sociohistorical time: The case of German individualisation. *International Journal of Behavioral Development*, 29 (3), 238–246.

Kelly, D.J., Liu, S., Ge, L., Quinn, P.C., Slater, A.M., Lee, K., Liu, Q., and Pascalis, O., 2007. Cross-race preferences for same-race faces extend beyond the African versus Caucasian contrast in 3-month-old infants. *Infancy*, 11 (1), 87–95.

Kelly, R., 2013. From the peaceful to the warlike: Ethnographic and archaeological insights into hunter-gatherer warfare and homicide. In: D.P. Fry, ed., *War, Peace, and Human Nature: The Convergence of Evolutionary and Cultural views.* New York: Oxford University Press, 151–167.

Keltner, D., 2009. *Born to Be Good: The Science of a Meaningful Life.* New York: W.W Norton.

Kharicha, K., Iliffe, S., Harari, D., Swift, C., Gillmann, G., and Stuck, A.E., 2007. Health risk appraisal in older people 1: Are older people living alone an 'at-risk' group? *The British Journal of General Practice*, 57 (537), 271–276.

Kiehl, K.A., 2006. A cognitive neuroscience perspective on psychopathy: Evidence for paralimbic system dysfunction. *Psychiatry Research*, 142 (2–3), 107–128.

Killgore, W.D.S. and Yurgelun-Todd, D.A., 2005. Social anxiety predicts amygdala activation in adolescents viewing fearful faces. *Neuroreport*, 16 (15), 1671–5.

Kim, H.S., Sherman, D.K., Sasaki, J.Y., Xu, J., Chu, T.Q., Ryu, C., Suh, E.M., Graham, K., and Taylor, S.E., 2010. Culture, distress, and oxytocin receptor polymorphism (OXTR) interact to influence emotional support seeking. *Proceedings of the National Academy of Sciences*, 107 (36), 15717–15721.

Kim, S. and Kochanska, G., 2012. Child temperament moderates effects of parent–child mutuality on self-regulation: A relationship-based path for emotionally negative infants. *Child Development*, 83 (4), 1275–1289.

Kimonis, E.R., Cross, B., Howard, A., and Donoghue, K., 2013. Maternal care, maltreatment and callous-unemotional traits among urban male juvenile offenders. *Journal of Youth and Adolescence*, 42 (2), 165–177.

Kimonis, E.R., Frick, P.J., Cauffman, E., Goldweber, A., and Skeem, J., 2012. Primary and secondary variants of juvenile psychopathy differ in emotional processing. *Development and Psychopathology*, 24 (3), 1091–1103.

Kimonis, E.R., Frick, P.J., Fazekas, H., and Loney, B.R., 2006. Psychopathy, aggression, and the processing of emotional stimuli in non-referred girls and boys. *Behavioral Sciences & the Law*, 24 (1), 21–37.

King-Casas, B., Sharp, C., Lomax-Bream, L., Lohrenz, T., Fonagy, P., and Montague, P.R., 2008. The rupture and repair of cooperation in borderline personality disorder. *Science*, 321 (5890), 806–810.

Kirman, A. and Teschl, M., 2010. Selfish or selfless? The role of empathy in economics. *Philosophical Transactions of the Royal Society B: Biological Sciences*, 365 (1538), 303–317.

Kirsch, P., Esslinger, C., Chen, Q., Mier, D., Lis, S., Siddhanti, S., Gruppe, H., Mattay, V.S., Gallhofer, B., and Meyer-Lindenberg, A., 2005. Oxytocin modulates neural circuitry for social cognition and fear in humans. *The Journal of Neuroscience*, 25 (49), 11489–11493.

Kiser, D., Steemers, B., Branchi, I., and Homberg, J.R., 2012. The reciprocal interaction between serotonin and social behaviour. *Neuroscience & Biobehavioral Reviews*, 36 (2), 786–798.

Klaus, M.H., Kennell, J.H., and Klaus, P.H., 1993. *Mothering the Mother: How a Doula Can Help You Have a Shorter, Easier, and Healthier Birth*. Reading, Massachusetts: Perseus.

Klein, M., 1998. *Love, Guilt and Reparation*. London: Vintage.

Knight, C., 2008. Early human kinship was matrilineal. In: N.J. Allen., H. Callan, R. Dunbar, and W. James, eds, *Early Human Kinship: From Sex to Social Reproduction*. Oxford: Blackwell, 61–82.

Kochanska, G. and Kim, S., 2012. Toward a new understanding of legacy of early attachments for future antisocial trajectories: Evidence from two longitudinal studies. *Development and Psychopathology*, 1 (1), 1–24.

Kochanska, G., Kim, S., Boldt, L.J., and Yoon, J.E., 2013. Children's callous-unemotional traits moderate links between their positive relationships with parents at preschool age and externalizing behavior problems at early school age. *Journal of Child Psychology and Psychiatry*, 54 (11), 1251–1260.

Kochanska, G., Woodard, J., Kim, S., Koenig, J.L., Yoon, J.E., and Barry, R.A., 2010. Positive socialization mechanisms in secure and insecure parent–child dyads: two longitudinal studies. *Journal of Child Psychology and Psychiatry*, 51 (9), 998–1009.

Koenigs, M., Young, L., Adolphs, R., Tranel, D., Cushman, F., Hauser, M., and Damasio, A.R., 2007. Damage to the prefrontal cortex increases utilitarian moral judgements. *Nature*, 446 (7138), 908–911.

Kogan, A., Saslow, L.R., Impett, E.A., Oveis, C., Keltner, D., and Saturn, S.R., 2011. Thin-slicing study of the oxytocin receptor (OXTR) gene and the evaluation and expression of the prosocial disposition. *Proceedings of the National Academy of Sciences*, 108 (48), 19189–19192.

Kohlberg, L., 1964. Development of moral character and moral ideology. In: M.L. Hoffman and L.W. Hoffman, eds, *Review of Child Development Research*. Vol. 1. New York: Russell Sage Foundation, 383–481.

——1976. Moral stages and moralization: The cognitive-developmental approach. In: *Moral Development and Behavior: Theory, Research, and Social Issues*. New York: Holt, 31–53.

Kok, B.E., Waugh, C.E., and Fredrickson, B.L., 2013. Meditation and health: The search for mechanisms of action. *Social and Personality Psychology Compass*, 7 (1), 27–39.

Konow, J. and Earley, J., 2008. The hedonistic paradox: is homo economicus happier? *Journal of Public Economics*, 92 (1–2), 1–33.

Konrath, S.H., O'Brien, E.H., and Hsing, C., 2011. Changes in dispositional empathy in American college students over time: A meta-analysis. *Personality and Social Psychology Review*, 15 (2), 180–198.

Koran, M.D., Faber, P.D., Aboujaoude, M.A., Large, P.D., and Serpe, P.D., 2006. Estimated prevalence of compulsive buying behavior in the United States. *American Journal of Psychiatry*, 163 (10), 1806–1812.

Kornfeld, D.S., 2012. Perspective: Research misconduct: The search for a remedy. *Academic Medicine*, 87 (7), 877–882.

Kringelbach, M.L., Lehtonen, A., Squire, S., Harvey, A.G., Craske, M.G., Holliday, I.E., Green, A.L., Aziz, T.Z., Hansen, P.C., Cornelissen, P.L. and Stein, A., 2008. A specific and rapid neural signature for parental instinct. *PLOS ONE*, 3 (2).

Krischer, M.K. and Sevecke, K., 2008. Early traumatization and psychopathy in female and male juvenile offenders. *International Journal of Law and Psychiatry*, 31 (3), 253–262.

Kronenberger, W.G., Mathews, V.P., Dunn, D.W., Wang, Y., Wood, E.A., Giauque, A.L., Larsen, J.J., Rembusch, M.E., Lowe, M.J., and Li, T., 2005. Media violence exposure and executive functioning in aggressive and control adolescents. *Journal of Clinical Psychology*, 61 (6), 725–737.

Kumsta, R., Sonuga-Barke, E., and Rutter, M., 2012. Adolescent callous–unemotional traits and conduct disorder in adoptees exposed to severe early deprivation. *The British Journal of Psychiatry*, 200 (3), 197–201.

Kunz, P.R. and Woolcott, M., 1976. Season's greetings: From my status to yours. *Social Science Research*, 5 (3), 269–278.

Kuzawa, C.W., Gettler, L.T., Muller, M.N., McDade, T.W., and Feranil, A.B., 2009. Fatherhood, pairbonding and testosterone in the Philippines. *Hormones and Behavior*, 56 (4), 429–435.

LaConte, S.M., 2011. Decoding fMRI brain states in real-time. *NeuroImage*, 56 (2), 440–454.

LaFrance, M., 1979. Nonverbal synchrony and rapport: Analysis by the cross-lag panel technique. *Social Psychology Quarterly*, 42, 66–70.

Lang, S., Af Klinteberg, B., and Alm, P.O., 2002. Adult psychopathy and violent behavior in males with early neglect and abuse. *Acta Psychiatrica Scandinavica*, 106, 93–100.

Lansford, J.E., Wager, L.B., Bates, J.E., Pettit, G.S., and Dodge, K.A., 2012. Forms of spanking and children's externalizing behaviors. *Family Relations*, 61 (2), 224–236.

Lawford, H.L., Doyle, A.B., and Markiewicz, D., 2012. The association between early generative concern and caregiving with friends from early to middle adolescence. *Journal of Youth and Adolescence*, 42 (12), 1847–1857.

Layous, K., Nelson, S.K., Oberle, E., Schonert-Reichl, K.A., and Lyubomirsky, S., 2012. Kindness counts: Prompting prosocial behavior in preadolescents boosts peer acceptance and well-being. *PLOS ONE*, 7 (12), e51380.

Leavitt,, K., Reynolds, S., Barnes, C.M., Schilpzand, P., and Hannah, S., 2012. Different hats, different obligations: Plural occupational identities and situated moral judgments. *The Academy of Management Journal*, 55 (6), 1316–1333.

Leimgruber, K.L., Shaw, A., Santos, L.R., and Olson, K.R., 2012. Young children are more generous when others are aware of their actions. *PLOS ONE*, 7 (10), e48292.

Lesch, K.P., 2011. When the serotonin transporter gene meets adversity: The contribution of animal models to understanding epigenetic mechanisms in affective disorders and resilience. *Molecular and Functional Models in Neuropsychiatry*, 7, 251–280.

Levinas, E. and Hand, S., 1989. *The Levinas Reader*. Oxford: Wiley-Blackwell.

Levine, M., Prosser, A., Evans, D., and Reicher, S., 2005. Identity and emergency intervention: How social group membership and inclusiveness of group boundaries shape helping behavior. *Personality and Social Psychology Bulletin*, 31 (4), 443–453.

Liberman, V., Samuels, S.M., and Ross, L., 2004. The name of the game: Predictive power of reputations versus situational labels in determining prisoner's dilemma game moves. *Personality and Social Psychology Bulletin*, 30 (9), 1175–1185.

Lieberman, A.F., Padrón, E., Van Horn, P., and Harris, W.W., 2005. Angels in the nursery: The intergenerational transmission of benevolent parental influences. *Infant Mental Health Journal*, 26 (6), 504–520.

Light, K.C., Smith, T.E., Johns, J.M., Brownley, K.A., Hofheimer, J.A., and Amico, J.A., 2000. Oxytocin responsivity in mothers of infants: A preliminary study of relationships with blood pressure during laboratory stress and normal ambulatory activity. *Health Psychology*, 19 (6), 560–567.

List, J.A., 2007. On the interpretation of giving in dictator games. *Journal of Political Economy*, 115 (3), 482–493.

List, J.A., Bailey, C.D., Euzent, P.J., and Martin, T.L., 2001. Academic economists behaving badly? A survey on three areas of unethical behavior. *Economic Inquiry*, 39 (1), 162–170.

Lockwood, P.L., Sebastian, C.L., McCrory, E.J., Hyde, Z.H., Gu, X., De Brito, S.A., and Viding, E., 2013. Association of callous traits with reduced neural responses to others' pain in children with conduct problems. *Current Biology*, 23 (10), 901–905.

Lorber, M.F. and Egeland, B., 2011. Parenting and infant difficulty: Testing a mutual exacerbation hypothesis to predict early onset conduct problems. *Child Development*, 82 (6), 2006–2020.

Lovelock, J. 2006. *The Revenge of Gaia: Earth's Climate in Crisis and the Fate of Humanity*. New York: Basic Books.

Luders, E., Kurth, F., Mayer, E.A., Toga, A.W., Narr, K.L., and Gaser, C., 2012. The unique brain anatomy of meditation practitioners: alterations in cortical gyrification. *Frontiers in Human Neuroscience*, 6 (34).

Lyubomirsky, S., Sheldon, K.M., and Schkade, D., 2005. Pursuing happiness: The architecture of sustainable change. *Review of General Psychology*, 9 (2), 111–131.

MacLean, P. D., 1973. *A Triune Concept of the Brain and Behavior*. Toronto: University of Toronto Press.

Maguire, E.A., Gadian, D.G., Johnsrude, I.S., Good, C.D., Ashburner, J., Frackowiak, R.S.J., and Frith, C.D., 2000. Navigation-related structural change in the hippocampi of taxi drivers. *Proceedings of the National Academy of Sciences*, 97 (8), 4398–4403.

Main, M. and George, C., 1985. Responses of abused and disadvantaged toddlers to distress in agemates: A study in the day care setting. *Developmental Psychology*, 21 (3), 407–412.

Main, M. and Solomon, J., 1990. Procedures for identifying infants as disorganized/disoriented during the Ainsworth strange situation. In: M.T. Greenberg, D. Cicchetti, and E.M. Cummings, eds, *Attachment in the Preschool Years: Theory, Research, and Intervention*. Chicago, Illinois: University of Chicago Press, 121–160.

Malamuth, N.M., Hald, G.M., and Koss, M., 2012. Pornography, individual differences in risk and men's acceptance of violence against women in a representative sample. *Sex Roles*, 66 (7–8), 427–439.

Mark, G.J., Voida, S., and Cardello, A.V., 2012. 'A pace not dictated by electrons': An empirical study of work without email. *Proceedings of the SIGCHI Conference on Human Factors in Computing Systems*, 555–564.

Marsee, M.A. and Frick, P.J., 2010. Callous-unemotional traits and aggression in youth. In: W.F. Arsenio and E.A. Lemerise, eds, *Emotions, Aggression, and Morality in Children: Bridging Development and Psychopathology*. Washington, DC: American Psychological Association, 137–156.

Marsh, A.A., Finger, E.C., Fowler, K.A., Adalio, C.J., Jurkowitz, I.T.N., Schechter, J.C., Pine, D.S., Decety, J., and Blair, R.J.R., 2013. Empathic responsiveness in amygdala and anterior cingulate cortex in youths with psychopathic traits. *Journal of Child Psychology and Psychiatry*, online.

Marsh, L., Pearson, A., Ropar, D., and Hamilton, A., 2013. Children with autism do not overimitate. *Current Biology*, 23 (7), R266–R268.

Martins, A.T., Faísca, L.M., Esteves, F., Muresan, A., and Reis, A., 2012. Atypical moral judgment following traumatic brain injury. *Judgment and Decision Making*, 7 (4), 478–487.

Marwick, H.M. and Murray, L., 2010. The effects of maternal depression on the 'musicality' of infant directed speech and conversational engagement. In: S. Malloch and C. Trevarthen, eds, *Communicative*

Musicality: Exploring the Basis of Human Companionship. Oxford: Oxford University Press, 281–300.

Mathur, V.A., Harada, T., Lipke, T., and Chiao, J.Y., 2010. Neural basis of extraordinary empathy and altruistic motivation. *NeuroImage,* 51 (4), 1468–1475.

McClure, S.M., Laibson, D.I., Loewenstein, G., and Cohen, J.D., 2004. Separate neural systems value immediate and delayed monetary rewards. *Science,* 306 (5695), 503–507.

McGilchrist, I., 2010. *The Master and His Emissary: The Divided Brain and the Making of the Western World.* Yale, Connecticut: Yale University Press.

McGuigan, N., Makinson, J., and Whiten, A., 2011. From over imitation to super copying: Adults imitate causally irrelevant aspects of tool use with higher fidelity than young children. *British Journal of Psychology,* 102 (1), 1–18.

McGuigan, N., Whiten, A., Flynn, E., and Horner, V., 2007. Imitation of causally opaque versus causally transparent tool use by 3- and 5-year-old children. *Cognitive Development,* 22 (3), 353–364.

Mehta, P.H. and Beer, J., 2010. Neural mechanisms of the testosterone–aggression relation: the role of orbitofrontal cortex. *Journal of Cognitive Neuroscience,* 22 (10), 2357–2368.

Meier, S. and Stutzer, A., 2008. Is volunteering rewarding in itself? *Economica,* 75 (297), 39–59.

Meins, E., Fernyhough, C., Wainwright, R., Clark-Carter, D., Gupta, M.D., Fradley, E., and Tuckey, M., 2003. Pathways to understanding mind: Construct validity and predictive validity of maternal mind-mindedness. *Child Development,* 74 (4), 1194–1211.

Meins, E., Fernyhough, C., Wainwright, R., Gupta, M.D., Fradley, E., and Tuckey, M., 2002. Maternal mind-mindedness and attachment security as predictors of theory of mind understanding. *Child Development,* 73 (6), 1715–1726.

Meltzoff, A.N., 1988. Infant imitation and memory: Nine-month-olds in immediate and deferred tests. *Child Development,* 59 (1), 217–225.

——2007. 'Like me': A foundation for social cognition. *Developmental Science,* 10 (1), 126–134.

Metcalfe, J. and Mischel, W., 1999. A hot/cool-system analysis of delay of gratification: Dynamics of willpower. *Psychological Review,* 106, 3–19.

Mikulincer, M. and Shaver, P.R., 2007. Boosting attachment security to promote mental health, prosocial values, and inter-group tolerance. *Psychological Inquiry,* 18 (3), 139–156.

——2010. Does gratitude promote prosocial behavior? The moderating role of attachment security. In: M. Mikulincer and P.R. Shaver, eds, *Prosocial Motives, Emotions, and Behavior: The Better Angels of our Nature.* Washington, DC: American Psychological Association, 267–283.

Mikulincer, M., Shaver, P.R., Gillath, O., and Nitzberg, R.A., 2005. Attachment, caregiving, and altruism: Boosting attachment security increases compassion and helping. *Journal of Personality and Social Psychology*, 89 (5), 817–839.

Mileva-Seitz, V., Afonso, V.M., and Fleming, A.S., 2012. Dopamine: Another 'magic bullet' for caregiver responsiveness? In: D. Narváez, J. Panksepp, A.N. Schore, and T.R. Gleason, eds, *Evolution, Early Experience and Human Development: From Research to Practice and Policy*. Oxford: Oxford University Press.

Mileva-Seitz, V., Steiner, M., Atkinson, L., Meaney, M.J., Levitan, R., Kennedy, J.L., Sokolowski, M.B., and Fleming, A.S., 2013. Interaction between oxytocin genotypes and early experience predicts quality of mothering and postpartum mood. *PLOS ONE*, 8 (4), e61443.

Milgram, S., 1974. *Obedience to Authority: An Experimental View*. London: Tavistock.

Milinski, M., Semmann, D., Krambeck, H., and Marotzke, J., 2006. Stabilizing the Earth's climate is not a losing game: Supporting evidence from public goods experiments. *Proceedings of the National Academy of Sciences*, 103 (11), 3994–3998.

Miller, J.G., Bersoff, D.M., and Harwood, R.L., 1990. Perceptions of social responsibilities in India and in the United States: Moral imperatives or personal decisions? *Journal of Personality and Social Psychology*, 58 (1), 33–47.

Miskovic, V., Schmidt, L.A., Georgiades, K., Boyle, M., and MacMillan, H.L., 2009. Stability of resting frontal electroencephalogram (EEG) asymmetry and cardiac vagal tone in adolescent females exposed to child maltreatment. *Developmental Psychobiology*, 51 (6), 474–487.

Mitchell, J.P., Macrae, C.N., and Banaji, M.R., 2006. Dissociable medial prefrontal contributions to judgments of similar and dissimilar others. *Neuron*, 50 (4), 655–663.

Moffitt, T.E., Arseneault, L., Belsky, D., Dickson, N., Hancox, R.J., Harrington, H.L., Houts, R., Poulton, R., Roberts, B.W., and Ross, S., 2011. A gradient of childhood self-control predicts health, wealth, and public safety. *Proceedings of the National Academy of Sciences*, 108 (7), 2693–2698.

Moll, J., Krueger, F., Zahn, R., Pardini, M., de Oliveira Souza, R., and Grafman, J., 2006. Human fronto–mesolimbic networks guide decisions about charitable donation. *Proceedings of the National Academy of Sciences*, 103 (42), 15623.

Moll, J., Zahn, R., de Oliveira Souza, R., Krueger, F., and Grafman, J., 2005. The neural basis of human moral cognition. *Nature Reviews Neuroscience*, 6 (10), 799–809.

Montag, C., Weber, B., Trautner, P., Newport, B., Markett, S., Walter, N.T., Felten, A., and Reuter, M., 2012. Does excessive play of violent first-person-shooter-video-games dampen brain activity in response to emotional stimuli? *Biological Psychology*, 89 (1), 107–111.

Moore, C. and Macgillivray, S., 2004. Altruism, prudence, and theory of mind in preschoolers. *New Directions for Child and Adolescent Development*, 2004 (103), 51–62.

Moore, G.A., 2010. Parent conflict predicts infants' vagal regulation in social interaction. *Development and Psychopathology*, 22 (1), 23–33.

Morgan, A.B. and Lilienfeld, S.O., 2000. A meta-analytic review of the relation between antisocial behavior and neuropsychological measures of executive function. *Clinical Psychology Review*, 20 (1), 113–136.

Morhenn, V.B., Park, J.W., Piper, E., and Zak, P.J., 2008. Monetary sacrifice among strangers is mediated by endogenous oxytocin release after physical contact. *Evolution and Human Behavior*, 29 (6), 375–383.

Morishima, Y., Schunk, D., Bruhin, A., Ruff, C.C., and Fehr, E., 2012. Linking brain structure and activation in temporoparietal junction to explain the neurobiology of human altruism. *Neuron*, 75 (1), 73–79.

Morris, A.S., Silk, J.S., Steinberg, L., Myers, S.S., and Robinson, L.R., 2007. The role of the family context in the development of emotion regulation. *Social Development*, 16 (2), 361–388.

Motzkin, J., Newman, J.P., Kiehl, K.A., and Koenigs, M., 2011. Reduced prefrontal connectivity in psychopathy. *The Journal of Neuroscience*, 31 (48), 17348–17357.

Murphy, J.M., 1976. Psychiatric labeling in cross-cultural perspective. *Science*, (141), 1019–1028.

Music, G., 2009. Neglecting neglect: Some thoughts about children who have lacked good input, and are 'undrawn' and 'unenjoyed'. *Journal of Child Psychotherapy*, 35 (2), 142–156.

——2010. *Nurturing Natures: Attachment and Children's Emotional, Social and Brain Development*. London: Psychology Press.

——2011. Trauma, helpfulness and selfishness: The effect of abuse and neglect on altruistic, moral and pro-social capacities. *Journal of Child Psychotherapy*, 37 (2), 113–128.

——2012. Selfless genes, altruism and trauma: Research and clinical implications. *British Journal of Psychotherapy*, 28 (2), 154–171.

Nairn, A. and Fine, C., 2008. Who's messing with my mind? The implications of dual-process models for the ethics of advertising to children. *International Journal of Advertising*, 27 (3), 447–470.

Narváez, D., 2009. Triune ethics theory and moral personality. In: D. Narváez and D.K. Lapsley, eds, *Personality, Identity and Character: Explorations in Moral Psychology*. New York: Cambridge University Press, 136–158.

——2013. The 99 percent – development and socialization within an evolutionary context: Growing up to become a 'good and useful human being'. In: D.P. Fry, ed., *War, Peace, and Human Nature: The Convergence of Evolutionary and Cultural Views*. New York: Oxford University Press, 341–358.

Narváez, D. and Gleason, T., R., 2012. Developmental optimization. In: D. Narváez, J. Panksepp, A.N. Schore, and T.R. Gleason, eds, *Evolution,*

Early Experience and Human Development: From Research to Practice and Policy. Oxford: Oxford University Press.

Nathanson, A.I. and Rasmussen, E.E., 2011. TV viewing compared to book reading and toy playing reduces responsive maternal communication with toddlers and preschoolers. *Human Communication Research*, 37 (4), 465–487.

Neave, N. and Wolfson, S., 2003. Testosterone, territoriality, and the 'home advantage'. *Physiology and Behavior*, 78 (2), 269–276.

Neff, K. and Germer, C., 2013. A pilot study and randomized controlled trial of the mindful self-compassion program. *Journal of Clinical Psychology*, 69 (1), 28–44.

Nettle, D., Colléony, A., and Cockerill, M., 2011. Variation in cooperative behaviour within a single city. *PLOS ONE*, 6 (10), e26922.

Niemiec, C.P., Ryan, R.M., and Deci, E.L., 2009. The path taken: Consequences of attaining intrinsic and extrinsic aspirations in post-college life. *Journal of Research in Personality*, 43 (3), 291–306.

Nisbett, R.E. and Cohen, D., 1996. *Culture of Honor: The Psychology of Violence in the South.* Boulder, Colorado: Westview Press.

Noble, K.G., Norman, M.F., and Farah, M.J., 2005. Neurocognitive correlates of socioeconomic status in kindergarten children. *Developmental Science*, 8 (1), 74–87.

Nowak, M. and Highfield, R., 2011. *Supercooperators: Evolution, Altruism and Human Behaviour or, Why We Need Each Other to Succeed.* Edinburgh: Canongate Books.

O'Connor, L.E., Berry, J.W., Lewis, T.B., and Stiver, D.J., 2012. Empathy-based pathogenic guilt, pathological altruism, and psychopathology. In: B. Oakley, A. Knafo, G. Madhavan, and D. Wilson, eds, *Pathological Altruism.* Oxford: Oxford University Press, 10–30.

Oakley, B., Knafo, A., Madhavan, G., and Wilson, D., eds, 2012. *Pathological Altruism.* Oxford: Oxford University Press.

Oberman, L.M., Hubbard, E.M., McCleery, J.P., Altschuler, E.L., Ramachandran, V.S., and Pineda, J.A., 2005. EEG evidence for mirror neuron dysfunction in autism spectrum disorders. *Cognitive Brain Research*, 24 (2), 190–198.

Oei, A.C. and Patterson, M.D., 2013. Enhancing cognition with video games: A multiple game training study. *PLOS ONE*, 8 (3), e58546.

Ogden, P. 2006. *Trauma and the Body: A Sensorimotor Approach to Psychotherapy.* 1st ed. London: W.W. Norton.

Ohtsuki, H. and Iwasa, Y., 2006. The leading eight: Social norms that can maintain cooperation by indirect reciprocity. *Journal of Theoretical Biology*, 239 (4), 435–444.

Olson, G., 2013. *Empathy Imperiled: Capitalism, Culture, and the Brain.* New York: Springer.

Oman, D., Thoresen, C.E., and McMahon, K., 1999. Volunteerism and mortality among the community-dwelling elderly. *Journal of Health Psychology*, 4 (3), 301–316.

Oosterbeek, H., Sloof, R., and Van de Kuilen, G., 2004. Cultural differences in ultimatum game experiments: Evidence from a meta-analysis. *Experimental Economics*, 7 (2), 171–188.

Opacka-Juffry, J. and Mohiyeddini, C., 2011. Experience of stress in childhood negatively correlates with plasma oxytocin concentration in adult men. *Stress*, 15 (1), 1–10.

Ophir, E., Nass, C., and Wagner, A.D., 2009. Cognitive control in media multitaskers. *Proceedings of the National Academy of Sciences*, 106 (37), 15583–15587.

Ostrosky-Solís, F., García, M.A., and Pérez, M., 2004. Can learning to read and write change the brain organization? An electrophysiological study. *International Journal of Psychology*, 39 (1), 27–35.

Over, H. and Carpenter, M., 2009. Eighteen-month-old infants show increased helping following priming with affiliation. *Psychological Science*, 20 (10), 1189–1193.

Pace, T.W.W., Negi, L.T., Adame, D.D., Cole, S.P., Sivilli, T.I., Brown, T.D., Issa, M.J., and Raison, C.L., 2009. Effect of compassion meditation on neuroendocrine, innate immune and behavioral responses to psychosocial stress. *Psychoneuroendocrinology*, 34 (1), 87–98.

Pagel, M., 2012. *Wired for Culture: The Natural History of Human Cooperation.* London: Allen Lane.

Paluck, E.L., 2009. Reducing intergroup prejudice and conflict using the media: A field experiment in Rwanda. *Journal of Personality and Social Psychology*, 96 (3), 574–587.

Pandey, A., Quick, J.C., Rossi, A.M., Nelson, D.L., and Martin, W., 2010. Stress and the workplace: 10 Years of science, 1997–2007. In: *The Handbook of Stress Science: Biology, Psychology, and Health.* New York: Springer, 137–149.

Panksepp, J., 2004. *Affective Neuroscience: The Foundations of Human and Animal Emotions.* Oxford: Oxford University Press.

Panksepp, J. and Biven, L., 2012. *The Archaeology of Mind: Neuroevolutionary Origins of Human Emotions.* New York: Norton.

Panksepp, J. and Panksepp, J.B., 2000. The seven sins of evolutionary psychology. *Evolution and Cognition*, 6 (2), 108–131.

Parker, K.J. and Maestripieri, D., 2011. Identifying key features of early stressful experiences that produce stress vulnerability and resilience in primates. *Neuroscience & Biobehavioral Reviews*, 35 (7), 1466–1483.

Pasalich, D.S., Dadds, M.R., Hawes, D.J., and Brennan, J., 2012. Attachment and callous-unemotional traits in children with early-onset conduct problems. *Journal of Child Psychology and Psychiatry, and Allied Disciplines*, 53 (8), 838–845.

Pastötter, B., Gleixner, S., Neuhauser, T., and Bäuml, K.T., 2013. To push or not to push? Affective influences on moral judgment depend on decision frame. *Cognition*, 126 (3), 373–377.

Patrick, C.J., Fowles, D.C., and Krueger, R.F., 2010. Triarchic conceptualization of psychopathy: Developmental origins of disinhibition, boldness, and meanness. *Development and Psychopathology*, 21 (3), 913–938.

Penner, L.A., Cline, R.J., Albrecht, T.L., Harper, F.W., Peterson, A.M., Taub, J.M., and Ruckdeschel, J.C., 2008. Parents' empathic responses and pain and distress in pediatric patients. *Basic and Applied Social Psychology*, 30 (2), 102–113.

Peters, W., 1987. *A Class Divided: Then and Now*. Yale, Connecticut: Yale University Press.

Pfabigan, D.M., Alexopoulos, J., Bauer, H., Lamm, C., and Sailer, U., 2011. All about the money – external performance monitoring is affected by monetary, but not by socially conveyed feedback cues in more antisocial individuals. *Frontiers in Human Neuroscience*, 5.

Piaget, J., 1965. *The Moral Judgement of the Child*. New York: Free Press.

Piff, P.K., Kraus, M.W., Côté, S., Cheng, B.H., and Keltner, D., 2010. Having less, giving more: The influence of social class on prosocial behavior. *Journal of Personality and Social Psychology,*, 99 (5), 771–784.

Piff, P.K., Stancato, D.M., Côté, S., Mendoza-Denton, R., and Keltner, D., 2012. Higher social class predicts increased unethical behavior. *Proceedings of the National Academy of Sciences*, 109 (11), 4086–4091.

Pinker, S., 2011. *The Better Angels of our Nature: Why Violence has Declined*. London: Penguin.

Polaschek, D.L., 2011. High-intensity rehabilitation for violent offenders in New Zealand: Reconviction outcomes for high- and medium-risk prisoners. *Journal of Interpersonal Violence*, 26 (4), 664–682.

Pope, A., Watson, J.S., Flaxman, J., Parnell, T., and Chapman, G., 1867. *The Odyssey of Homer*. London: G. Bell & Sons.

Porges, S.W., 2011. *The Polyvagal Theory: Neurophysiological Foundations of Emotions, Attachment, Communication, and Self-regulation*. New York: Norton.

Poulin, M.J., Holman, E.A., and Buffone, A., 2012. The neurogenetics of nice receptor genes for oxytocin and vasopressin interact with threat to predict prosocial behavior. *Psychological Science*, 23 (5), 446–452.

Poythress, N.G., Skeem, J.L., and Lilienfeld, S.O., 2006. Associations among early abuse, dissociation, and psychopathy in an offender sample. *Journal of Abnormal Psychology*, 115 (2), 288–297.

Pradel, J. and Fetchenhauer, D., 2010. Why most theories get it wrong. In: U.J. Frey and C. Stormer, eds, *Homo Novus – A Human Without Illusions*. New York: Springer, 79–92.

Prinz, J.J., 2011. Is empathy necessary for morality? In: A. Coplan and P. Goldie, eds, *Empathy: Philosophical and Psychological Perspectives*. Oxford: Oxford University Press, 211–229.

Prior, V. and Glaser, D., 2006. *Understanding Attachment and Attachment Disorders: Theory, Evidence and Practice.* London: Jessica Kingsley.

Putnam, R.D., 2000. *Bowling Alone: The Collapse and Revival of American Community.* New York: Simon & Schuster.

Qiao, Y., Xie, B., and Du, X., 2012. Abnormal response to emotional stimulus in male adolescents with violent behavior in China. *European Child & Adolescent Psychiatry,* 21, 193–198.

Raine, A., 2011. An amygdala structural abnormality common to two subtypes of conduct disorder: a neurodevelopmental conundrum. *American Journal of Psychiatry,* 168 (6), 569–571.

Rakow, A., Forehand, R., McKee, L., Coffelt, N., Champion, J., Fear, J., and Compas, B., 2009. The relation of parental guilt induction to child internalizing problems when a caregiver has a history of depression. *Journal of Child and Family Studies,* 18 (4), 367–377.

Ramachandran, V.S., 2000. Mirror neurons and imitation learning as the driving force behind 'the great leap forward' in human evolution. *Edge.* Available from: www.edge.org/3rd_culture/ramachandran/ramachandran _p1.html.

Rand, A., 1984. *Philosophy: Who Needs It.* New York: Signet Books.

Rand, D.G., Greene, J.D., and Nowak, M., 2012. Spontaneous giving and calculated greed. *Nature,* 489 (7416), 427–430.

Reddy, V., 2008. *How Infants Know Minds.* Harvard: Harvard University Press.

Rekers, Y., Haun, D., and Tomasello, M., 2011. Children, but not chimpanzees, prefer to collaborate. *Current Biology,* 21 (20), 1756–1758.

Reyniers, D. and Bhalla, R., 2013. Reluctant altruism and peer pressure in charitable giving. *Judgment and Decision Making,* 8 (1), 7–15.

Richardson, K. and Norgate, S., 2005. The equal environments assumption of classical twin studies may not hold. *British Journal of Educational Psychology,* 75 (3), 339–350.

Richins, M.L. and Dawson, S., 1992. A consumer values orientation for materialism and its measurement: Scale development and validation. *Journal of Consumer Research,* 19 (3), 303–316.

Rifkin, J., 2010. *The Empathic Civilization: The Race to Global Consciousness in a World in Crisis.* Cambridge: Polity Press.

Rindfleisch, A., Burroughs, J.E., and Denton, F., 1997. Family structure, materialism, and compulsive consumption. *Journal of Consumer Research,* 23 (4), 312–325.

Rizzolatti, G., Fogassi, L., and Gallese, V., 2006. Mirrors in the mind: Mirror neurons, a special class of cells in the brain, may mediate our ability to mimic, learn and understand the actions and intentions of others. *Scientific American,* 295 (5), 54–61.

Roberts, J.A., 2011. *Shiny Objects: Why We Spend Money We Don't Have in Search of Happiness We Can't Buy.* New York: HarperCollins.

Roberts, J.A. and Pirog, S.F., 2013. A preliminary investigation of materialism and impulsiveness as predictors of technological addictions among young adults. *Journal of Behavioral Addictions*, 2 (1), 56–62.

Robertson, L.A., McAnally, H.M., and Hancox, R.J., 2013. Childhood and adolescent television viewing and antisocial behavior in early adulthood. *Pediatrics*, 131 (3), 439–446.

Rosenhan, D.L., Underwood, B., and Moore, B., 1974. Affect moderates self-gratification and altruism. *Journal of Personality and Social Psychology*, 30 (4), 546–52.

Rosenthal, R. and Rosnow, R.L., 1975. *The Volunteer Subject*. New York: Wiley.

Rousseau, J.J., 1754. *Discourse on the Origin and Foundations of Inequality among Men*. 1985. London: Penguin.

Sääksvuori, L., Mappes, T. and Puurtinen, M. 2011. Costly punishment prevails in intergroup conflict. *Proceedings of the Royal Society B: Biological Sciences*, 278 (1723), 3428–3436.

Sahlins, M.D., 2008. *The Western Illusion of Human Nature: With Reflections on the Long History of Hierarchy, Equality and the Sublimation of Anarchy in the West, and Comparative Notes on Other Conceptions of the Human Condition.* Chicago, Illinois: University of Chicago Press.

Salekin, R.T., Worley, C., and Grimes, R.D., 2010. Treatment of psychopathy: A review and brief introduction to the mental model approach for psychopathy. *Behavioral Sciences & the Law*, 28 (2), 235–266.

Sandel, M.J., 2012. *What Money Can't Buy: The Moral Limits of Markets.* London: Allen Lane.

Saxe, R. and Haushofer, J., 2008. For love or money: A common neural currency for social and monetary reward. *Neuron*, 58 (2), 164–165.

Scheele, D., Striepens, N., Güntürkün, O., Deutschländer, S., Maier, W., Kendrick, K.M., and Hurlemann, R., 2012. Oxytocin modulates social distance between males and females. *The Journal of Neuroscience*, 32 (46), 16074–16079.

Schindler, K., Van Gool, L., and de Gelder, B., 2008. Recognizing emotions expressed by body pose: A biologically inspired neural model. *Neural Networks*, 21 (9), 1238–1246.

Schmidt, M.F.H. and Sommerville, J.A., 2011. Fairness expectations and altruistic sharing in 15-month-old human infants. *PLOS ONE*, 6 (10), e23223.

Schmidt, M.F.H. and Tomasello, M., 2012. Young children enforce social norms. *Current Directions in Psychological Science*, 21 (4), 232–236.

Schnall, S., Haidt, J., Clore, G.L., and Jordan, A.H., 2008. Disgust as embodied moral judgment. *Personality and Social Psychology Bulletin*, 34 (8), 1096–1109.

Schneiderman, I., Zagoory-Sharon, O., Leckman, J.F., and Feldman, R., 2012. Oxytocin during the initial stages of romantic attachment:

relations to couples' interactive reciprocity. *Psychoneuroendocrinology*, 37 (8), 1277–1285.

Schor, J., 2006. *Born to Buy: The Commercialized Child and the New Consumer Culture*. New York: Simon & Schuster.

Schore, A.N., 2009. Right-brain affect regulation. In: D. Fosha and D. Siegel, eds, *The Healing Power of Emotion: Affective Neuroscience, Development & Clinical Practice*. New York: Norton, 112–144.

Schreier, H.M., Schonert-Reichl, K.A., and Chen, E., 2013. Effect of volunteering on risk factors for cardiovascular disease in adolescents. *JAMA Pediatrics*, 167 (4), 327–332.

Schulz, K., Rudolph, A., Tscharaktschiew, N., and Rudolph, U., 2013. Daniel has fallen into a muddy puddle – Schadenfreude or sympathy? *British Journal of Developmental Psychology*, 31 (4), 363–378.

Sektnan, M., McClelland, M.M., Acock, A., and Morrison, F.J., 2010. Relations between early family risk, children's behavioral regulation, and academic achievement. *Early Childhood Research Quarterly*, 25 (4), 464–479.

Seligman, M.E., 2012. *Flourish: A Visionary New Understanding of Happiness and Well-Being*. New York: Simon & Schuster.

Sennett, R., 2012. *Together: The Rituals, Pleasures and Politics of Cooperation*. London: Allen Lane.

Shahrokh, D.K., Zhang, T.-Y., Diorio, J., Gratton, A., and Meaney, M.J., 2010. Oxytocin–dopamine interactions mediate variations in maternal behavior in the rat. *Endocrinology*, 151 (5), 2276–2286.

Shamay-Tsoory, S.G., Fischer, M., Dvash, J., Harari, H., Perach-Bloom, N., and Levkovitz, Y., 2009. Intranasal administration of oxytocin increases envy and schadenfreude (gloating). *Biological Psychiatry*, 66 (9), 864–870.

Shamay-Tsoory, S.G., Harari, H., Aharon-Peretz, J., and Levkovitz, Y., 2010. The role of the orbitofrontal cortex in affective theory of mind deficits in criminal offenders with psychopathic tendencies. *Cortex; A Journal Devoted to the Study of the Nervous System and Behavior*, 46 (5), 668–677.

Shand, N., 1985. Culture's influence in Japanese and American maternal role perception and confidence. *Psychiatry*, 48 (1), 52–67.

Shannon, C., Schwandt, M.L., Champoux, M., Shoaf, S.E., Suomi, S.J., Linnoila, M., and Higley, J.D., 2005. Maternal absence and stability of individual differences in CSF 5-HIAA concentrations in rhesus monkey infants. *American Journal of Psychiatry*, 162 (9), 1658–1664.

Sharot, T., 2012. *The Optimism Bias: Why We're Wired to Look on the Bright Side*. New York: Vintage.

Shaw, A., Montinari, N., Piovesan, M., Olson, K.R., Gino, F., and Norton, M.I., 2012. *Children Develop a Veil of Fairness*. Harvard Business School Working Paper.

Sheldon, K.M., Gunz, A., Nichols, C.P., and Ferguson, Y., 2010. Extrinsic value orientation and affective forecasting: Overestimating the rewards, underestimating the costs. *Journal of Personality*, 78 (1), 149–178.

Sheldon, K.M. and McGregor, H.A., 2000. Extrinsic value orientation and 'The tragedy of the commons'. *Journal of Personality*, 68 (2), 383–411.

Shirtcliff, E.A., Vitacco, M.J., Graf, A.R., Gostisha, A.J., Merz, J.L., and Zahn Waxler, C., 2009. Neurobiology of empathy and callousness: Implications for the development of antisocial behavior. *Behavioral Sciences & the Law*, 27 (2), 137–171.

Siegel, D.J., 2012. *The Developing Mind: Toward a Neurobiology of Interpersonal Experience*. New York: Guilford Press.

Simons, L.G., Simons, R.L., Lei, M.-K., and Sutton, T.E., 2012. Exposure to harsh parenting and pornography as explanations for males' sexual coercion and females' sexual victimization. *Violence and Victims*, 27 (3), 378–395.

Simpson, J.A. and Belsky, J., 2008. Attachment theory within a modern evolutionary framework. In: J. Cassidy and P.R. Shaver, eds, *Handbook of Attachment: Theory, Research, and Clinical Applications*. New York: Guilford Press, 131–157.

Singer, T., Seymour, B., O'Doherty, J.P., Stephan, K.E., Dolan, R.J., and Frith, C.D., 2006. Empathic neural responses are modulated by the perceived fairness of others. *Nature*, 439 (7075), 466–469.

Sivanathan, N. and Pettit, N.C., 2010. Protecting the self through consumption: Status goods as affirmational commodities. *Journal of Experimental Social Psychology*, 46 (3), 564–570.

Sloane, S., Baillargeon, R., and Premack, D., 2012. Do infants have a sense of fairness? *Psychological Science*, 23 (2), 196–204.

Slutske, W.S., Moffitt, T.E., Poulton, R., and Caspi, A., 2012. Under-controlled temperament at age 3 predicts disordered gambling at age 32: A longitudinal study of a complete birth cohort. *Psychological Science*, 23 (5), 510–516.

Small, G.W., Moody, T.D., Siddarth, P., and Bookheimer, S.Y., 2009. Your brain on Google: Patterns of cerebral activation during internet searching. *American Journal of Geriatric Psychiatry*, 17 (2), 116–126.

Smith, C.E., Chen, D., and Harris, P., 2010. When the happy victimizer says sorry: Children's understanding of apology and emotion. *British Journal of Developmental Psychology*, 28 (4), 727–746.

Smith, K.B., Oxley, D., Hibbing, M.V., Alford, J.R., and Hibbing, J.R., 2011. Disgust sensitivity and the neurophysiology of left-right political orientations. *PLOS ONE*, 6 (10), e25552.

Sperry, R.W., 1961. Cerebral organization and behavior. *Science*, 133 (3466), 1749–1757.

Sroufe, L.A., 2005. *The Development of the Person: The Minnesota Study of Risk and Adaptation from Birth to Adulthood*. New York: Guilford Press.

Stanton, S.J., Beehner, J.C., Saini, E.K., Kuhn, C.M., and LaBar, K.S., 2009. Dominance, politics, and physiology: Voters' testosterone changes on the night of the 2008 United States presidential election. *PLOS ONE*, 4 (10), e7543.

Steinbeis, N., Bernhardt, B.C., and Singer, T., 2012. Impulse control and underlying functions of the left DLPFC mediate age-related and age-independent individual differences in strategic social behavior. *Neuron*, 73 (5), 1040–1051.

Stout, M., 2007. *The Sociopath Next Door*. New York: Broadway Books.

Strathearn, L., 2011. Maternal neglect: Oxytocin, dopamine and the neurobiology of attachment. *Journal of Neuroendocrinology*, 23 (11), 1054–1065.

Strathearn, L., Fonagy, P., Amico, J., and Montague, P.R., 2009. Adult attachment predicts maternal brain and oxytocin response to infant cues. *Neuropsychopharmacology: Official Publication of the American College of Neuropsychopharmacology*, 34 (13), 2655–2666.

Stringer, C., 2011. *The Origin of Our Species*. London: Allen Lane.

Strobel, A., Zimmermann, J., Schmitz, A., Reuter, M., Lis, S., Windmann, S., and Kirsch, P., 2011. Beyond revenge: Neural and genetic bases of altruistic punishment. *NeuroImage*, 54 (1), 671–680.

Stuckler, D. and Basu, S., 2013. *The Body Economic: Why Austerity Kills*. London: Allen Lane.

Sturge-Apple, M., Skibo, M.A., Rogosch, F.A., Ignijatovic, J., and Heinzelman, W., 2011. The impact of allostatic load on maternal sympathovagal functioning in stressful child contexts: Implications for maladaptive parenting. *Development and Psychopathology*, 23, 831–44.

Sutter, M., 2007. Outcomes versus intentions: On the nature of fair behavior and its development with age. *Journal of Economic Psychology*, 28 (1), 69–78.

Swing, E.L., Gentile, D.A., Anderson, C.A., and Walsh, D.A., 2010. Television and video game exposure and the development of attention problems. *Pediatrics*, 126 (2), 214–221.

Tajfel, H. and Turner, J.C., 1979. An integrative theory of intergroup conflict. In: W. Austin and S. Worschel, eds, *The Social Psychology of Intergroup Relations*. Monterey, California: Brooks/Cole, 33–47.

Takahashi, H., Kato, M., Matsuura, M., Mobbs, D., Suhara, T., and Okubo, Y., 2009. When your gain is my pain and your pain is my gain: Neural correlates of envy and schadenfreude. *Science*, 323 (5916), 937–939.

Tamayo, T., Herder, C., and Rathmann, W., 2010. Impact of early psychosocial factors (childhood socioeconomic factors and adversities) on future risk of type 2 diabetes, metabolic disturbances and obesity: a systematic review. *BMC Public Health*, 10 (525).

Tankersley, D., Stowe, C.J., and Huettel, S.A., 2007. Altruism is associated with an increased neural response to agency. *Nature Neuroscience*, 10 (2), 150–151.

Tapscott, D., 2009. *Grown Up Digital*. New York: McGraw-Hill.

Tarter, R.E., Kirisci, L., Gavaler, J.S., Reynolds, M., Kirillova, G., Clark, D.B., Wu, J., Moss, H.B., and Vanyukov, M., 2009. Prospective study of the association between abandoned dwellings and testosterone level on the development of behaviors leading to cannabis use disorder in boys. *Biological Psychiatry*, 65 (2), 116–121.

Tassy, S., Oullier, O., Duclos, Y., Coulon, O., Mancini, J., Deruelle, C., Attarian, S., Felician, O., and Wicker, B., 2012. Disrupting the right prefrontal cortex alters moral judgement. *Social Cognitive and Affective Neuroscience*, 7 (3), 282–288.

Terris, E.T., Mahoney, N., Vercoe, M.J., and Zak, P.J., 2010. The impact of childhood trauma on oxytocin release and trustworthiness. Available from: www.sfn.org/am2010/press/OmniPress/data/papers/17578.htm.

Thoits, P.A. and Hewitt, L.N., 2001. Volunteer work and well-being. *Journal of Health and Social Behavior*, 42, 115–131.

Thompson, K.L. and Gullone, E., 2008. Prosocial and antisocial behaviors in adolescents: An investigation into associations with attachment and empathy. *Anthrozoos: A Multidisciplinary Journal of The Interactions of People & Animals*, 21 (2), 123–137.

Thornton, L.C., Frick, P.J., Crapanzano, A.M., and Terranova, A.M., 2012. The incremental utility of callous-unemotional traits and conduct problems in predicting aggression and bullying in a community sample of boys and girls. *Psychological Assessment*, 25 (2), 366–378.

Tither, J. and Ellis, B., 2008. Impact of fathers on daughters' age at menarche: A genetically and environmentally controlled sibling study. *Developmental Psychology*, 44 (5), 1409–1420.

Tomasello, M., 2009. *Why We Cooperate*. Cambridge, Massachusetts: MIT Press.

Tost, H. and Meyer-Lindenberg, A., 2010. I fear for you: A role for serotonin in moral behavior. *Proceedings of the National Academy of Sciences*, 107 (40), 17071–17072.

Trevarthen, C. and Aitken, K.J., 2001. Infant intersubjectivity: Research, theory, and clinical applications. *The Journal of Child Psychology and Psychiatry and Allied Disciplines*, 42 (1), 3–48.

Trivers, R., 2002. *Natural Selection and Social Theory: Selected Papers of Robert L. Trivers*. Oxford: Oxford University Press.

Trumble, B.C., Cummings, D., Rueden, C., O'Connor, K.A., Smith, E.A., Gurven, M., and Kaplan, H., 2012. Physical competition increases testosterone among Amazonian forager-horticulturalists: A test of the 'challenge hypothesis'. *Proceedings of the Royal Society B: Biological Sciences*, 279 (1739), 2907–2912.

Turiel, E., 1983. *The Development of Social Knowledge: Morality and Convention.* Cambridge: Cambridge University Press.

——2002. *The Culture of Morality: Social Development, Context, and Conflict.* Cambridge: Cambridge University Press.

Turkle, S., 2012. *Alone Together: Why We Expect More from Technology and Less from Each Other*. New York: Basic Books.

Twenge, J.M. and Campbell, W.K., 2009. *The Narcissism Epidemic: Living in the Age of Entitlement*. New York: Atria.

Umphress, E.E., Bingham, J.B., and Mitchell, M.S., 2010. Unethical behavior in the name of the company: The moderating effect of organizational identification and positive reciprocity beliefs on unethical pro-organizational behavior. *Journal of Applied Psychology*, 95 (4), 769–780.

Unternaehrer, E., Luers, P., Mill, J., Dempster, E., Meyer, A.H., Staehli, S., Lieb, R., Hellhammer, D.H., and Meinlschmidt, G., 2012. Dynamic changes in DNA methylation of stress-associated genes (OXTR, BDNF) after acute psychosocial stress. *Translational Psychiatry*, 2 (8), e150.

Uslaner, E.M. and Brown, M., 2005. Inequality, trust, and civic engagement. *American Politics Research*, 33 (6), 868–894.

Uvnas-Moberg, K. and Petersson, M., 2005. Oxytocin, a mediator of anti-stress, well-being, social interaction, growth and healing. *Z Psychosom Med Psychother*, 51 (1), 57–80.

Vaish, A., Carpenter, M., and Tomasello, M., 2009. Sympathy through affective perspective taking and its relation to prosocial behavior in toddlers. *Developmental Psychology*, 45 (2), 534–543.

——2010. Young children selectively avoid helping people with harmful intentions. *Child Development*, 81 (6), 1661–1669.

Vaish, A., Missana, M., and Tomasello, M., 2011. Three-year-old children intervene in third-party moral transgressions. *British Journal of Developmental Psychology*, 29 (1), 124–130.

Van Baaren, R.B., Holland, R.W., Kawakami, K., and van Knippenberg, A., 2004. Mimicry and prosocial behavior. *Psychological Science*, 15 (1), 71–74.

Van der Meij, L., Almela, M., Hidalgo, V., Villada, C., IJzerman, H., van Lange, P.A.M., and Salvador, A., 2012. Testosterone and cortisol release among Spanish soccer fans watching the 2010 World Cup final. *PLOS ONE*, 7 (4), e34814.

Van 't Wout, M., Kahn, R.S., Sanfey, A.G., and Aleman, A., 2006. Affective state and decision-making in the Ultimatum Game. *Experimental Brain Research*, 169 (4), 564–568.

Van Vugt, M. and Iredale, W., 2012. Men behaving nicely: Public goods as peacock tails. *British Journal of Psychology*, 104 (1), 3–10.

Viding, E., Jones, A.P., Paul, J.F., Moffitt, T.E., and Plomin, R., 2008. Heritability of antisocial behaviour at 9: Do callous-unemotional traits matter? *Developmental Science*, 11 (1), 17–22.

Viding, E. and McCrory, E.J., 2012. Why should we care about measuring callous–unemotional traits in children? *British Journal of Psychiatry*, 200 (3), 177–178.

Viviani, D., Charlet, A., van den Burg, E., Robinet, C., Hurni, N., Abatis, M., Magara, F., and Stoop, R., 2011. Oxytocin selectively gates fear responses through distinct outputs from the central amygdala. *Science*, 333 (6038), 104–107.

Vohs, K.D., Mead, N.L., and Goode, M.R., 2006. The psychological consequences of money. *Science*, 314 (5802), 1154–1156.

Voors, M., Nillesen, E., Verwimp, P., Bulte, E., Lensink, R., and van Soest, D., 2011. Violent conflict and behavior: A field experiment in Burundi. *American Economic Review*, 102 (2), 941–964.

Wain, O. and Spinella, M., 2007. Executive functions in morality, religion, and paranormal beliefs. *International Journal of Neuroscience*, 117 (1), 135–146.

Wallman, J., 2013. Stuffocation. Surrey: Crux Publishing Ltd.

Walters, G.D., 2009. Anger management training in incarcerated male offenders: Differential impact on proactive and reactive criminal thinking. *International Journal of Forensic Mental Health*, 8 (3), 214–217.

Walum, H., Westberg, L., Henningsson, S., Neiderhiser, J.M., Reiss, D., Igl, W., Ganiban, J.M., Spotts, E.L., Pedersen, N.L., and Eriksson, E., 2008. Genetic variation in the vasopressin receptor 1a gene (AVPR1A) associates with pair-bonding behavior in humans. *Proceedings of the National Academy of Sciences*, 105 (37), 14153–6.

Warneken, F. and Tomasello, M., 2008. Extrinsic rewards undermine altruistic tendencies in 20-month-olds. *Developmental Psychology*, 44 (6), 1785–1788.

——2009. Varieties of altruism in children and chimpanzees. *Trends in Cognitive Sciences*, 13 (9), 397–402.

Webster-Stratton, C., Reid, M.J., and Hammond, M., 2004. Treating children with early-onset conduct problems: Intervention outcomes for parent, child, and teacher training. *Journal of Clinical Child and Adolescent Psychology*, 33 (1), 105–124.

Wedekind, C. and Milinski, M., 2000. Cooperation through image scoring in humans. *Science*, 288 (5467), 850 –852.

Weierstall, R., Schalinski, I., Crombach, A., Hecker, T., and Elbert, T., 2012. When combat prevents PTSD symptoms – results from a survey with former child soldiers in Northern Uganda. *BMC Psychiatry*, 12 (1), 41.

Weierstall, R., Schauer, M., and Elbert, T., 2013. An appetite for aggression. *Scientific American Mind*, 24 (2), 46–49.

Weinstein, N. and Ryan, R.M., 2010. When helping helps: Autonomous motivation for prosocial behavior and its influence on well-being for the helper and recipient. *Journal of Personality and Social Psychology*, 98 (2), 222–244.

Weisman, O., Zagoory-Sharon, O., and Feldman, R., 2012. Oxytocin administration to parent enhances infant physiological and behavioral readiness for social engagement. *Biological Psychiatry*, 72 (12), 982–989.

Weng, H.Y., Fox, A.S., Shackman, A.J., Stodola, D.E., Caldwell, J.Z.K., Olson, M.C., Rogers, G.M., and Davidson, R.J., 2013. Compassion training alters altruism and neural responses to suffering. *Psychological Science*, 24 (7), 1171–1180.

Whitaker, R., 2011. *Anatomy of an Epidemic: Magic Bullets, Psychiatric Drugs, and the Astonishing Rise of Mental Illness in America*. New York: Broadway Books.

Wiessner, P., 2009. Experimental games and games of life among the Ju/'hoan Bushmen. *Current Anthropology*, 50 (1), 133–138.

Wilcox, K. and Stephen, A., 2013. Are close friends the enemy? Online social networks, self-esteem, and self-control. *Journal of Consumer Research*, 40 (1), 90–103.

Wilkinson, R., 2005. *The Impact of Inequality: How to Make Sick Societies Healthier*. London: Routledge.

Wilkinson, R. and Pickett, K., 2009. *The Spirit Level: Why More Equal Societies Almost Always Do Better*. London: Allen Lane.

Williams, K.D. and Nida, S.A., 2011. Ostracism: Consequences and coping. *Current Directions in Psychological Science*, 20 (2), 71–75.

Wilson, E.O., 2012. *The Social Conquest of Earth*. New York: Norton.

Wiltermuth, S.S. and Heath, C., 2009. Synchrony and cooperation. *Psychological Science*, 20 (1), 1–5.

Winnicott, D.W., 1958. *Through Pediatrics to Psychoanalysis: Collected Papers*. New York: Basic Books.

——1971. *Playing and Reality*. New York: Basic Books.

——1996. *The Maturational Processes and the Facilitating Environment: Studies in the Theory of Emotional Development*. London: Karnac.

Wood, H., 2011. The internet and its role in the escalation of sexually compulsive behaviour. *Psychoanalytic Psychotherapy*, 25 (2), 127–142.

Wright, N.D., Bahrami, B., Johnson, E., Di Malta, G., Rees, G., Frith, C.D., and Dolan, R.J., 2012. Testosterone disrupts human collaboration by increasing egocentric choices. *Proceedings of the Royal Society B: Biological Sciences*, 279 (1736), 2275–2280.

Wright, N.D., Hodgson, K., Fleming, S.M., Symmonds, M., Guitart-Masip, M., and Dolan, R.J., 2012. Human responses to unfairness with primary rewards and their biological limits. *Scientific Reports*, 593.

Yip, J.J. and Kelly, A.E., 2013. Upward and downward social comparisons can decrease prosocial behavior. *Journal of Applied Social Psychology*, 43 (3), 591–602.

Zahn, R., de Oliveira Souza, R., Bramati, I., Garrido, G., and Moll, J., 2009. Subgenual cingulate activity reflects individual differences in empathic concern. *Neuroscience Letters*, 457 (2), 107–110.

Zahn-Waxler, C., Park, J-H., Usher, B., Belouad, F., Cole, P., and Gruber, R., 2008. Young children's representations of conflict and distress: A longitudinal study of boys and girls with disruptive behavior problems. *Development and Psychopathology*, 20 (01), 99–119.

Zak, P.J., 2012. *The Moral Molecule: The New Science of What Makes Us Good or Evil.* London: Bantam Press.

Zak, P.J., Matzner, W., and Kurzban, R., 2008. The neurobiology of trust. *Scientific American Magazine*, 298 (6), 88–95.

Zak, P.J., Stanton, A.A., and Ahmadi, S., 2007. Oxytocin increases generosity in humans. *PLOS ONE*, 2 (11).

Zhong, C.B., Bohns, V.K., and Gino, F., 2010. Good lamps are the best police. *Psychological Science*, 21 (3), 311–314.

Zhong, C.B., Strejcek, B., and Sivanathan, N., 2010. A clean self can render harsh moral judgment. *Journal of Experimental Social Psychology*, 46 (5), 859–862.

Zimbardo, P.G., Maslach, C., and Haney, C., 2000. Reflections on the Stanford Prison experiment: Genesis, transformations, consequences. In: T. Blass, ed., *Obedience to Authority: Current Perspectives on the Milgram Paradigm.* Mahwah, New Jersey: Laurence Erlbaum Associates, 193–237.

Index